Praise for *The I*

"Here is the honest, unvarnished story of a life of great challenges and great joys. Israel's voice comes through the pages to touch the reader's heart."

—David Wolpe, Max Webb Rabbi Emeritus of
Sinai Temple, Los Angeles, California

"A remarkable man... a gifted storyteller. I think historians will welcome this account of one immigrant Jew's struggles to make it in the new land... I have never read anything quite like this diary."

—Arnold Eisen, Chancellor Emeritus and Professor,
The Jewish Theological Seminary

The Inheritance
(Yurusha)

Israel Rosen

Translated by Dr. William Glicksman
Edited by Elliot Rosen
Foreword by Neal Karlen

Minneapolis

Minneapolis
FIRST EDITION September 2023

The Inheritance (Yurusha)
Copyright © 2023 by Elliot Rosen and Israel Rosen.
All rights reserved.

No part of this book may be used or reproduced in any manner whatsoever without written permission except in the case of brief quotations used in critical articles and reviews. For information, write to Calumet Editions, 6800 France Avenue South, Suite 370, Edina, MN 55435.

Printed in the United States of America

10 9 8 7 6 5 4 3 2 1

ISBN: 978-1-960250-98-8

Cover and interior design: Gary Lindberg

Table of Contents

Foreword by Neal Karlen. 1
Introduction by Elliot Rosen 7
Part One: From Birth to Marriage 13
Part Two: Marriage – Divorce – Love – Family 31
Part Three: Family and Business Life and Suffering in the Old Country . 47
Part Four: My Difficult Journey to America 57
Part Five: Becoming a Griner – Adjusting to Life in America 73
Part Six: Settling in Philadelphia – A Griner No More. 91
Part Seven: My Nightmare and Finally Gaining My Family. 107
Part Eight: Trials and Tribulations – My Real Life in America 127
Part Nine: My Search for a Better Life Continues. 191
Part Ten: My Life Becomes Beautiful. 213
Postscript 229
(My Confession of Sins, Before Death)
    Better Expressed: My Poor Testament? 233
Additional Notes 237
Epilogue. 241
Zayda's Book Episode One: The Blood Libel of R'Yosele 245
Zayda's Book Episode Two: The Two
    Rich Men from Our Town Vishnevets 257
Zayda's Book Episode Three: A Man in the Middle Years
    with all the Virtues by the Name of Leyb Mazer 259
Zayda's Book Episode Four: Shabes in the Old Country 265
Zayda's Book Episode Five: The Story of Binyomin the Convert. 269
Zayda's Book Episode Six: The Fantasy of R'Itshel 275
Zayda's Book Episode Seven: The Lessons of
    Dr. Shmaryohu Levin and How I Saved a Life 279
Zayda's Book Episode Eight: The Message of R'Tsvi Hirsh Maslansky. 285
Zayda's Book Episode Nine: Foreman of the Jury. 289
Zayda's Book Episode Ten: My Atlantic City Mitzveh. 293
Acknowledgments 297

In loving memory of David, Vera and Lewis Rosen

The Inheritance
(Yurusha)

FOREWORD
by Neal Karlen

What makes Israel Rosen's *The Inheritance* so transcendentally artful is precisely the fact that his memoir was never intended as an act of art. When Rosen detailed the details—in Yiddish, with a fountain pen—of his immigrant's odyssey from Eastern Europe to America, he didn't aspire to make literature meant to survive the ages.

So Israel Rosen may not have been a "literary" writer in the traditional sense (as understood by the lofty-minded, often pretentious purveyors of said "art"). However, that is all for the good. Unfortunately, there have seemingly been more brilliant literary Yiddish artists in just the last two hundred years than there are people now alive who can read and understand the language used by the authorial likes of Sholom Aleichem, Isaac Bashevis Singer, and Chaim Grade.

Rather, Rosen, who died in 1948 at seventy-eight, hoped, at most, that his scribbled memories might be fashioned into a manuscript that might, *somehow*, simply survive *him*. Perhaps, he mused with his pen, his memories might serve as a humble legacy to his own descendants, an ordinary gift meant merely so his own bloodline could know *what happened*, how, between the nineteenth and twentieth centuries, *these* particular Rosens got from Russia (Czarist) to Pennsylvania (Philadelphia).

This is the "inheritance" of the title: one modest man's modest story of the past. It was a story meant to reach, if he was lucky, the author hoped, one particular family in the future. His.

Luckily, by aiming his words no higher than his own experience, Rosen has contributed, with the help of several collaborators, a work that will not just be seen by a few of his forthcoming relatives. Rather, it will be remembered by multitudes of readers who don't, as they say, have skin in the game.

In hoping that his memories be remembered, Israel Rosen's best move was having Elliot Rosen as a grandson. Elliot was only seven when his grandfather died in 1948; it would be decades before he took possession of the manuscript from assorted relatives. And for help in translating his Zayda's (grandfather's) penned Yiddish words into English, he turned to the distinguished Philadelphia-based Yiddishist and scholar Dr. William Glicksman.

Glicksman was the esteemed author of many ethereal highbrow articles and monographs on Yiddish as a language, culture and world view. He saw the beauty of what Rosen, the poor immigrant, had written. And unlike most experts in most anything, Glicksman wisely didn't try to improve what Rosen's simplicity had wrought. His grandfather's book, Elliot Rosen remembered Glicksman telling him, was a "treasure."

Glicksman, Rosen also remembers, told him that in these words, his grandfather had authentically rendered himself as "a pious man, a humble man, a poor man, a stubborn man and a man without mazel [luck]."

Piety, humility, poverty, stubborn lessness? Has a greater prescription for a historically enduring book's protagonist ever been written in any manual? Just as smartly, Glicksman told the author's grandson he'd "translated word for word without correcting the grammar or editing the text so that we would not lose [Israel Rosen's] meaning, feelings, and sensitivity."

It was an act of genius, for in doing so, Glicksman made Yiddish itself a co-conspirator with Rosen in committing a work of true art. Yes, Yiddish is a character. Glicksman turned Rosen's Yiddish into English—and yet the English he gave back was astonishingly Yiddish in its attitude, irony, fatalism, romance and humor.

It was an act of linguistic alchemy. In translating Rosen's Yiddish into English, he actually made the Yiddish come alive in full flower of the magic it once was.

Ah, Yiddish. The oft-considered "gutter" language of the Eastern European uneducated ghetto and shtetl Jew, spoken by thirteen million people at the dawn of World War II, a language whose own story through the centuries was in itself a mirror of Jewish history, thought, and practice—for better and worse, in good days and holocausts.

Yet, alas, the language was reduced to virtual extinction first, most obviously by genocide. And what the Nazis couldn't wipe out, Jews themselves tried to linguistically erase after the Holocaust. Yiddish was repressed by its own as the language of the forever victimized, ghettoized, Wandering Jew. To replace Yiddish would come a modernized, secularized version of Hebrew, the holy language, used before 1948 only for prayer in devotion. Suddenly, Hebrew was reborn as the lingua franca of a new independent and strong Jew, the language of Israel, the tongue not of a historic victim but of a proud, Biblical people.

Pity the loss of Yiddish, dagnabbit. Though the language has rebounded in the academy and some boisterous allied institutions. But today, the only people on the planet who speak Yiddish are Chasidic Jews.

Such history!

In the beginning, Yiddish was a minor dialect in medieval Europe that helped peasant Jews live safely apart from the marauders of the First Crusades. Incorporating a large measure of antique German dialects, Yiddish also included little scraps of French, Italian, ancient Hebrew, Aramaic, the Slavic and Romance languages, and a dozen other tongues native to the places where Jews were briefly given shelter. One may speak a dozen languages, all of them Yiddish. The language was beautiful, as they say in the tongue, a "mish-mosh." (Never a mish-mash!)

And to begin to understand the soul of Yiddish, one needn't understand the homely language as much as its bipolar worldview. Mere answers of how this gutter language saved and mirrored the Jews over the last thousand years don't begin to tell the tale of the *mamme loshn* (mother tongue) any more than the correct answers on *Jeopardy!* reveal anything beyond the memorization of trivia.

Over the centuries, experts have thought Yiddish had as many linguistic meanings as the word *oy*. At various times, it was considered a jargon, dialect, vulgar street language, secret code, medium of high art, punishment, Jewish Esperanto, or even an embarrassment to its people. Yet, it's always been anything but trivial.

And so, (with the help of a large cast of enablers, including his grandson Elliot and a Yiddishist and translator named William Glicksman), Israel Rosen makes the world anew, in Yiddish rendered into pitch-perfect English.

In Israel Rosen's world, death to a good man or woman who believes there must be more to existence than just THIS doesn't just stop breathing; he or she "went to the true world."

In Yiddish, "LIFE" stories can be tragic and hilarious—simultaneously. One doesn't just laugh so as to not cry: one wants to wail mournfully and laugh boisterously—at the exact same moment. Writes Rosen, making this notion real in also perfect translation:

> From the age of twenty-two till thirty-seven, I had an understanding that God gave me a fine and decent wife and beautiful children and wisdom [and I] came to this land. I am healthy and strong and forgot my weakness. I will try to sweeten my life. I love the beautiful world and people. I did not let myself down, got stronger, had more confidence, and went forward. I looked far ahead, full with love, and tried to make even the worst for the best.

And then he takes a beat.

Here I really began to suffer.

Not, "and then I began suffering." No... after all those swell existential happenings, *really* came the suffering. That is the grand, virtually unexplainable irony of Yiddish.

Further, how does Rosen evoke the feeling of a memory he shall never forget? By saying, "I will never forget?"

Feh! (Properly spelled with an exclamation mark.) Rather, the episode he is recalling "is still located in my bones until this very day." Beautiful.

And how does one make another *feel* the history of one's own poverty? "He knew very well," writes Rosen, "the taste of rags."

The "taste of rags." THAT is Yiddish!

A world where, according to Israel Rosen, you know a friend

because "they take interest in my joy." Or, the author continues, "in this life, on this planet, one can't ever be *too* geographically or spiritually lost, as long as you have a place, even in your mind, where you think you *should* be."

"If you have the address, you will find it," says Israel Rosen.

And neither Kierkegaard nor Wittgenstein ever posed the Divine dilemma better. And with that, Rosen fulfills the prime Yiddish commandment of all: "Be a *mensch!*"—a phrase every Yiddishe mamma infinitely implores every Yiddishe boychik and girlchick, from cradle to grave: "be a mensch!"

Mensch is a beautiful word; it has no translation. It is sort of related to the German word "mensch," which means "human being" or "man" in the general sense. But the Yiddish word is completely different. Mensch has no gender. And "calling someone a "mensch" is the ultimate compliment, expressing the rarity and worth of another person's qualities.

Mensch is the Nobel Prize of words. It's a title bestowed upon you and one you can't bestow upon yourself. It has nothing to do with accrued wealth, fame or official honors. The key to being "a real mensch" is nothing less than character, rectitude, dignity, a sense of what is right, responsible and decorous. Being a mensch is the highest aspirational goal one can set for oneself and one's children.

It means—everything. And yet, the word has no translation.

Thankfully, the inheritance has one translation—into a beautiful, simple English that mimics Yiddish precisely.

Israel Rosen, in transmitting your memoir *The Inheritance*, you've given the world not only a work of original, almost aboriginal, art— you've proven yourself a real mensch.

Mazel tov, Rosens! Mazel tov, reading world!

INTRODUCTION
by Elliot Rosen

This project has been a long time coming to fruition. As *The Inheritance* goes to print for the first time, I am 82 years old and as excited as a child. And relieved. There have been many starts and stops over the years in sharing my Zayda's legacy. In September 1979, I wrote an article for the *Main Line Jewish Expression* as a High Holidays piece, which is printed below. I offer it is a fitting foundation for what will follow.

> September 26, 1979
>
> For many years, I have been haunted by the soul of my Zayda. Although he died in 1948 when I was seven years old, his image has grown ever stronger in my memory bank. This is the result of my Bubba living with us until her death in 1960 and all the stories and anecdotes we heard about him over the years. However, the main reason his image and memory have impacted on me so greatly is because of his autobiography.
>
> I remember clearly and vividly in our home in Strawberry Mansion, watching my Zayda writing in Yiddish "his story." I used to marvel at his use of the old-fashioned fountain pen, especially his beautiful line drawings of lions, fish, birds, and designs. When he died, this autobiography was placed somewhere in the house and collected dust. When my Bubba "went to the true world" (his words to

describe death), my father's oldest brother (Max) took the book.

Over the years, Uncle Max indicated there was much in the book that should not be revealed, and it always piqued my curiosity. Last winter, my parents went to visit Uncle Max and Aunt Dora, who were living in York, Pennsylvania. Aunt Dora was dying of cancer, and my parents drove up through terrible winter weather one Sunday. Uncle Max (who was 83 at the time) handed my father the book he had so closely guarded as if he had a premonition.

The next day we received a call from York that Uncle Max had been rushed to the hospital and had died. Earlier in my life, in the summer of 1966, my wife was visiting her parents, who live out of town, and I had dinner at my parents. I was told that my Aunt Reba (my father's oldest sister) was in bed with a cold, so after dinner, my brother Lewis and I drove the few blocks to my aunt's home in Wynnefield. We had a great visit and really laughed, as my aunt had a super sense of humor. She once came to our house having just left the beauty parlor in disgust. She said she went in and asked for a Jackie Kennedy hairdo but came out looking like Mamie Eisenhower. She also once looked at our pet poodle relaxing and enjoying life like a queen and said, "Even a dog has to have mazel."

The next morning at 7:30, I received a call from my mother that Aunt Reba had died during the night. The word I can think of to explain these coincidences is intuition. But there is a much better word in Yiddish, and that word is "beshairt" (fate). At this time of the year, it is very easy to think about "beshairt."

When my father brought the book back last winter, he gave it to me. After much investigation and inquiry, it was recommended that I see Dr. William Glicksman, who lives in Overbrook Park. He is a survivor of the Holocaust and is a world-recognized expert on Polish Jewry and a Yiddish scholar. Thus far, we have translated about two-thirds of my Zayda's writings.

When Dr. Glicksman called me to come over to pick up the first thirty pages, I had no idea what to expect. Before Dr. Glicksman gave me the translation, he spoke to me about the "treasure" that this book was. He told me my Zayda was a pious man… a humble man… a poor man… a stubborn man and a man without mazel. He told me he translated word for word without correcting the grammar or editing the text so that we would not lose my Zayda's meaning, feelings and sensitivity.

The word treasure doesn't even come close to describing what this book means to us. We can't wait to receive each new installment. I have made copies and sent them to the rest of the family. There are many gaps in the story that my parents, aunts and uncles are trying to fill in, but the depth of the story of this Jewish immigrant's struggle is the most meaningful substantiation of my heritage I could have ever found.

Much of his story is filled with melancholy, always very moving, with some tragic humor and irony reminiscent of *Fiddler on the Roof*. Hopefully, it will be published someday so everyone can share this very human story. However, all that really matters is that I have been able to receive my Zayda's yurusha (inheritance). We Jews live with the word Zachor (remember). In this season of Teshuvah (repentance), Tephilah (prayer) and Tzdakah (charity), my remembrance is to acknowledge the blessing and gift of my Zayda (Israel Rosen) of bequeathing Tshuvah, Tephilah and Tzdakah to me.

The complete translation was finished shortly after the article was published. My Zayda did not include names and dates, which has made it difficult to create the timeline, and he does repeat himself frequently. I agree that the charm of his phrasing is important; I have taken the liberty to selectively make the flow more readable. This is clearly not a book of historical significance but is a glimpse into one man's story and his immigrant experience. I'm sure it mirrors the stories of hundreds of thousands, if not millions, of immigrants, but this is MY ZAYDA'S STORY!

I originally wanted to call it *The Kesslegarden*, which is the way I transliterated what I thought was a Yiddish term depicting a scene of chaos. I have since found out that what I thought was Yiddish was really, The Castle Garden, the chaotic immigration holding center in Battery Park, New York, that is also known as Castle Clinton or Fort Clinton. As these years have passed and this project remained on the back burner, I have, from time to time, re-read my Zayda's book. It is not easy to read as Dr. Glicksman handwrote the translation on a yellow legal pad, and I frequently need help interpreting his handwriting. I also typed a few of the episodes (very short stand-alone vignettes) and made copies to give to the family one Pesach Seder a few years ago. But the impact of Dr. Glicksman's words to me that first time he gave me translated pages has never faded. This is MY YURUSHA! It is my INHERITANCE.

NOTE: Elliot also provided additional clarifications and explanations with names and dates. (Wm. G. = Dr. William Glicksman's commentary when he did original translation of text)

The Inheritance (Yurusha)

Map of Ukraine in 2014

Part One
From Birth to Marriage

As a small child, when I suckled the milk from my mother's breast, it was sour and not good for me, and therefore much of my life has been bitter. Many people maintain, in their older years, that they should feel as good from the taste as when they (*the people,* Wm. G.) suckled the milk from their mothers' breasts. Unfortunately, I can't say this, for when my mother gave birth to me, I already had eight siblings. During my younger years, my father was well up, but this didn't last long. When I came into this sinful world, my mother was very sick. We did not have anything to save her. I suffered more than ordinary children in the first months with hunger because my mother did not have with what to feed me, not even sweet milk from her breast.

When I got older, my mother began to bring me up. She used to cook for me buckwheat with milk or with butter and used to feed me. This I remember until today and which I can still taste. I can also still hear the sweet tune she used to sing to me with a warm and tender kiss. With the words "ZUNINU" (*my little son,* Wm. G.), "KASHINYO" (*"KASHINYO" a local description of a beloved child of a Slavic root. It could also be from the Yiddish KISHN-to kiss or pillow a KISHN,* Wm. G.), not one time but many. All of this makes me feel such a love that I can never forget. When I recall this, I feel such an unusual pleasure and love that I can't bring it out from the depths of my heart. It is now, thank God, fifty years since my beloved mother z"l (*Hebrew letters meaning of blessed memory,* Wm. G.) is in the true world. I have thought of her almost every day and always with a warm love. I am now, thank God, sixty years old, K'AYN HORE (*the evil eye,* Wm. G.). I have, K'AYN

HORE, six children, five of them are, thank God, married; the three daughters and two sons. I did not have yet one good day. I, therefore, consider it my duty to describe everything—my life, my trials, my adventures, my pain but most of all, my story. Although in the beginning, it will sound childish, I hope that my further writing will be interesting. I'm not writing this for anybody, only for myself and for my wife and children. They didn't know me during my life. They didn't know anything. They should know after my death what I have gone through and who were my parents; from the cradle, they cared about me, and they loved me.

I was the ninth child, something unusual in those years with us in the old country; the youngest son (*pinky,* Wm. G.). Until the age of eight, everything was good for me. They gave me everything as if I was the only one (*the only child,* Wm. G.). When I became eight, I had a severe cold and got pneumonia, my parents knew a doctor should be called. But ours was a small town where there was not a doctor who would not be needed very often. So, we trusted in God that he will help, and he really helped. I was told that I could not talk and could not open my eyes. They had already put a feather to my nose. They had already considered me as dead. Then my mother ran to my bed and began to scream that she donated the years of the rest of her life to me. Her screaming and noise made me open my eyes, and I asked for a drink of water. This I was told by my father and mother. So, it took enough time until I recuperated a little bit, for they took from me much blood. In the old country, years before, they took blood from the veins. This was the last resort.

It took a long time until I became well and regained my health. There was much happiness and joy for my parents. They loved me very much, especially since I escaped death and became again alive. Everything was done to regain my health. Perhaps it would be so if not for the coincidence that my mother was confined to bed very sick. She could no longer recuperate from her sickness; she used to stay more in bed than walking around. This way, she used to watch me since nobody could do it. My father was depressed. He needed to work for a livelihood. Then I began to sense my bad situation. What could I have done, a child of nine years? My mother's health got worse. We were poor. We didn't have anything to save her. We were all together, the older and younger ones. Even those who were married lived together. We didn't know much. It was our parents' fault. They did not let us go.

Thus, we grew without knowledge. What could we do at that time, especially since I was a little child? This was going on, and it depressed me. I may say that from that time until today, I suffer. When I reached the age of ten, my mother could no longer leave the bed. When I used to approach her, she did not let me go away; she kissed me and covered me with her cold tears. She used to say, "My child, I am dying, but with whom am I leaving you? Such a weak child you are. How dear you are to me, but, my child, they call me, and I must go..."

What could I, then a child of ten, understand? It didn't last long. It was Passover, after the first Seder; I even remember that the first Seder was on a Friday (*March 26, 1880,* ER); she died, left this sinful world to go into the right world. After her death began the very hard days, and months, particularly the death anniversaries that I will describe in true detail, not to omit the wickedness and the goodness. Everything is right; it will come out, and everything will be interesting, even the smallest, the most weak, the most poor. For I see that I have not achieved anything until now, and I will not leave anything. Why? Nobody knows. I, therefore, want to leave at least my own description (*autobiography,* Wm. G.) not for anybody, only for myself.

16   Israel Rosen

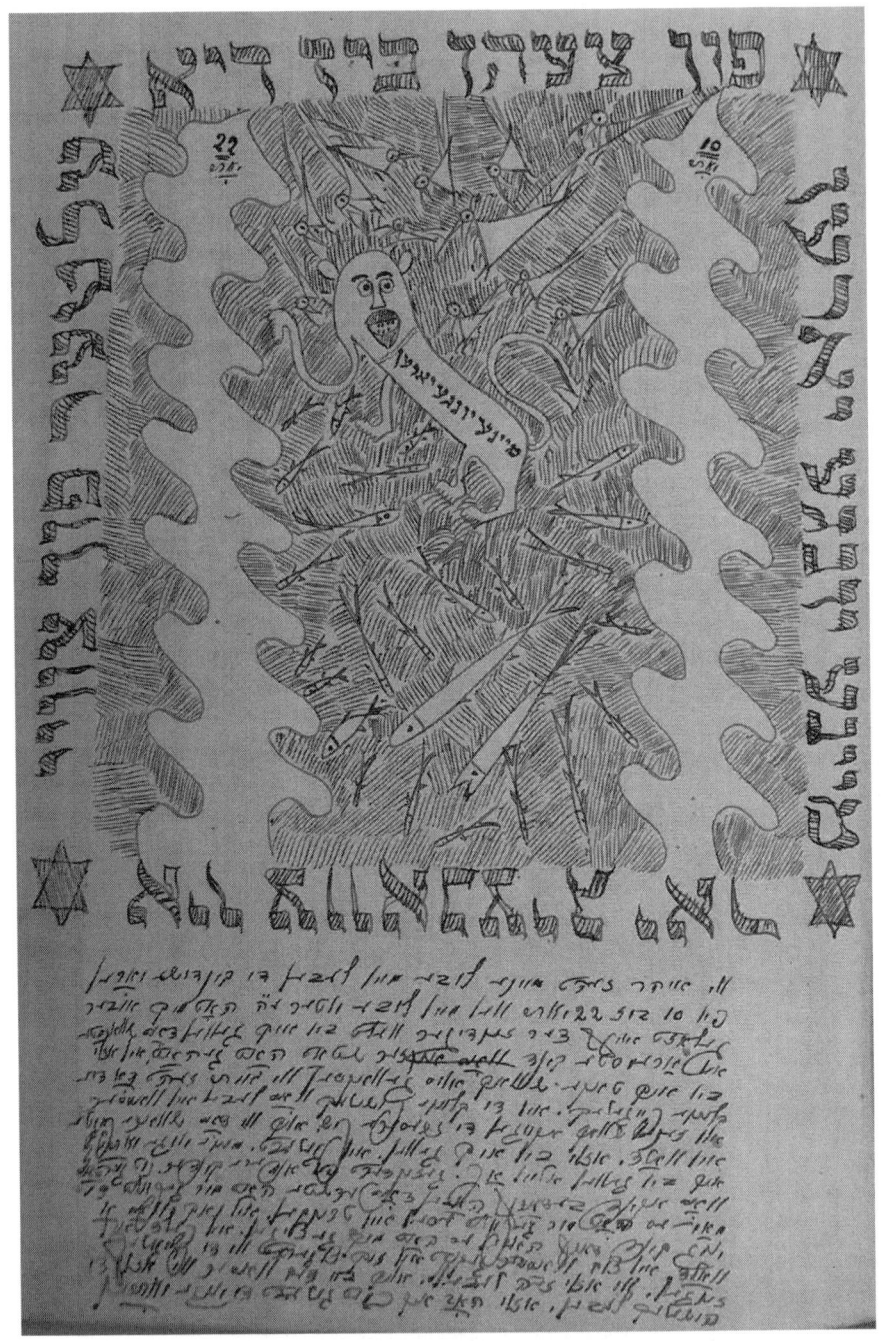

**Page drawing and inscription, my young years
from ten until the age of twenty-two years.**

The Inheritance (Yurusha)

Translation: As you can see, my dears, my life the younger years from ten to twenty-two when my dear mother, (Hebrew word – Ayin, Yod, Hey), blessed be her memory, left me in this sinful world, I was the weakest and poorest child in the town. Thus, I grew up weak as you see here the little birds and the little fish that live in the water, and are weak against the bigger fish, also, as the weak bird in the forest. So, I was and lived during my younger years. I was by myself, separated from other children. I didn't have what a child ought to have. The final thing lacking was my mother. I didn't have enough to eat and to drink and everything that a young child should have. I was longing for the fields, forests, and to the river myself and heard the birds singing, how they live and at the water, and how the fish live. This way, I almost lived all my young years.) Written inside the animal (it could be a lion) in the middle of the drawing are the Yiddish words **MY YOUNGER YEARS**.

When I write about my life, I feel relieved. Perhaps when this is read, I will not be accused and ridiculed so much. Maybe, a good word will be heard about me. Money is not the main thing, nor is luxury. A good word is appreciated during our lifetime, let alone after death. I would like to live very much. I didn't live yet (*in Yiddish, this means that he was not yet useful,* Wm. G.), not for myself, not for my family, and not for strangers (*in the sense for other people,* Wm. G.). I am, thanks God, sixty years old, but I have not accomplished anything. I believe if better people than I am should be inclined, everyone should describe his life; it would certainly be important. It would be something to read. Since, however, I am the smallest (*in the socioeconomic classification and also in terms of modesty,* Wm. G.), it is exactly why I want to describe everything, from my birth till my leaving this world. If my writing is too weak; (*in the sense insufficient in style, in composition, in grammar, etc.,* Wm. G.), it is for two reasons. First, because I don't know; secondly, I feel that my days are numbered, given to me by grace (*God's will,* Wm. G.), as everything was given by grace until today. Such I will write and will endeavor not to omit anything. I must do it for myself, my family, and even for strangers.

After my mother's death, it wasn't long until I began to feel my precarious situation. Nobody looked (*in the sense of caring,* Wm. G.) after me. My father was depressed. He had to earn a livelihood for such a family of, K'AYEN HORE, grown up and small children as I already described. In his younger years, my father was an efficient man, a businessman. But in his older years, he was left with a big house with three stores. From all this, he derived a half subsistence of the rent. Furthermore, in winter, he used to sell all kinds of paint. In the summer, he used to sell scythes to cut the grain from the fields.

So it was, living the poor life. What could I, a child, understand? My older brothers stayed at home, and in addition, I was weak! I went to HEYDER (*the traditional European Jewish school-elementary,* Wm. G.) and learned how to read and write Yiddish, but my learning did not last long. It was discontinued at the age of twelve. My father did not have with-what to pay *(tuition,* Wm. G.). I didn't have any of the delights a child my age should have, not even proper nourishment and sleep (*conditions,* Wm. G.). Nobody took care of me. But I had a will to live! I envied other children who had a mother and a home and who were mainly healthy—everything I didn't have. But I could not help myself. I did not have a job since I was still a little boy in a small town, abandoned. I was walking around idle, and life became miserable for me. The summer days were very long and tedious. What did I do? What all children, big and small, would do. In our town, there was a big river, a deep one. Thus, everyone could swim. So, I also learned how to swim, and I became an excellent swimmer. I went to the river to swim almost every day. There, at the river, I saw people every day. Some would sit day by day and catch fish, small and big, with angling rods. I enjoyed sitting there watching them catch fish. Who were these people who devoted their time to catching fish? Were they the big men of the city, the Count, the Priest, or the city clerk and common smallest (*in the sense of socio-economics,* Wm. G.)? Poor Christians, poor Jews, I fit right in and would sit day by day watching and admiring their patience and skill. I used to forget about everything, even about eating.

Since I was seen every day sitting, eventually they asked for my service. One gave me his angling rod to attach a crumb of bread or a worm; the other a small fish. Thus, I received for this a couple of GROSHEN (*100 GROSHEN = 1 ruble, i.e., 100 cents = 1 dollar,* Wm. G.). Often, after a full day of catching fish, they would give me some to take home. When I came home, my father used to yell at me and became angry because I was not home all day; not just one time did I get a good beating, for he felt very lonely without my mother. He used to reproach me with the words, "Because of you, your mother died and left this world. She would still live now! She donated you her years!" Not one time I was thinking: what does it mean? "She donated you her years," and there used to descend upon me such a melancholy that I despised my life.

And so, the days passed into weeks, and the weeks faded into months, and my greatest pleasure and satisfaction came during the summer just sitting and catching fish. I used to sit a whole day before I caught a fish, and even so, it was a small one. If a stranger gave me his rod to hold, I caught the greatest fish. In order to quiet down my father's anger that he should not beat me, I used to bring the fish home. Then he saw that I don't want to go around idle a whole day and let it be this way. Hence during the summer, my pleasure was to catch fish or to see how the other catches.

But during the winter, it was already entirely different. I used to sit every day and all evening in the synagogue near older children, boys, also poor, that used to study by themselves. So, I also listened. In addition to this, I learned to draw and make "KVITLEKH" (*usually a slip of paper 1/8 of a notebook page, on which was written a number. This replaced playing cards that were prohibited in a house of prayer. The game was usually called 21, i.e., one who reaches the highest number without going over 21 wins. The students studying rabbinic literature, mainly Mishnah or Talmud, played such games during recess time; KVITL is singular, KVITLEKH is plural,* Wm. G.). I was experienced in beautiful handwriting. Everyone liked my KVITLEKH. Don't ask. I used to write two sets of KVITLEKH daily. I received 25 GROSHEN for each set. Thus, I earned 50 GROSHEN a day. And in the evening, I had extra (*i.e., additional,* Wm. G.) sets, my own—which I gave (*i.e., rented,* Wm. G.) to play for ten games for 2 or 3 GROSHEN, which brought in an additional 25 GROSHEN. My father began to look at me differently and was indeed proud of me and of my great achievement of being able to write and draw beautiful KVITLEKH. Not everybody can do this, but I really think he looked at me differently because of the money I made and brought home.

Such was my occupation: in the summer to catch fish, and in the winter to write and draw KVITLEKH. However, I did not play the game. I used to save every GROSHEN I earned. Thus, I made a few rubles to dress myself as the children of the rich. With this business, I supported myself from the age of twelve until I was sixteen. At sixteen, I began to comprehend better that this is not the proper way of life for a young boy. Only in my thoughts could I dare imagine being able to achieve the utmost. It was at this time that many Germans came to town to erect a large sawmill plant. They installed the biggest machines I had ever seen that could cut the greatest oaks and make all kinds of boards and wood. Hence laborers were needed, young and old. As usual, the rich didn't apply, only the poor. The pay was between fifty and seventy-five GROSHEN a day. In those years, that was a great deal. The first couple of weeks I worked, I felt my strength declining from day to day. But to have work and to be equal to the others gave me courage. However, not for long. One day I fainted. They had to bring me home, and a doctor was called. I had already saved a couple of rubbles. He ordered me not to go to work anymore.

I was in bed for months. I had a lot of aggravation that I can't be like others. What could I do, to go again and catch fish and write "KVITLEKH"? So, I felt I have something to invent. This thought was on my mind every day. I was doing nothing, and my father should give me everything, I could not expect. So, I suffered and kept quiet until I complained to my father that I was not satisfied with such a life. I wanted to travel the world and go to larger cities. I already was big (*i.e., an adult*) BOHUR (*young man*) with understanding. He answered that not even one child left the home and especially since you are such a weak child. Life became miserable. Everything that I am writing here is not so important; it sounds childish. For I write everything that I went through as a child, but later in my writing, everything with God's help will be justified. It will be more coherent; it will be understood better. I felt an urge to travel in this big world. But I didn't have the courage. It was a weakness on my side and the fault of my father and sisters and brothers. I used to always envy those who used to travel and come, especially those who were not illiterate, who could learn (*i.e., were educated,* Wm. G.) and write. I had an uncle, my mother's brother, who lived in a larger city than ours, all together it was four miles. It was a commercial city, there was a train. This attracted me. So, I would go there many times during the summer to spend two or three weeks there. They did not do anything for me, although my uncle was well up. I don't remember whether or not he gave me any money. I went back by foot. I loved the green fields in summer. This was my greatest pleasure to think about the world. I also had an aunt, my mother's sister, also in a small town, even smaller than ours. I used to go often by foot, usually during the summer and stay there a couple of weeks. But again, no one did anything for me. Thus, passed my years, the best ones which a child should have are those years, but not I. Yes, it was gnawing because there was a young desire to live. But there was not the right person to care about me. For not one time did I complain about such a life. Thus, the answer came from myself. Whatever, you have to be satisfied; it is donated anyway. Your years are donated. After all, how long can you live? So, I suffered and kept silent. I could not do better, and nobody cared about me, and I made peace with my thoughts.

In the meantime, I reached the age of eighteen. I came in contact with many big (*in the author's view, socially higher or even economically,* Wm. G.) people, also decent from whom one could learn. I, myself, knew very little. I did not learn anything. I, therefore, liked those few who knew. At the age of eighteen, I tried another occupation. I had beautiful handwriting. Indeed, nothing more. This was not meant to deceive anyone. I began to teach little children. Thus, I made a living. I already had everything I needed. At the time, when I already made a living for myself, came my friend of the same age as me. He didn't have a father. He could learn (*in the sense that he was educated,* Wm. G.) and write and he was healthy. For his mother took better care, although she was poor, but yet a mother. My friend was (*i.e., lived,* Wm. G.) in a village where he taught children to read and write, and he received a hundred rubles with food and lodging per Z'MAN (*a Hebrew term used in Yiddish which indicated the time from SUCCOS to PASSOVER and the time from PASSOVER to SUCCOS. In American terms it may be called a semester,* Wm. G.). Thus, he had it good. Thus, he tried for me also. For a few Jews from another village also needed a boy (*i.e., a young man,* Wm. G.) to teach their children: younger ones and for less money. This made me happy, and I went with him, actually walked by foot, for this was my best pleasure. It was four miles from us...

The Inheritance (Yurusha) 23

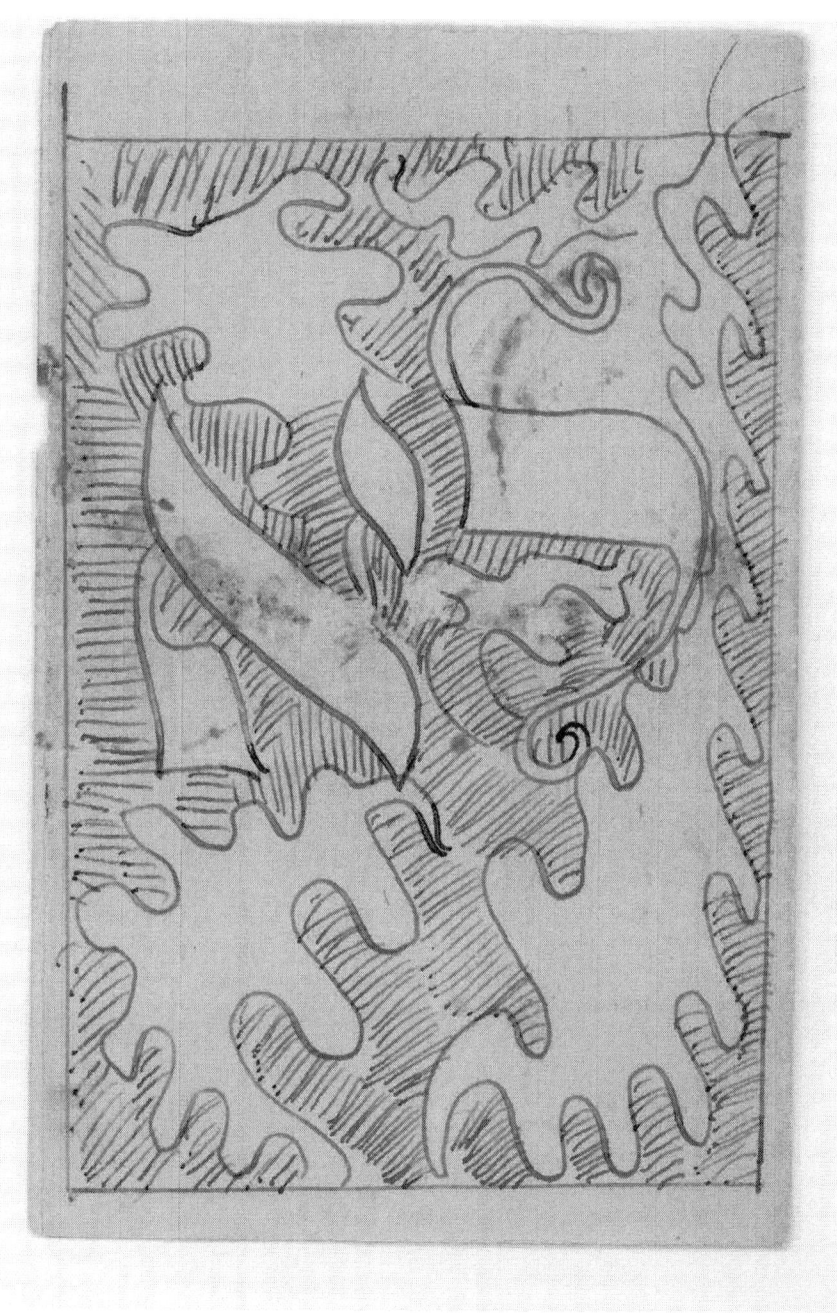

Example of Israel Rosen's KVITLEKH.

24　　　　　　　　　　　Israel Rosen

Example of Israel Rosen's KVITLEKH.

The Inheritance (Yurusha) 25

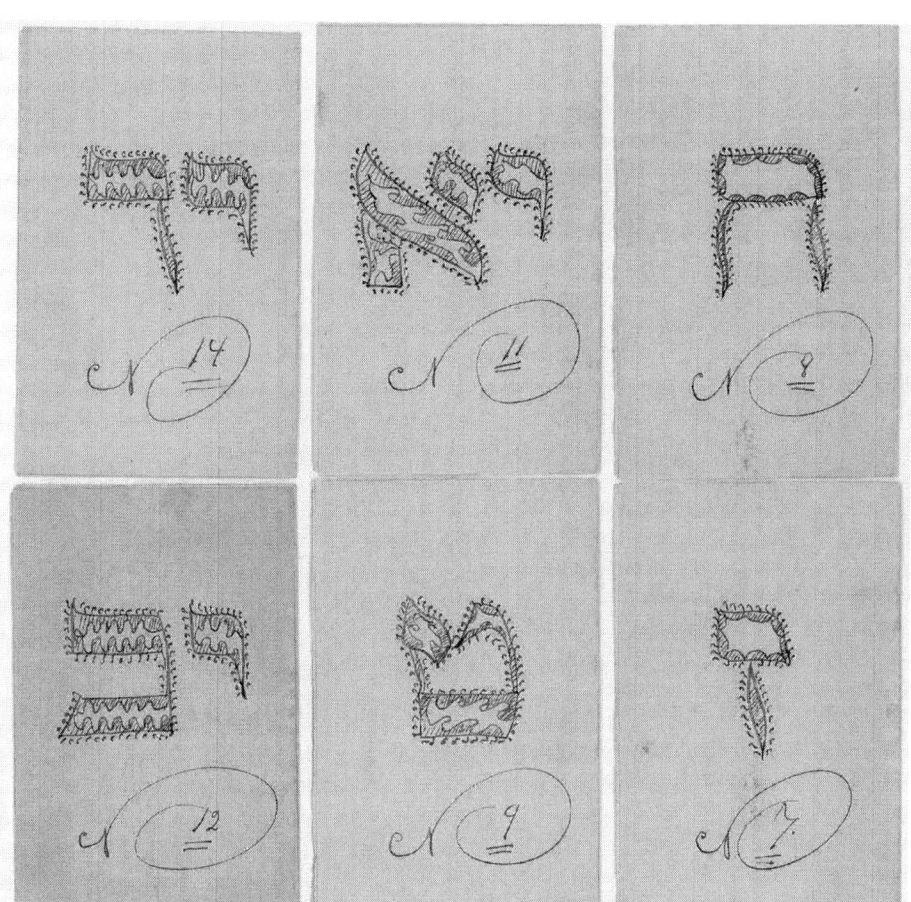

Example of Israel Rosen's KVITLEKH.

When I came, they were pleased with me. For with my clothing and appearance, I could cover (*in text deceive*) what was going on in me inside. It would take time for me to feel competent. Thus, I got the job at the age of eighteen. I was satisfied and happy. First of all, I had enough food and a place to sleep and mainly to what my heart was striving for—fresh air, green fields, and trees, clean small rivers and streams with various fish which I used to catch in my free time so quiet and serene as I listened to the songs of the various birds. I felt that every day of the week brought me health. I eat well and sleep well, and indeed to receive after my stay a couple of dollars (*i.e., rubbles,* Wm. G.) and to come home for Passover to my father and family and friends. Let them see that I am also already a grown-up person and, indeed, a fine person and teaching fine children; two boys and two girls. They saw that I can write beautifully, that's all. With this I deceived them. However, it brought me aggravation because I didn't know how I could teach another one (*or others,* Wm. G.). Thus, I had to go twice a week to my friend that he should study with me in order that I could transfer it to my pupils as long as I have taught them how to pray or a PARASHA (*a weekly portion of the Pentateuch,* Wm. G.). Perhaps if I have learned more and I could teach more but when the talk began about RASHI and GEMORAH (*TALMUD,* Wm. G.) I got scared. For I was afraid, God forbid, to lose my job, although my friend encouraged me and assured me that everything, with God's help, will be good. I felt that I was well off and felt that I am healthy from the fresh air and everything which was dear to my heart.

Thus, a year passed where I was, and I had almost everything. I spent the time with many fine people. They treated me as their own children. And the fresh air and the forests made me feel that they did me a lot of good. The only thing I was afraid of was that the children will have to learn after Passover, RASHI and GEMORAH. My friend did not let me think about this. "Everything will be good. We will have to travel to your father for Passover." Why I say travel—to walk by foot. This was my greatest pleasure to walk through fields. A week before Passover, there was much rainwater filling the rivers and creeks, and it was muddy. I could not get a horse and wagon. So, I went by foot. I had a little bit more strength and indeed had my friend. What did it mean for such young boys to go four times over the big waters and various creeks? To walk alone was too difficult. But with the friend walking home, I didn't feel it. Thus, thanks God, we came home. However, I caught a cold in the waters, and I had to stay in bed on Passover and a couple of weeks after Passover. Thus, I could not go and keep my job, although it was for me so dear. Furthermore, I knew that I can't deceive the good people.

So, my friend went by himself, and I remained at home. I decided to forget traveling and to be away from home in order to be equal to others. They have life, health, and years. I have donated years; how long can I live since my mother donated me her later years? This thought, whenever I began to think, was the only one that came to my mind. This was my only thought, such a weakness. This ruined the best and young years. But my low courage I did not lose. As soon as I recuperated a little bit, I again had some children (*pupils,* Wm. G.) in town to teach to write. Thus, I continued to have for myself (*i.e., to earn,* Wm. G.) and was busy all days. The rest of my time, in the evenings, when I had time, I used to go to Abe. who was at least eight years older than me. with his younger brother my age. We became friends. Thus, I had the opportunity to get acquainted with him. He used to write PROSHENIES (*entreaties to a local or central government office,* Wm. G.) or various official letters. Here I had the opportunity to spend my evenings, eat together and sleep. Their father was still alive. At that time, nothing was lacking for me. I came in contact with all kinds of people, I had an income, was well dressed as the biggest (*i.e., the richest,* Wm. G.). The years were running; after all, this was not an occupation for me. Something was urging me. My heart was telling me that there is a big and beautiful world with great people with judgment in life. But I didn't have the courage. When I used to tell it to my father, he became angry at me and blame me for his whole life, and this was painful for me. Actually, he was right. It was very sad for him to be without my mother, to earn a living, K'AYN HORE, for such a family.

In America, the children help if they are good: if not for the parents, at least for themselves. In the old country, one had to marry off his children and give a dowry. Here in this country, the children marry off themselves. Now you can understand how terribly my father suffered. People did not understand it could be different. My father was not the only one. I understood it very well, but I could not help myself. With my thoughts, I wanted to accomplish a lot, the result was that I didn't do anything; I remained satisfied (*interesting is here his conception about the process of marriages here and in the old country. Apparently, his children married off themselves and generally did not become a burden, at least too much to the parents.* Wm. G.).

Thus, I became twenty years of age: looked at life, and wanted to live. I had a heart and felt as all boys of my age. Our town was small (*in original SHTETL,* Wm. G.) and possessed everything; forests and rivers and fruit gardens. In the evenings of the summer, particularly on Saturdays and Holidays, youth were strolling. But nobody dared, actually was afraid that if he would be seen, his parents would be told. This was so. If one loved, it was only with his eyes and also with his heart. Not like here in this golden land (*a critical observation,* Wm. G.). I am not inclined to express too much of my opinion whether in the old country was better or here is better. But this is true, especially if one was not in love like me. Perhaps the rich who had everything. Thus, came the time when I reached the age of twenty-one and to be drafted into the army as everyone who reaches the age of twenty-one in my time. As you had to appear for military conscription, the healthy boys would not eat so much, not drink, not to sleep at night two or three months before in order not to be drafted. Many impaired their eyes and did whatever they could do. It was exactly I who wanted to be drafted. You will ask why, so I will explain to you: because I was a weak man. I was afraid (*that I will not be drafted,* Wm. G.). I concluded that those returning from service are handsome and healthy. The weakest came home healthy. Hence, I wanted very much to be taken as a soldier, but I didn't have the luck, they didn't want me. For the first time, they gave me a green ticket (*indicating to be called again,* Wm. G.). The second time they let me free with a blue ticket. My father was very happy that they let me free, got free from "FONYEN" (*the nickname Jews used to call the Russians, a cryptonym for Russia,* Wm. G.). But I, myself, was not satisfied, for they don't let free healthy men hence I am a sick man. So, I was very upset. I wanted to go in military service for two reasons; first, I would

The Inheritance (Yurusha)

become healthy, and second, I would see the world and indeed would learn a lot.

Thus, I remained in our small town and was continuously upset. But my father was most happy. It was not a small thing. It costs other fathers a lot of money (*i.e., bribery,* Wm. G.) to get their child free, and here I had a blue ticket without a cent. Hence, I am free with a blue ticket. If you know a boy who was freed with a ticket in the old country, it became very important. They wanted to buy him (*i.e., to marry him,* Wm. G.) and give a dowry and clothing and KEST (*room and board, keep especially that is offered by a family to its new son-in-law to enable him to continue his studies, usually at a Yeshiva, without financial worries,* Wm. G.). The one who returned from service was not paid so much. Thus, indeed, my father was proud of me. It was not a small thing – a blue ticket. As a boy, I could not serve as an example. I could cheat as when I pretended to be the teacher. Still, now, it is all I can say in my older years.

Part Two
Marriage – Divorce – Love – Family

In the first week after being freed by my blue ticket, they began to get for me brides. There was a time when the parents decided without money (*i.e., dowry,* Wm. G.), my father did not even want to talk. He did not care whether I liked the girl or not. This was the way of the parents at that time. They suggested a girl three miles away from our town with six-hundred-ruble dowry and four years KEST. This meant a lot. When I went with my father to look (*the term "look" is closer to the Yiddish original than "see,"* Wm. G.), everything pleased me—the parents, the sisters, the brothers who were there. Their house was almost the most beautiful in town but not the bride. My father asked me my opinion, to which I answered him, "I am pleased with everything but not with the girl." So, he became angry and said, "Look where you are coming in, in richness. They will make from you a respectable person. You are so poor and sick. You need to have such a house. The love will come later after the marriage." Yet I was displeased. First, she was ugly, second, her way of talking one could not understand. That is, she was not to my liking as one which I hoped to find, although I did consider myself not important, that I am not even worthy of those (*i.e., the girl he went to see,* Wm. G.). But my soul desired and liked people with whom you could converse, also to learn something. I liked to learn even from the smallest child who said something important even until this day. I like to hear from those who understand. I answered my father. "No, father, I can't be connected with such (*people,* Wm. G.), who I don't like." My father was displeased with my answer. His answer was, "Of what are you so proud, you are poor and naked (*i.e., poor in clothing,* Wm. G.), you are also sick. And here you can get lucky—not a usual thing—six-hundred-ruble dowry with a heritage and KEST and clothing." But I did not want to hear. We went home. There were plenty of girls in the old country. A boy who had a ticket had not to care (*about a bride,* Wm. G.).

I saw many girls, poor and rich. The first were after me every day—my own father and the whole family almost forced me. I was displeased because of my poverty, scared of further suffering, and became engaged for the good fortune, rather for the misfortune. And in fact, it changed a lot, but here I would have to describe much of my writing. So, I will make it short. How I did not want to get married later, although I was also engaged. I wanted to send back the engagement contract (*T'NOYIM*). My father said that this is not the way to do it; better to get divorced after the wedding than to disrupt the engagement. I have attempted to go to her several times to get to know her better. Perhaps she has good virtues, the main thing is not a pretty face, but I could not find anything; not a conversation, a word of writing or reading… only a healthy body that's all. So were the parents very rich. When I came home, again the same, I don't want to get married. Now I thought I want to get far away from home; thus, nothing will come from this SHIDUKH (*an arranged marriage,* Wm. G.). I went to BERDICHEV, which was very far from us. Now why should I get married? So, I really took upon myself to be NAVENAD homeless, wandering. If at least I could get some work, it would not bother me. But I suffered. Actually, I should not have been worried, for I didn't have anything to sell (*in the sense that he didn't have any trade, education and the like qualities to offer,* Wm. G.). You can't work, and you are very poor (*he's talking in the third person and goes on saying,* Wm. G.) you have a bride, what can I lose by coming back and I was very much upset and thought that I will not be wanted any more.

But I had good luck and indeed got married without love. Perhaps love will come after the marriage. To describe what kind of wedding we celebrated, how rich and beautiful and good I am not interested to describe it sufficiently for you. It will suffice for me to write that immediately the first day after the HUPEH (*wedding ceremony,* Wm. G.) I could not look at her, particularly talk to her. I cursed my years (*a popular expression of deprivation,* Wm. G.); this means the years donated to me by my mother. I took it very much to my heart and became sick. I was confined to bed for a couple of weeks. A doctor was called, but a doctor could not do much for me. He could not have for me a medicine which only myself could feel that I needed.... The best for me was to return home; the sooner, the better. As a boy, I didn't have a home, especially now that I am FARISHET (*this term is the author's description of being married and probably is a combination of a Yiddish word and a Hebrew word,* Wm. G.). Now I suffered more, for I was ashamed. But this is the way it was, and I took to my poor occupation. After I regained my stature from the terrible dream, I tried at first to forget about everything. I also tried to figure out how to get free (*from the marriage,* Wm. G.), but there were always friends who liked to make peace in order to have a MITZVAH. They did not let me have my peace, why I don't want to be together with her? After all, why am I so proud and particular? So, I will try in a good way to get free, but how? It will not help me. At the end (*as a way-out,* Wm. G.) I will take the medicine which everyone takes. But taking the medicine made bitter my life and poisoned my whole body for a time. I feel it until today. This medicine, you will excuse me, every human being must take. It is a cure for the human being—for the man as well as for the women—which are in love. Not for those who don't love. It is good to take the medicine which restores health, and it is a cure for him. Nor one which makes sick and makes bitter and has poison. But I could not help myself. I suffered and kept quiet and tried, but I could not get separated. It was very difficult. It came what had to come whether sweet or bitter. Nature does not make any exceptions. It catches and affects you; the bitter medicine quicker than the sweet one... she was with child.

The parents had seen that from now on I will adjust, but not me. I was only thinking of getting free. There would be too much to describe now. I will leave out much for not so quick did it happen as it is being written. I went through a lot. In me remains a memory until today, which you read, with God's help, in my writing. Ordinarily, much will be left out, for it is impossible to describe everything. You need a lot of strength and strong nerves and indeed to be able to transfer everything... (*It seems to me the term "poison" must be referring to the institution of getting married,* Wm. G.). About this I thought, to get the dowry into my hands. How I got them, it is, again, too much to describe, but as I wrote, how to cheat I know until today. So, I cheat the people with the world together. But I don't want to stray away from my road, not to hurry, to go straight, and I wrote that if they don't free me to get divorced, I will go away to America. I didn't take, and I returned everything, the money, the clothing, and we got divorced, and I wrote that the child, the girl belongs to me when she gets older. I became free. At that time, I began to think differently about myself and about my life, that I don't need to get married again. After all, who will be willing to take care of me? Prior to this, when I was a bachelor, it was different. Now I am a young man. I began forgetting about everything as everything was a dream for me, a bad one but a dream. I used to daydream with myself. For here in America, such a person as I would never get married again. But not in the old country, years ago. This way I lived.... I came in company with various people, indeed bigger (*in the sense of more learned,* Wm. G.), who knew much more than me, and thanks God, I learned from them.

However, in spite of the fact that I was incapable to do anything, they did not cease to talk me into getting married. Yes, here I must stop to write about the young men (*i.e., the boys,* Wm. G.) who were called to service together with me. They served all the years, and coming from rich parents, they got married to rich girls. They had all right, everything. But almost all of them died after they got married, some even before the wedding. Do you know why? They got involved in all kinds of drinking and wild behavior. Nobody remained. I, the feeble and weak, went through everything; I got married and divorced and endured pains, but I felt good. So, I grew myself stronger, in spite of the words from my father, sisters, and brothers; words and talk that I have donated years.

I finally began to laugh and became convinced that I am healthy and strong and forgot my weakness. My aim was to begin a new life. I will try to sweeten my life. I love the beautiful world and people. I did not let myself down, got stronger, had more confidence, and went forward. How did I feel not having one good day from the cradle onwards? I looked far ahead, full with love, and tried to make even the worst (*i.e., adjust to the situation,* Wm. G.) for the best. Indeed, I had many suggestions to get married, girls but mainly married women (*widowed or divorced,* Wm. G.). But I already took time and didn't look for money or for a beautiful house or nice in-laws. Of course, I wanted all of this, but what I looked for mainly was love. I should love her, and she should love me. If one looks, he will find it. 90 percent, not?

I already used to travel to the small towns. I had an opportunity to meet many girls and families. I needed company. So, I traveled to a SHTETL, a few miles from ours and stayed in a tavern (inn). There I met a young girl and a beautiful one with all virtues. From my conversation with her, I got informed that she got married at the same time as me and also without love. Her parents wanted it. He was learned (*in the text "he could learn" which in colloquial language meant that he was versed in Judaic studies as the Bible, perhaps Talmud and similar subjects or also in secular studies,* Wm. G.) and write and he had money. But she did not live with him even one day, and she got divorced. She was also forced to marry by her parents. This girl, my present wife, she should be in good health, was much to my liking. Also, the parents and sisters and brothers and the house was still more beautiful than the one I saw before. In short, everything is okay, and I thought here would be good for me. The main thing that I should be welcomed.

In the same tavern lodged with me a man from my SHTETL who was a matchmaker. He began to REDN (*i.e., REDN-to talk up SHIDICHIM looking for brides,* Wm. G.). He took me around to take a look at some girls. They were not to my liking. I was only thinking about the girl I met at the tavern. I heard that in previous years, many years ago, her parents were very rich. They held property (*grounds,* Wm. G.) but lost a lot of money when the harvest in the fields was not good and even got burned. All together, these events left them poor. She was the oldest child, and she was twenty-one years old, and I was the youngest of my father's children. So, I thought for myself, even if they don't give me a cent dowry, I will take this girl. So, she was to my liking. This could be called love and was what I was looking for. Usually, I didn't say anything, I kept everything for myself. I was there one night and one day.

I went home and thinking only about her. I was to her liking too. Do you know why? I don't! But this is the way it was. I must write the truth as I look upon myself. Write about myself and about all those that I mention (*remember,* Wm. G.) now and will mention further.

The first question to be asked is if you have decent parents, whether you come from a respected family, which in the old country was called LAYTISH (*respectable,* Wm. G.), turns out to be today not so important. However, that is the way it was in those days in the old country. Everyone wanted to be equal (*i.e., in society,* Wm. G.). When I came home and told my father, sisters, and brothers that in LONIVITS at ELIEZER KATZ (*the owner of the tavern/inn and her father*), I saw a young woman of twenty-one years, who all together lived with her husband a couple of days, there. If they would like me, I would be satisfied without money. I will send a matchmaker. This is the way I am thinking. Traveling there about my business is a secondary matter, it does not mean much... my trip will only be because of her. It so happened that I met a man from the same SHTETL who says that he was sent from the house where I lodged, that they all like me. If their daughter is to my liking, then they want me for as a HOSN (*bridegroom,* Wm. G.), and they will give me dowry and KEST, everything what I want. How happy I was feeling and thought that even if they give a hundred rubles, I would be satisfied. This would encourage me very much.

I reached the day when a fair had to take place in town. I wanted to stay in the same house and get better acquainted and be able to talk to her. And so, it was, I came, already not as a stranger. We were talking and spent some time. I was very happy. They proposed to me some girls from the same city, but I was thinking only about her. I didn't want to know about any other. I was under the impression that I am fooling them (*i.e., considering himself as not worthy of the girl,* Wm. G.). They thought that they were fooling me. They promised me NADN (*dowry,* Wm. G.), while they don't have it to give to me. Such was my luck, I was thinking, here you have all the good before I show up. When I came, everything came to an end. My father was rich before I came into this world, but he became poor. It is the same here, and so it was going on, which I will, with God's help, prove in my further writings.

I am, God forbid, afraid that this is the way it is going to be. But after me, it will come the best, but I am satisfied. I am not worthy of even this. The end was that we both fooled each other, but not me. I am satisfied still today. Perhaps, not she. She has to be asked; she herself will answer. When I was in the house, there were a few merchants from my town. Very fine, pleasant people. They were asked about me. They could not say anything wrong, but also not anything good. Each one of them knew me. Everyone could see me many times as a little boy, and not too much could be said about me. But I knew myself very well and know until today. But who will humiliate himself? So, I will not elaborate on this too much, although it is very interesting in life (*of a person,* Wm. G.). I didn't ask anybody, even my father. Her father came to us in order to get acquainted with my father and family. My father approved of my engagement. Yes, everything is good to which he is skilled. In the old country, they didn't ask about a queen (*i.e., about the pedigree,* Wm. G.), but they asked about the grandfather—if he was of a respected lineage. That is all that was required.

Nevertheless, I know the two fathers were asking for what is he fit and for what will he be fit after the wedding. After all, you have to make a living. My father's answer was amazing. "He knows how to make good KVITLEKH and to rewrite PROSHENYES, and he can sell VIGRISHE (*tickets*). The main thing, you will excuse me, he is fit for children both producing and teaching, which is a great profession. How many couples are getting divorced because of not having children? They are turning to GUTE YIDN (*i.e., ultra-orthodox extremely pious REBES who prayed for childless women,* Wm. G.) and to doctors. But my youngest (*in original MUZINIK,* Wm. G.) he is all right, although he didn't love his wife, he fathered a daughter. Nevertheless, today, especially since he is in love"... They wrote the engagement contract and they promised to give me a few hundred dollars (*rubles,* Wm. G.) dowry, and the SHIDUKH (*the match*) was concluded. As far as I was concerned, I was happy with a lot of hope. The wedding was set all together at two months. She has everything, only I needed clothing. There came the time at which they had to give me the couple of hundred dollars (*rubles,* Wm. G.) dowry. I understood that they will give it, but they did not. I agreed to everything. For them, it was pleasant. I knew that I didn't deceive them, neither they me. There is much more to describe, but I must go on as things were going on in reality... and so I will try until the end in order that I should not appear disguised. My mask should be taken off, not to take it with me into the grave as others do. This is my obligation, for I owe much to my family as well as to strangers (*others,* Wm. G.).

I got married the second time, although my first marriage was with music and was greeted with honors and riches, this one took place in a quiet way. I was a young man, and she was a married woman. She was twenty-one years, I was twenty-four, but joy was in our hearts, thanks God, until today. The fact that we are old people, but not with all can the sinful human being be happy and satisfied with his life. Although I went through much, and also now I am going through, yet I can't express my feelings, how I was feeling after my second marriage. It sweetened my life. I forgot about everything from before, I got courage in life. I loved my wife very much; I loved my father-in-law and mother-in-law and all their children. With one word (*in short,* Wm. G.), everything. It is, therefore, to be understood that not just from love came a child; especially if one is in love which was still known in the old country. Here in America, they try to make a decent living first, fix up a home, and other good things before they have a child. If you have everything, then you can afford to have a child, but indeed only a child. If two, it is already an exception. One does not feel the pleasure of a large family. But in the old country, they didn't know what they know here. Perhaps some didn't want or didn't know what is known today.

I must record here what happened in our SHTETL. An episode, which I remember when I was a boy. A couple got married; very young and were on KEST as it was the custom, and the love was great. So, she had every year a child, six years KEST, and they had six children. The parents had to support them with the children, but in the end, what are going to be the results, what could be done back then fifty-five years ago? Here is the mother, but at home is the love so great... a healthy couple from a healthy home (*the author used the Russian term ZAVOD, i.e., a factory enterprise it means from financially healthy parents,* Wm. G.). Do you know what? It was decided by the parents, with the approval of the couple, that about a yearlong, they should be separate, not to sleep together, rather in one HEYDER (*the author used the Hebrew term to indicate "room,"* Wm. G.). And they endured it.

After a year, it was a pity to look at them. I don't, God forbid, exaggerate. So it was. But when the year passed, to the day, here I don't need to describe the first thing that a Jewish daughter does when the husband comes home from a long journey? So also, they from a year being at home and not being together, so God helped and how, with a pair, a girl and a boy. Now you understand. The parents finally saw that it does not help. Thus, they had, K'AYN HORE, twelve children. He could not make a living until God helped and a few children grew up, and they came to America, and they brought over the parents with the whole family. Here the children were working and brought the mother PAYDE (*a strong expression in Eastern Europe for pay,* Wm. G.) every week. And the father used also to earn by teaching children, and he was very well off. Many of his children had already children (*of their own,* Wm. G.) and lived in a beautiful house, K'AYN HORE, healthy persons at the old age and healthy children. When I came to America, he was already a long time here. I used to come to him to borrow money which he used to give me (*in original he uses the Hebrew term G'MILES HESED a loan without interest,* Wm. G.). But he used to attach a condition that I should return the amount of the loan in gold coins. And this is the way it was. He had a large safe where he put the money; very rich now. Not one time he used to remind me of the episode. I could write and write about this man. He and she died a few years ago in an old age and left the money to the children and children's children.

Now back to my life after my second marriage. Time was not at a standstill, and I didn't make a living yet. I didn't do anything. I didn't have with what to do business (*the author uses the Hebrew word MISHER,* Wm. G.) one needs money. I didn't have a trade either. But there was love. I want to make it short. She gave me a boy, (*in America, his name is Max,* ER) a very beautiful child who made our life sweeter. But to all these pleasures, it is good to have PARNOSE (*livelihood,* Wm. G.). This was very much lacking, and this is the main thing in this country, PARNOSE. As I have already mentioned several times, my father-in-law was once well-to-do, but not now when I am here. He promised me a couple hundred rubbles and actually wanted to give me more than he promised. He did not have anything, and he didn't possess anything. We were together, lived together, and suffered together. Even with money, I didn't know about MISHER (*business*), let alone without money... I could not take it. They were very good to me, to everybody. I, therefore, suffered a lot, and also my wife, and we kept quiet.

Here I would like to mention that my brothers and sisters were all storekeepers. So, I wanted to be a storekeeper, but regrettably, I didn't have with what. Here one helps the other but not in the old country. Perhaps yes, there were other families who did help each other but not mine. I was punished with such a family. But here, I would have to write much about each family individually. Almost half of them are already in the true world (*the author uses the Hebrew term EMESER,* Wm. G.). I could not help myself and didn't have anybody who could help me. Therefore, I took to poor business where my father-in-law was acquainted in a big village five or six miles away. We considered a mile a VIORST (*Russian measure,* Wm. G.) about six VIORSTS from our SHTETL. There I used to go to buy grain or anything that I could buy with money from a couple of mills. I used to take in advance from a merchant, and this way, I used to do business as a middleman as a broker.

The whole world was open for me. The whole week I used to spend in the village and come home Friday morning for the SHABES, which is impossible for me to describe; to see my wife and child and everyone. The whole world belonged to me. I loved very much my wife and child. I got involved in MISHER (*business,* Wm. G.) very diligently, and I showed my abilities. God used to help me. Other young men who got married at the same time envied me. I without money made better than they with money. So, I lived very satisfied, it encouraged me very much. Also, my father-in-law liked to live so, nice and clean (*in the moral and ethical sense,* Wm. G.). They never recognized that we live (*i.e., that we operate our business,* Wm. G.) without money. The finest merchants from the surrounding SHTETLIKH (*towns and villages*) used to come to our house. I used to pity my father-in-law. He was once very rich, he had everything, but the wheel turned over. In the small town, when you turn from rich to poor, one feels completely fallen (*lost his socio-economic position in society,* Wm. G.), his credit was cut off, but as a young man, I could get credit. So, I used to do business and help him out, and we both together made a very poor life. But for others, our life looked very rich. We suffered but kept silent.

So, this was the way our happy time was going on week by week. Who knew about something better as long as I made an account of my assets? Nothing for me and nothing for you (*a way of thinking of the average not wealthy Jew in the SHTETL who was satisfied with the minimum existence,* Wm. G.). I was the happiest man in the world. And so, until now, when I write these words. For I don't have money now either, and so I am now also satisfied. From this happy time came, thanks God, a child, a girl (*RIFKA, Reba when she was in America,* ER). Again, happiness and hope for the better. I tried out various businesses, but I never had much luck. Everything that came out from under my hands with small profits went over to the other. He made it better, for I could not keep up with my few dollars (*rubles,* Wm. G.) the other's property and I knew… if grain was profitable on the market, I bought grain, if there were other products, so I bought them. Indeed, everything what my eyes saw, I tried. For a long time, people used to come to me that I should go in partnership with them, I refused. I used to explain to everybody and teach them how to conduct business.

Thus, everyone liked me in the old home. I never used, God forbid, to offer more than the other, not to spoil the other as it was the custom. Only to look for my PARNOSE like a bird for the grain; far, far, not to outbid and take away from the other. Thus, I used to be, thanks God, until today, even here in America, what I am doing. Nobody can say that I am doing wrong to the other. Morals and ethics are the most important things. I praise God with songs as the bird sings, and it is not being understood, so am I. There are many who don't understand me, that I come not from those who call themselves MENSHN (*decent people,* Wm. G.) and talk like people (*a critical remark of people, I would say snobs,* Wm. G.), but when I begin to talk with my singing, they don't understand me. Not one time I am getting FARDINST (*literarily earnings, but in folks tongue, it also meant to be bothered, beaten up. I assume that on the roads to the villages, the author was attacked by village boys: my second thought is that the author might have encountered difficulties from his business competitors. Both of my theories might clear up in further reading.* Wm. G.). I thank God that I am getting unhurt with my poor belongings and my FEYRDELKH (*small horse,* Wm. G.). How many times I remained naked, hardly got away with my life. It took a long time until it grew back (*i.e., until he came back to normal,* Wm. G.). But I used to be able to forget. You will read in my further and last chapters, actually in my writing, you will, with God's help, find out everything correctly. I, therefore, adopted as my friend, my equal, this feeble and poor bird.

Time was running, more, K'AYEN HORE, was needed. We lived fine as human beings need to live, not just for oneself. At home (*i.e., in the old country*), they used to respect a good Jew (*in colloquial language, to respect a good, decent, pious Jew,* Wm. G.) and give him a ruble. Interest from money was also an expense. In the old country, they used to give a good interest. I was not a great hero, as I mentioned in the beginning of my writing, but what I went through, the greatest hero would not be able to accomplish. I was very strong in my mood, and I used to do everything openly. And God indeed helped me at all times. The years were sweet for me. Every time came a new child. Equally came various situations, which I didn't want to suffer (*to endure,* Wm. G.), but I could not help myself. Others used to seek their luck in the bigger cities or to emigrate to America. I used to go to the village and be there usually for a whole week. I could not eat the thick food and have a good place to sleep.

The Christians (*i.e., the peasantry,* Wm. G.) from the village had a good opinion about me. They told me to move with my family to the village, then everything would be better for me. I knew this, but what to do? As it is, I enjoy life when I come home for the SHABES and see people. Equally, my wife and children, how will they be without her parents? In addition to this, it was restricted (*for a Jew,* Wm. G.) to reside in the village. The old ones (*Jews,* Wm. G.) who lived there for a long time were not allowed, let alone a new one (*the author refers here to a restriction for Jews to live in the villages. This was mainly applied in the Ukraine, where the density of the Jewish population was well known. Jews were, in addition to the big cities as KIEV, BERDICHEV, KHARKOV and others, living in the Pale of Settlements of which the main element were the SHTETLEKH,* Wm. G.). They (*the peasants,* Wm. G.) promised me that they will see that everything should be in order. And I did it. It is not being done as quickly as it is being written. I had to go through plenty, but I didn't stop.

We moved to the village and left the SHTETL, not far, altogether about five or six miles away. There they knew me. From the little that I had, I bought everything, and that I had grocery products; we made, thanks God, a poor life. When the SHABES came, we used to cry very bitterly, but what could we do? The PARNOSE got better. I bought a beautiful horse and wagon. We used to come to the SHTETL as important people, tenant farmers and received more credit and the feeling (*i.e., mood,* Wm. G.) was better. My father-in-law and mother-in-law and the children used to come to us. A year later, we showed up more in the village. Prior to this, we were afraid to show up. In the center of the village was the Inn. Everyone already knew about us. It used to cost me (*i.e., bribery,* Wm. G.) a couple of rubles for the chief of police and the village clerk. So, it was in Russia with money and again money. Thus, we were settled for three years. Later came a manifesto that whoever resides beginning that year receives PRAVOZHITELSTVO (*i.e., the right to reside,* Wm. G.).

And we really received it and were not afraid (*apparently, the author refers here to the trends of liberalization—although still very much limited—building up to and after the abortive Russian revolution of 1905,* Wm. G.), and we were happy. We already had four children (*MORECHAI, RIFKA, BLUMA and HAYKE*), K'AYN HORE. Some needed already to learn, and it was unpleasant to remain among the GOYIM. What else could we do? PARNOSE was not an easy matter. My hopes were for something better in life. I was hoping to stay a couple of years more and save a few hundred dollars (*rubles,* Wm. G.) and move back to the city and take up something else. But, instead, again to travel day by day from the town to the village and back, it is rather better to live in the village. The RIBONO SHEL OYLEM (*The Master of the World,* Wm. G.) listened to our prayers, but in a different way, not as I used to think. There came the war with Japan (*1903/4,* Wm. G.), and great reserves were called. I was not afraid since I had a blue ticket. But in the village, things got worse from day to day. There were robberies and fighting every day. So, I got scared, and I and my family left and went to the town of her parents until the call of the reserves will be over, and I left everything ownerless, only to secure our life. We made a great mistake. A few years later, we returned, they did not let us back in. I didn't want to argue with them. We didn't want, in fact, we could not, and to rent another house we didn't want. So, I thought that this is God's will. Perhaps it is better so. So, we came back to our SHTETL, but poorer than before. Even the cow, which we possessed for milk for our children, was killed before our eyes.

This is only in writing. It is too much pressure on the little man. With limited comprehension, it is impossible to describe our life and what we went through in the four to five years' time that we spent in the village, especially from the hooligans. Upon our return to the SHTETL, we, as usual, stayed in my father-in-law's house and continued to suffer. I used to explain to my wife that we have seen how many young men of my age were drafted into the war (*army,* Wm. G.) and never came back home until today. No matter how I suffer, I can only get down—not up. And indeed, see much worse than I am, and I see everything is being led by a great powerful God, not from anyone else. If there are such people who don't believe in him, let them not believe. I, God forbid, am not like them now, and I wish to continue so for the future. I see every minute and every hour and every day and every month and every year that we have a dear God even though I suffer so much. When wicked people are doing me wrong, it is really then that I love them. I love the world. I love everything that God created.

My duty of writing is only for myself and for my family. But I also have to mention those few with whom I came in contact in business and in other connections. For as a little man, I was restless and kept looking and never stopped. If they cheated or deceived either in money or they just did something wrong to me, I was not from those who stayed away not to have anything to do, not to get together with someone. Just the contrary, every time, I learned more about the human being's character.

If somebody did to me something wrong, I tried to do something good to him. This was my way of life. And indeed, therefore I must in my writing (*mention,* Wm. G.) those few whom I used to meet every day and connected with them in business or just (*acquainted,* Wm. G.) despite that some are already in the OYLOM HOEMES (*the true world,* Wm. G.) let them rest there, but I want to keep their memory.

Part Three
Family and Business Life and Suffering in the Old Country

At the same time that I got married the second time, my father-in-law's brother also got married. He came back from service, served four years for FONYE (*a cryptonym among Jews in Russia for the Russian Empire, i.e., Tsar, government, army, etc.,* Wm. G.). He came home healthy and had money that his parents left for him as an inheritance. He also took dowry as was the custom at that time. After the wedding, we used to travel for trade into the same village, indeed into the very same one to which I used to travel and live. I used to borrow money or take an advance, but I paid interest for borrowing or to give my merchandise for less. To hold out, as it was the custom, I could not.

He, blessed should be his memory, accomplished (*his aim,* Wm. G.) and kept the grain, and did good business. His hand was larger than my whole body. I could not lift a bushel of grain as he did, only with strain to carry as he did. Not one time it used to affect my health which I never had. I, therefore, wound up in bed to recuperate. He was blessed with everything—with health, with money, and especially with luck. He did the greatest business with the GOYIM. I also did business, but I was weaker, shorter, and poorer. He used to come to the village every day and every day return home. I, no. I used to be two days or even a whole week. He used to come to the village during the winter dressed in sheepskin fur with one gray sleeve and the other black, and he looked worse than the worst beggar. At the same time, his horse and wagon were also that of the poorest kind of person. Also, at home, he lived in a house inherited from his father, which was fixed up as if he was the poorest Jew in the SHTETL. Otherwise, he was very wise and not a tough guy. But his character is impossible to describe. I realize that I do not have to write about his accomplishments, especially since he is already in the right world. But I must, it will fit into my writing, he is my example, he should forgive me. We usually met all the time, almost every day, in the village. He used to smoke a lot but never took his own. He was afraid that he will have to give some to a fellow Jew or to a GOY, LEHAVDL (*he made a distinction in this case between a Jew and a Goy,* Wm. G.). Thus, he used to get from the GOYIM plain tobacco.

I was entirely different. When I began to travel to the village, first, I bought the best horse and wagon and made for myself a good and nice sheepskin fur and had with me the best cigarettes. I had prepared this for myself and for everyone who will ask. If I did not have sufficient (*cigarettes,* Wm. G.), it was for me worse than not to have bread. To smoke tobacco, who could do this? I already wrote several times before that to cheat, I could do, and nobody would know, but I could not deceive myself, for I knew myself very well. I did business not to go around idle, but I could not live this way. I used to suffer because of this, but I could not do otherwise. I used, very often, to envy because of this. If one has money only to live as I, it is not good but to live like he used to live, with money, I certainly couldn't. Not necessarily just he, for there were many like him. Thus, we were traveling, and we used to meet each other several times during the day. When I used to travel to the village in the morning, I used to meet on the road many GOYIM traveling with bundles of grain. When I used to ask them, "Where are you going?" they answered me, "To DAVID KATZ." Already sold; I didn't want to envy, but one is only a human being and not an angel. I used to think that we have a good God; he gives to one too much what he actually does not need; the more he has, the worse he gets. I would like to live (*i.e., to make a living,* Wm. G.). This is the way I live. It is hard for me my life, but I live a modest and decent life.

But what is the result of all this? We suffer too much, and I immediately began to think otherwise. I am satisfied with my life. Only good health for all of us. So, I kept traveling. Hence, I am richer than he is and many more like him. Yes, when I used to come, we used to meet each other. Sometimes in the morning, sometimes during the day, and quite often after having bought some grain or something else. For I used to buy everything that came to my attention. I used to enjoy myself until the evening. God is a father, and I traveled or walked in the village only thinking about good and being satisfied. When he met me, the first question was, "What is new? Did you already have a PETSHATEK?" (*A Slavic expression for a first business deal*, Wm. G.) And as the custom was, my answer was thanks God for this. He then would look at me as if he had an even worse opinion than you can imagine. It was as if I were naked in his eyes, and I should have taken the purse out of my pocket to prove to him my worth, and then he would say, "Give me a cigarette so I can smoke. Let my wife at home not worry. I never denied anything to her when I had something in my pocket." And thus, often that he would complain, and I would listen and see how worried he was. Not one time I thought, what is wrong with this man? I didn't want to ask him. I didn't want to go too much into conversation with him. Let it be this way. Perhaps it must be so, not otherwise. If all people would be so, the world would not be able to exist. I only prayed to God he should predestine my purchases, so I would not encounter him.

I looked for any way to feed my seeds (*i.e., his family,* Wm. G.). As I have already mentioned, I learned from this poor bird and praised, first of all, God. But it sometimes happened that I did not follow my good intentions and went to his GOY, the one who wanted to sell to me but that my uncle should not find out. It was usually my bad luck that he would show up, one should not have envied me. My situation was already in his hands. I could never stand up to him. So he was healthy and strong and also in money. Thus, I used to try to avoid him and looked for my PARNOSE not to encounter his customers. The more I tried to avoid him, the more he met me. I didn't want to argue with him. After all, he is an uncle, but I couldn't hold it in me anymore. One time he came over to me as usual and, as always, began first with a cigar. I wanted to avoid him this time, and he began to talk, "You are all right. You already have a few sacks with grain…" that he didn't have yet a PETSHATEK (*the first deal,* Wm. G.). I was really angry. I said, "I can only tell you that you are an UM-MENTSH (*a person of indecent behavior,* Wm. G.). You were born a sinner and cause other people to sin. You don't want to live, and you don't afford it to others. That's all, please leave me alone. I want to be joyful. Nothing, God forbid, is lacking to me. Only health for my whole family. And what about the grain which I encountered on the road driving to you yesterday and this morning, the GOYIM STAKA and NAVA? This is nothing?" "If so," he answers me, "you don't understand business MISHER. The grain which they were carrying was paid long ago," and he laughed at me. "I consider only what I buy today, for I saw with whom I am dealing." And I answered him, "Now I understand you, uncle!"

I used almost to avoid him, not to get together. He, however, had me in mind, in the village, in the shtetl to talk much more and make fun how I conduct myself. But he got richer every day. In the shtetl, he was considered a rich man. I used to think, according to his life (*style,* Wm. G.), he should have a couple of thousand rubles. I and my father-in-law got poorer every day. We could not lower ourselves. I stopped to travel to the village, for everyone was in debt to him. And furthermore, as I mentioned before, I could not come back where I once lived... it became troublesome for me. So, I looked in town for various business opportunities. I did everything, it was not easy.

I dealt in eggs and delivered them myself to VALITSHIK (*a name of a town,* Wm. G.). I borrowed money and paid a big interest. At that time, the good uncle also traveled less. He began to feel weaker. He used to give payment in advance, so they brought (*the goods,* Wm. G.) home. I used to be at peace with him. I never asked him for a favor, for I knew what would happen if I had. And this was true about someone who asked and approached him, someone who was close to him to lend him a GMILUS-HESED, a loan. Then he (*the author's uncle,* Wm. G.) took out his purse from the pocket and showed him: "See, I have money, but my heart does not let me to lend you." The same way my father-in-law, his older brother, once came to him on the eve of PESACH to ask for a loan of ten rubles for he didn't have anything to prepare for PESACH. He (*the father-in-law,* Wm. G.) could not go to a stranger. He is the prominent BALEBOS (*proprietor, owner; in our case, however, it should be interpreted as the prominent member of the Jewish community, but the author used it in a sarcastic implication,* Wm. G.) in the shtetl. He didn't want to lend him unless he will bring him as a pawn the silver spoons, forks and knives. "How come, brother, you know how PESACH is being observed in my home, and you want to insult my table (*i.e., the holiday,* Wm. G.), and my wife and my children. "So, bring me another pawn." I remember that he (*the author's father-in-law,* Wm. G.) had a good wagon from the old times when he had a horse, so he drove it to him. It is much to write. One could write a book only of this single man's life. So about him and so about his wife. But do you know what their end was and what happened to this man? To my deep regret, he was my uncle, and I don't have the power to describe. He is probably already thirty years in the right world (*dead,* Wm. G.). I only write what I need in order that people should know how to live, not to be foolish, although he thought he was smarter than anyone else. It should be remembered that the other person is also a MENTSH. The one who does not know whether or not he knows too much and with insufficient knowledge is being punished good.

And so, the end of the story from their being so stingy and hard work of so many years, was that his wife began to be sick and had to stay in bed a year's time, and she died. She left two children, a boy and a girl, also spoiled by this, they didn't afford them to eat enough, or just didn't allow them to live, and she died at a young age. I thought that he would reconsider his way of life. They proposed to him decent SHIDUKHIM (*matchmaking*). After all, he was a big merchant, genteel and rich man. So many (*women*) wanted him, but he was afraid that he might take somebody who would like him to conduct his life differently. So, he took his wife's sister, who also lived in the same way. I will make it short, it didn't take long, he lived with her all together two years and became sick, and he was in bed a couple of months. I must say the truth, all the time we didn't visit him. My father-in-law was estranged (*in text far,* Wm. G.), let alone me. He called for us, his brother and me. When we came to him, we saw that he is very sick, and he begged us to save him. But to see that money should not go away (*i.e., that too much should not be spent,* Wm. G.). But we saw that money will not help for the doctors said that his lungs are burned from smoking too much of a low-quality tobacco and similar things which were not allowed (*permitted*) to him, which took away from his life.

When he saw that he was dying, he was yelling to his brother not to spare his money and save him. But it was too late, and he died at a young age. He didn't live, not for himself and not for nobody. Perhaps you may think that he left a lot of money, so I can tell you that. In whole, his possessions were twelve to fifteen hundred rubles and this not in cash only among what the GOYIM owed. He left a broken home (*i.e., dilapidated,* Wm. G.), which had a value of 200 rubles, a broken bed for 50 cents (*the author valued in American currency,* Wm. G.) and a horse and wagon perhaps worth 10 rubles and two sick children; a boy, a cripple. The way this man could have lived, a man, a healthy one and a rich one who was learned (*i.e., versed in general terms, in scripture,* Wm. G.) and could write and especially that he was a wise man. He could live, and his family could live, and could help a brother and a stranger. When he died, I had a pain in my heart (*a popular Jewish expression for sorrow,* Wm. G.) for I already understood life and wanted to live. I felt equally for my father-in-law. His brother was a man who killed (*i.e., did a lot of harm,* Wm. G.) himself and also his family. This episode of my father-in-law's life, I will never forget.

Perhaps I think, not one time, it is possible that if I would have money, I would perhaps be the same. Since I am always alert and watchful to the surroundings and situation, I have learned to think differently. But as you have read and seen, I strain for my life since my young years. As a weak and poor person, I still want to live and provide a life for my family. And it is strange after what happened to my uncle and his family that I began to think in terms as I thought that one should not envy the other. Only try to do your best. It will, with God's help, come. You will go through this world with difficulties, but this will bring you life (*i.e., experience,* Wm. G.). The more you will go through, the more you will understand. If you don't understand anything, you will always look for more. Look, you foolish human being, you are weak and poor. And the other one was a giant, and everything was against you. And in the end, look!

I opened indeed my eyes, first of all to the RIBONO SHEL OLAM (*Master of the World,* Wm. G.) and saw how he leads the sinful man and, thanks God, my beloved father-in-law lives until today (*or until this day,* Wm. G.) with the mother-in-law together with the children in

The Inheritance (Yurusha)

the old country. And, thanks God, we here lived very fine in this world. He, K'AYN HORE, married off children very fine and lived to see grandchildren and great-grandchildren. Let him (*apparently his father-in-law,* Wm. G.) and all live to have a lot of NACHES and luck. We receive letters from the old man written in his own handwriting, thanks God, until this present day. Now I will go over to my own writing of facts about my life. I did everything, not hesitated no matter whether the work was hard or easy for me. Whatever was negotiable, I mean whatever was on the market, I bought. But I must stop on one thing. Whatever I did for myself, I did not have luck. I don't know why. But considering, I knew to give, and I give until the present day. In that, I do have luck, thanks God. For what I possessed, Thanks God, K'AYN HORE, the other one does not possess. Perhaps even if I would have everything, I would, God forbid, forget God, and I would be worse than the other. Why am I privileged with this, after all, I am a little man (*little in the sense of modesty,* Wm. G.). Everything that God gave to me was for me, and it is until today a gift (*the gift is the strong belief in God,* Wm. G.).

Listen to what I call not to have luck. As it is known to you, that I repeated doing, I traded in eggs (*here the author used the Yiddish term EYER and the Hebrew one BAITZIM,* Wm. G.) and would drive with them to VOLOTSHISK (*a town in prewar Czarist Russia,* Wm. G.) packed 150 dozen eggs. I will describe this episode, and it is worthy that you should read and know as I remember until today what happened on that trip to VOLOTSHISK with the 150 dozen eggs. Read and laugh. I made a mistake, not a dozen but a SHOK (*a measure of 60 units,* Wm. G.) consisted of sixty eggs, and I paid for a SHOK, 85 KOP (*a contraction of the monetary unit KOPEYKA in Yiddish KOPIK. One ruble consisted of 100 KOPIKS,* Wm. G.). I packed them and was ready to travel the ten miles from us to VOLOTSHISK.

I used to take with me a man to be for me more joyful to travel and indeed not to be alone in case if something happens, especially in the old country many years ago. As usual, I didn't take money for the trip. You know very well if you look, you find it. Thus, one time came a man whom I knew very well to introduce him to you. He was known to be capable to do everything. He traded in everything, a very wise man. I was very satisfied with him. I will have to whom to talk, especially to spend some time together. It was before ROSH HASHANAH. We started our voyage at sunset, and we were traveling the whole night. While on the road, he chanted for me the prayers for ROSH HASHANAH and YOM KIPPUR. He was very well prepared to be a HAZN. As soon as it became day and light, not far from the town, egg dealers (*or dealers in eggs,* Wm. G.) began to return home. They already sold their eggs. Naturally, I wanted to know the price they obtained. I asked a Jew, or a young man, "What is new, and how is the price? How much did you take, a ruble?" He told me they already were paying a ruble and 5 KOPIKS for a SHOK. I was very delighted. It is not a small thing, a profit of 20 KOPIKS on each SHOK

The man traveling with me stopped singing and began thinking and counting. He turned to me with a question, "R'YISROEL, how much do you have on this wagon?" My answer was the truth, "150 SHOK." "How much did you pay for a SHOK?" But the answer he himself answered. He knew very well the price. "If so, you have 30 rubles earnings, profit." I kept silent. Not good that a stranger figures out and make for me the score. Further on within a couple of VIORSTS (*a Russian measure, 7 VIORSTS was a mile,* Wm. G.) I met another one. I didn't need to ask. He himself asked (*this refers to the author's companion,* Wm. G.) "R'YID or YINGERMAN (*Yiddish for young man,* Wm. G.), how did you sell your eggs, what price did you take?" "I took a ruble and 10 KOPIKS, but as soon as I sold, they already paid 15 KOPIKS more." My cantor was deeply involved in the account and makes me as a rich man. And actually, this is the first time that I should hear about such a price. He says to me, "This is because I am traveling with you! Let it be as it is. God should help you. You are a decent Jew, a good one and respectable one." And he continues to enumerate all my virtues, so I will make it short. I have already counted on the 5 KOPIKS more. My heart began to flow out from me before and now even more as the price increased. I finally reached the town. Whoever met me was calling to me that I am most lucky, and I am a man with a wagon full of eggs being looked at as if exalted? Besides making a lot of money (*i.e., profit,* Wm. G.) that I came B'SHOLEM (*i.e., in good conditions, not harmed by anyone, not robbed and the like,* Wm. G.). I had there an uncle, my father's brother, younger than he. He is also already in the right world (*i.e., Deceased,* Wm. G.), a very fine and wonderful man R'MOSHE LUZER from VISHNEVETS, blessed be his memory. When he noticed me, he was very delighted. I asked my uncle, "How is the price?" "A ruble and 20 or 25 KOPIKS." I became scared. It was not a small thing. I used to earn 3 or 5 KOPIKS on a SHOK. Even if I threw out a couple of SHOKS, not fresh ones, or a little bit broke because of the road, I used to earn 5 rubles, 10 rubles was already a lot. My uncle unpacked (*opened,* Wm. G.) the cover, then I noticed a HASENE (*here is the meaning, a scene, something unexpected used in the colloquial Yiddish,* Wm. G.). The whole top of the eggs was broken, a sum of a couple of SHOKS, which had to be thrown out even if it amounts to a few rubles profit. But at such prices, it will pay the damage. My Jewish passenger had made himself comfortable (*in text, spread out comfortably,* Wm. G.), and when he saw what he had done, did not want to remain anymore. I gave the wagon over to my uncle since I didn't DAVEN (*pray,* Wm. G.) yet. This was not a little thing in our old home. Eating whenever you could, but to DAVEN came first and time to praise God. At that time, I was in a happy mood, comes my uncle and tells me that one horse from my two remained lying (*fell on the ground,* Wm. G.). I already forgot about eating and brought a doctor, and the horse doctor took blood from him. I was in a state of shock, couldn't think straight and finally told my uncle that I will go to the office later, he should have the HESHBON (*bill, accounting,* Wm. G.), and I will receive the money. I worked very hard and cost me a couple of rubles. The end was that the horse didn't get up anymore. In addition, I had TSU ZINGEN UN TSU ZOGN (*a popular expression to describe one's troubles,* Wm. G.) that my horse should be taken away. During that day, I didn't even have water in my mouth.

    Only in the evening I ate something, and I went to sleep, but I could not fall asleep. On my bed, I made an account that, after all, something should remain. And the next day, in the morning, the first thing was to DAVEN, and after that, I went to the office to have an account. You should not ask how many eggs were broken and how many were not good that from all my figuring almost nothing remained for me except that I was worn out. At home, they were already expecting me as for the messiah before they finally lived to see me. For my wife was informed (*in text she took regards in the sense of information,* Wm. G.) what price I obtained. Hence, they began to make plans what to do with so much profit. But my return home took a lot (*of time,* Wm. G.) because I drove with one horse. Also very much upset and so it was understandable that the whole story was unpleasant for me and the whole business.

Now my dears, how do you like my experience, as you say in the American vernacular, the episode which is still located in my bones until this very day? But (*the author asks,* Wm. G.) listen to my further life, rather my efforts in order that I should live. Not for me but for you to go through everything as the little man. The big one, if they want, will write about their life and probably it will be more interesting. One could learn something. But I went through it and made further efforts (*to continue,* Wm. G.) my feeble life against the great world with everything that happened, I remained on my post and tried further. But truly, what was lacking was luck. If not luck, then I don't know what other name to use. Perhaps in my further chapters, I will call it differently.

After the trip, I began to feel that I am working indeed hard, and at the end, I didn't have (*i.e., I didn't earn,* Wm. G.) anything. But if it would be, then it would not be so bad. I began to feel that I am healthy and not, God forbid, sick. That one can get sick from such a life, after all, what will be the end? One gets older, the family should be healthy and with years, gets larger, K'AYN HORE.

I was not a good friend to my father, who kept all his children with him at home, especially I, who always desired and kept my eyes open to go away into the big world, which I used to see every day before and after I came back. Here I began to feel that I am becoming a debtor each time. As long as I had other's money, I didn't care much. But when I experienced that it is getting worse, not better, I had a dilemma. It is true my wife and children were very dear to me, but to leave (*i.e., them,* Wm. G.), I myself was never abroad, but I have to try for my children because I brought them into this world. I began to think much during the day and night about a long journey only to America. But this depends on money. I was in debt in the SHTETL a couple of hundred rubles. I didn't have enough to give back. I had only a horse and a wagon which the value was 65 rubles.

Part Four
My Difficult Journey to America

I used to talk over with my wife about traveling (*i.e., emigrating,* Wm. G.). She didn't want to hear. She didn't have the possibilities to stay with somebody, only what she had where to be. If I would have for myself for the trip, I would try to persuade her. So, I wanted to forget. But in the meantime, I thought about America. I had a sister and a brother and an uncle and nephews there. I wrote to everybody almost all about my situation, that they should rescue me. Some didn't even answer. The one who answered me was a brother. He wrote to me to knock out America from your head. America is not for you, even for a healthier person. He himself is suffering. He can't help me. This way they wrote to me, without any help.

But I didn't lose my mood to emigrate—only to America. To borrow money and to leave without saying keep well, I could not do, although this would be the best. I, God forbid, could not take away from anybody, and this, I think, was my misfortune all the years in everything. Now I understand it. But I can't help myself. My father was already old, but he could not help me. I even had three rich brothers; two lived in the same town as my father. The older one lived ten miles farther, the richest in ZASLAW. But I have to write the truth here; he was very stingy. If one is stingy, he is bad, not so much to others as his own. Perhaps I would also be so, but as a poor man, I was good. Nevertheless, I went first to my older brother, after that, I will speak to my two brothers, but I expected help from the richest and, if not, from them (*with their help,* Wm. G.) I will be able to come to America. And from America, I didn't have any answer.

At the same time, a niece wrote to me that she received SHIFSKARTN (*i.e., travel permits,* Wm. G.) from her husband and also money for the trip and that she should immediately leave. Hence, she went to see me before she leaves. Her husband is my sister's son. I went to her and told her about my situation and how bad it is. If I would only have to travel with something (*i.e., money,* Wm. G.), I could go with her together. A woman by herself with three children, moreover from a village who never in her life traveled outside a small town, let alone a voyage to America, would benefit having someone with them. We talked it over. I spent a few days with her, and it was decided that I will go with her. It was understood to begin to write her husband, my nephew, that I want to travel with his wife and that he should send a SHIFSKARTE. Was this not right? I wrote to him several times before that he should help me. Perhaps if he would know that I want to go with his family, it would be diffcrent. But the answer was not now, only that I should go with them until the port, and there I should remain until they left. When she will arrive B'SHOLEM (*in peace,* Wm. G.) to her husband, she will try that a ticket should be sent to me. Perhaps I would be able to help myself. But I must go with them, then my wife will let me go. But here I must say a lie to my wife and her parents that my nephew sent also a SHIFSKARTE for me that I should go with his family, then everything will come out good. If not, I will not be able to get out so quick. For me, it was very unpleasant to deceive and say that I have a SHIFSKARTE especially since I knew that I didn't have it. I showed such a paper, but it was only related to my niece, and it was decided that they should come to me and that she should say that a ticket was sent for me.

And I went home, but before I went home, I wrote a letter to my nephew, her husband, and also to others. Perhaps he or someone will be able to send me a SHIFSKARTE before we will arrive in ANTWERP in order that I will be able to go with his wife and the children. I wrote to him that since you can't do that, so see to it that your uncle can do it for you, and others will know you did the right thing. I wrote a good letter, and this way, it remained in my thoughts as well as his. It can't be any other way. This is the best plan, to go with them now.

When I came back home, I still had my horse and wagon. My wife asked me what I have accomplished there; with my trip. "You look in a mania in your thoughts. For the time being, you don't have anything in your mind? What will be the end?" Ordinarily, she was right; let alone I by myself, my heart hurt me very much (*i.e., had a lot of guilt and aggravation,* Wm. G.). And to bring it out and tell the truth, I could not, never until this very day. Indeed, if something was good, yes! But to cause someone aggravation, something that no one could help me, I didn't want to bring to anyone. So, I have done all my life, to keep myself happy. At the same time, she (*his wife,* Wm. G.) should learn that my trip was not in vain. I took out from my pocket the envelope. See this is the SHIFKARTE that my nephew sent for me, only that the SHIFSKARTE won't be good. Only when I go together with the family (*the SHIFKARTE will be good,* Wm. G.) will it be of value. When I began to talk about going to America (*she said,* Wm. G.), "You are a weak man, and I, with little children, will remain here alone?" K'AYN HORE there were four children, and the fifth was about to come, as was the style in the old home. One might not be capable of anything, but please excuse me, to have children, we are capable.

I began to comprehend my responsibility, that I don't have the right anymore to conduct such a life. I must try regardless of anything, no matter how hard it would come to me to rescue myself. My father and mother-in-law told her that she is not the only one (*as an example,* Wm. G.) and that his niece and the children are also going. And there are many such women with children going.

She (*his wife,* Wm. G.) finally admitted that I am right. I tried to convince her, look at your parents, they have children all with them and suffer, K'AYN HORE beautiful and decent girls who in America would achieve a lot and help your parents. Furthermore, I also saw what my father did for me (*an ironic remark,* Wm. G.). I suffer very much until this very day. I, therefore, wish (*in text want,* Wm. G.) that my children should not suffer because of me. I must go (*in text travel,* Wm. G.). It can't be otherwise. "Do me a favor (*he turns to his wife,* Wm. G.) don't drain blood from me for nothing (*a popular Yiddish expression "TSAP MIR NIT DOS BLUT,"* i.e., don't give trouble and cause aggravation, Wm. G.). God knows the truth, that I am not going for myself to have a good time, only for your sake" (*i.e., our welfare and a decent life,* Wm. G.). She finally saw that I am right. I will have with whom to travel (*until now, the text indicates that the person with whom he will travel is the wife of his nephew in America,* Wm. G.), and there she will also take care of me. For truthfully, she is a faithful person (*my wife*) without any hypocrisy. She knew that I am overworked, not so much from labor as from bad times, and there in America, I will have to work. She, therefore, didn't want me to go. I knew it very well. Here I couldn't endure that I knew I was deceiving her. I didn't have a SHIFSKARTE. Therefore, I will have to wait long and suffer before they will send it to me. But it has to be this way. There is no other way, and I will have to wait until the time I will receive a letter from her (*i.e., the wife of his nephew,* Wm. G.) letting me know when she will begin her voyage. That I should make everything ready for the trip. Thus passed a few weeks, and I received a letter that she is coming (*this explains that she, his nephew's wife, was preparing herself and the family for the trip,* Wm. G.).

At the same time, I was in touch with good friends, those to whom I owed from all my years about 2,000 rubles, the good friends (*in text, it is described with the Yiddish expression GUTE BRIDER,* Wm. G.). Here I didn't want that this should be known. It was not feasible for me. So, I kept silent. I only possessed the horse and wagon, so I sold them and took in 65 rubles. I gave my wife 35 rubles, and I was left with 30 rubles. I would have taken only twenty if I would have had the SHIFSKARTE, but I didn't, so I needed some money for who knows how long I will have to sit there idle and wait. I made myself ready to go. In the SHETL, they found out. Some had pity with me as it is customary with our Jews, some envied me that I was leaving the SHETL, but I felt where I am going and to whom, that nobody sent me even one dollar about what I used to write and request almost every day.

And now, I am undertaking a journey without a SHIFSKARTE, deceiving my wife and children and everyone. But I consoled myself that I am compelled to go on this way, that I can't do otherwise. God will therefore help me. I am not going because I want to be free, only because of my family and our future. So certainly God will help me. I rejected the pressing on me of melancholy. I must do it this way. My niece with her three children came to me in the SHETL where they spent a few days, and we had to travel several times to my native SHETL VISHNEVETS (*the name of the SHETL indicates to me it was named after the Polish nobleman COUNT KORYBUT WISHNOVIETSKI, well-known Polish hero in the 17/18 century Poland. It's in the eastern part of the UKRAINE,* Wm. G.), where my two brothers lived and my whole family.

My father died during the time of my departure one month before. I didn't have the privilege to part with him. He knew that I wanted to go. Also, there is a lot to write when a husband leaves his wife and children, whom I love and deserve a lot from, it is not easy to depart. One can understand how one feels, what I was going through those days, but which I was counting, even the hours. I was no exception; everybody goes through this. But I still consider myself as an exception. Why was it so? I didn't have in mind only money and to live big (*i.e., as a rich man,* Wm. G.). My greatest delight was my wife and children, especially when I came home and met my wife and children in a good mood. At the same time, not to owe anyone. Even to be in debt but it has to show that the possibility to pay the sum is here and most likely then the whole world was for me, especially that I felt that all of us, thanks God, are well, as it is until this very day.

Now you can well understand how reluctant it was to depart from home. But PARNOSE (*this term indicates in Yiddish to make a living, to earn a livelihood is top priority. There is no word of explanation following this expression. It by itself indicates the meaning,* Wm. G.). Furthermore, the thoughts that I brought children into this world overwhelmed me. Now they are small, when with God's help, they will grow up, what would they do in a small SHETL? I felt it very well. I, therefore, did it (*i.e., to depart for America,* Wm. G.) for my children and indeed for myself and my wife. I was thirty-six years old, soon to be thirty-seven, and my wife thirty-four. We began to say goodbye, which I can't forget until today how much pain it caused to my heart. It is impossible to describe it, to relate it, especially with words. Yet some important words have to be mentioned.

How difficult was my parting with my wife and children, with everyone separate? But it had to be this way and not different. When I was ready to depart, my wife was crying and spoke to me with words, I should not forget her, that I should not be more than a year or two in America, and as soon as I will make a couple of hundred dollars, I should immediately come home. "Do you hear my husband? Do you promise me this? For without you, I will not be able to live. You should not consider to remain in America!" I listened very carefully to her words and told her that my departure from my family was very difficult for me. My feeling and pity for them can't be described, and I completely forgot whether I will succeed or not. But my mood was good in me that God will help me in virtue of my family and traveling all that night, I didn't speak to my niece or her children. They were happy. She's going to her husband and the children to their father. I only thought about my wife and children, how I left them with 35 rubles, and I travel without a SHIFSKARTE.

Who knows if I will reach my destination and what will be my destiny? If yes, I will not return home. I deceived my wife and children and promised (*to return home,* Wm. G.). But my aim is to rescue them from such poverty and from the small town. But to carry out my plan is very difficult for me, twisted with thorns, which I have to clean out on my way. I could not fall asleep and at the same time not to forget them even for a minute, I only heard the sound of her words, "My beloved husband, don't forget what I am telling you. I take from you an oath that you should stay there a year or two and after that, to come home. Not to think to remain in America." My niece was comforting me, why am I so worried? I answered her, "You know very well how I left my wife and children, and also deceived them that I have a SHIFSKARTE. Not them I misled, but mainly myself. What will I do?" She used to comfort me, "Don't worry, uncle, God will help."

When the day began to come, we reached my native SHETL and stopped at the young man who took upon himself to bring us over the border. I left them and went to the synagogue to pray. I said KADISH after my father. In the synagogue, I met my brother. He saw me and asked how do you come here so early? I told him that I am going with our nephew's wife and children to America, that I myself don't have a SHIFSKARTE, how I deceived my family in order that I should get out. And that I believe and think this would be the right way, that you as a brother should help me to reach America together with them.

His answer to me was that the other brother can help me. He does not have children; he is richer than he. In short, I went to the brother who has no children. He envied me that I go to America. I answered him yes, perhaps you should envy me, but when I don't have a SHIFSKARTE and to buy one I don't have the money, then there is no reason to envy me. And there is the duty that one brother should help the other brother. One should help even the stranger let alone a brother... what happened during our conversation is terrible to mention, and I am ashamed to let you know that something like this should take place between brothers of the same blood and flesh.

I realize that I will have more pains in my heart than their help for me, and I realized that this is only my own fault, nobody else's, that my road is so full of thorns wherever I will turn, something is indeed in myself that people are so bad and so corrupt to me. It seems indeed that these are donated years (*he uses his mother's phrase that she donated her years to him,* Wm. G.). I should be satisfied with my life and not to desire to run and look for better. But at the same time, my mind dictates me different. I want everything for myself (*he apparently means to have a decent life, sufficient of everything needed for him and his family. It does not look from the text that he desired from or envied others,* Wm. G.). Isn't this true? As for myself, I am satisfied, but my wife and children, which I brought into this world, deserve better. Why should it happen to them? I was encouraged at the same time when I had a conversation with my brothers. For it could be that I am better situated than them. One has no children; money does not mean anything. The other one has a malicious wife, and I don't have to envy him either, as my heart dictated, don't envy them.

You will tell everything with God's help in pleasure (*in text he uses the Hebrew term NACHAT in colloquial Yiddish NACHES,* Wm. G.), which I will describe in my final chapters. Then you will see that the world does not govern itself, that we have a good God, but one must believe in him at all times. You should not be too delighted when things are going good for you and not to be despaired when things are going bad. The main thing is to be a human being (*in text MENTSH which in colloquial Yiddish means to be a decent person,* Wm. G.).

I saw that I should not argue with them, not that I am the punished one, but exactly them. I said farewell to them, and I was ashamed to tell this to others, although I felt that I should go to others from my SHETL who knew me and grew up with me, tell them everything, and hope they would certainly help me. Here was my defect and wickedness that I never wanted to tell the other that he should know until this very day but so that you, my family, should know the truth. I didn't even tell my family (*niece*), although I suffered a lot and kept silent.

We left our native SHETL and moved out the next evening. We were not far from the border. I don't need to write that we were not exceptions. Good or bad, we, thanks God, crossed the border. Our first stop was ZBARZ, the second TARNOPOL (*both cities were then part of the Austrian-Hungarian Empire. After WWI, they went over to Poland. It was in the region of Eastern Galicia,* Wm. G.). I didn't have time to see TARNOPOL. The representatives (*I assume of the Jewish community,* Wm. G.) with whom we came in contact were not to my liking. We found ourselves between strange Jews with long beards and ear locks (*in text PEYES,* Wm. G.). They saw a Russian Jew, especially an immigrant, so they want to eat him all up (*in Yiddish colloquial OYFESIN meant to absorb him totally for themselves,* Wm. G.) the couple of rubles which one had with himself should remain with them (*a very right observation,* Wm. G.). But thanks God that I soon left them on my way to Vienna.

Coming to Vienna, we also didn't find everything good, that I should already see something new and good for me. The bigger the city, the greater was the swindle, and indeed from our fellow Jews, they should be in good health, and I hoped that in America, it is different ... another world. I saw it as other immigrants who were detained there for various reasons. I, myself, was holding onto my niece with her little children, a woman who never left her home, a pity she was very depressed. So, I cared about her and her children. We stayed there a few days, and from there (*Vienna,* Wm. G.), we were about to go to Antwerp, but we stopped on the way and had to wait an hour. A man came over to me, took me under my hand and said to me, "Come with me." I got scared, but he said to me, "Don't be afraid, I will bring you back in time, don't be frightened." He brought me to a hall and gave me a drink, two glasses of beer. I didn't want to eat, after that he brought me back and took out 5 silver francs and gave it to me and kissed me and gave me his card, when I will come in peace to America, I should write him about myself. This man gave me a lot of courage. I don't know until today who this man was, a Jew or a Christian (*in the text GOY,* Wm. G.), but a person who I cannot forget, and this gave me life.

We came to Antwerp, for it is there that will come the notice about SHIFSKARTE, which they (*i.e., the immigrants,* Wm. G.) are to receive. Coming to Antwerp, my niece went to the office to get the SHIFSKARTEN in order that she should know when they will be able to depart. Yes, and she said to me, "Uncle, I am very happy that you went together with us. If not for you, I don't know how I would manage to do everything having with me the children, especially on the boat, I indeed need you. Hence, I didn't want to tell you on the way, but now I am telling you that I have an extra 100 dollars, I mean rubles, which I know that I will bring them to my husband. However, since I know your situation and that you helped me a lot during the whole trip, I will buy for you a SHIFSKARTE, and you will go together with us. I will not leave you here. I am not allowed to leave you." Out of great joy, I could not get up. "Yes, yes, Uncle, you are going with us, with me and the children." In the office, we heard first all the following words. "What, this young man is also going? But Madame," she was told, "you yourself can't go yet." "Why?" my niece asked. "Because you have only in this office a recommendation. We should receive from there notice that your SHIFSKARTEN are paid in full. And as long as we will not have this, you can't go." It is easier to write about it than as to talk or witness it.

When would we know, tomorrow or a few days later? Not one tomorrow passed and not one week. They already forgot about me. I wanted to live to see the moment of them departing. But nothing happens. The woman and children were worn out, not talking about the money, which they had. From all sides, they took advantage of us. Every day we went to the office three or four times daily to ask. But they forget about it. I could not endure their suffering, let alone talking about myself. I denied myself a cent for food, only to have for paying to stay overnight. After a few weeks there, I reached a good man asking him to draw from her the poor little money that it should be less expensive. And she used to write every day to her husband in New York, also to her sister in Philadelphia and to a brother, to every friend but without an end. They didn't have the strength or mood to walk around. Here it is too much to describe. But God had mercy, he helped us, the woman, her children, and me.

After staying a few weeks came an answer with a couple of dollars that they can already go. I remained lonely without a cent. But she swore that as soon as she will arrive, she will make a turmoil (*she will scream and shriek,* Wm. G.) that a SHIFSKARTE should be sent to me with a couple of dollars. Her separation with the children from me is not easy to describe. They were so attached to me. But what could they do to help me or I them? We said goodbye to each other, and they traveled away, thanks God.

During my stay by myself in Antwerp, I used to see friends and walk every day in the streets to get acquainted with the city. My few cents came completely to an end. I used to walk around for days. In the evening, I used to write letters to America; they could have awakened even a dead person. I had to whom to write. When I left, they gave me addresses. My uncle, blessed be his memory, gave me to his children and my mother-in-law to her rich brother who was already for a long time in New York. Also, my sister and a brother. I had to whom to write.

To my deep regret, I didn't receive from anybody an answer. Until today, I can't understand it. Why was it so? I didn't want to write home in order not to aggravate them. I only wrote that we are waiting for the SHIFSKARTEN. That we only had recommendations, therefore, we wait here. In Antwerp, I was not any more a GRINER (*i.e., newcomer not acquainted with the place and living conditions,* Wm. G.). Once I was walking in the street, I saw men and women sitting at tables and drinking beer. They called me, they told me to sit down and gave me to drink a glass and a second one. They talked to me, but I could not understand them. Then I experienced again that they are decent people. They did not make fun from me. If I could only talk with them and tell them, they would help me with a couple of francs. But since I could not understand them and they me, so I left them with nothing gained but the friendship shown to me, which encouraged me, and I came to the conclusion that there are still good people and decent ones without beards and not Jews.

I used to go around day and night, hungry; nevertheless, my heart was full of good hope. I used to write to America every day and waited for help. But it took a long time, and I was walking constantly in the street and contemplating maybe a miracle will happen to me. Here, again I encountered a few people sitting and drinking. This time there were some who could speak German-Yiddish. I assume they were Jews. They recognized that I am an immigrant from Russia, they understood, I told them. They treated me with dinner and bid them goodbye. They gave me a couple of francs or crowns; I don't remember how much, and they consoled me that I will find a good life in America, and they really wished me good from the bottom of their hearts. This led further my eyes that I am going to a new and good world where I will forget all minor things, even those that I live on donated years. This is one of the old silly things that is always in my mind. Somehow, I felt proud of myself that I got out. It is true that my road was full of heavy stones, but with God's help, I will overcome them. Here I want to tell you how I got through.

I washed my clothing, a clean collar, a beautiful suit and good shoes, everything should be complete as I was used to all my years at home and especially now when I know that I am going to the great world, America. I went through plenty, the time I spent in Antwerp until God helped, and on a certain day came the SHIFSKARTE with 10 dollars from my nephew whose wife travelled with me. And he writes to me that I should not spend a cent from these 10 dollars. I have to bring this money to show it when I will come to KESSLEGARDEN (*Castle Garden point of immigration in New York*). I thanked God. It was three weeks before Rosh Hashanah. Also, that I don't have the extra couple of dollars for the trip annoyed me. After all, I am a human being.

My heart dictated that as soon as I will depart, money for me will arrive from my sister, or my brother, or from my uncles or from a cousin. All the time I was writing letters such which could tear down mountains. To wait another few weeks, I didn't want. I was afraid that I may wait in vain. I got tired to stay in Antwerp. One thing consoled me, that I have clothing equal to an American. I bought everything before I left, a suit and a hat. The man with whom I lived all the time I was in Antwerp was friendly to me. He and his wife were really exceptions. They were immigrants from Warsaw but were very fine people. So, I left them my address where I will stay in New York, if they receive something for me, they should send it to me for my heart dictated that it should be this way. Such a MAZL I always have had since my childhood until this very day, as I have already described many times that everything good came before me or after me but never directly to me.

I had to go travel by a small boat from Antwerp to Liverpool. Everyone had to go to a doctor before getting on the ship. I pretended that I didn't know and relied upon God that he will help me. None of my acquaintances left with me from Antwerp. Thus, as I left Antwerp, I said goodbye to the family with whom I stayed all the time. They wished me a happy and healthy trip and that I should arrive B'SHOLEM (*in peace, lucky and in good conditions,* Wm. G.). They will follow my instructions if something will come for me, they will send it to me and write to me. Also, from the old home letters used to come to them.

There is a lot to describe; the small boat on which we travel for a night, but since I was not the only one, it is not interesting to write. If it was not good for me, it was certainly not good for many. I was not an exception, to travel all night in this small boat. It was like the taste of death, equally to be the two days in a stall where they kept us, I would like to talk about this. When the doctor examined everybody, I saw everything and I also saw who he detained some people, so my soul went out from me. I felt very weak. However, I passed, thanks God, B'SHOLEM, but only because I kept myself clean and neat. He made a good gesture that I can go. So, I was very much delighted. About a few days later, we departed from Liverpool on a big ship named LUCANIA, which would be on the high seas about ten days. About this, only miracles could be written. But for this are big people, not me. I looked on everything with open eyes, being always on the deck seeing the good and not good, but I never missed to look at the huge ocean with much hope and courage, and I believed that God will help me. I didn't have the strength even of the smallest child.

The Inheritance (Yurusha)

I was aware that I am going to a land known as a golden land, that soon I will be there and earn and send the first couple of dollars to my wife. This revived in me another spirit and life. As usual, I traveled third class. During the day, I met people on the deck. These were Americans who traveled and spoke AMERIKANISH (*i.e., English,* Wm. G.). I looked on everyone with great love. The ship came constantly closer, and my thinking about the new land came to me closer every day, and I made all kinds of plans, but the best were during the days of the voyage.

We observed Rosh Hashanah on the ship according to everything how a Jew observes. Even a HAZN (*a cantor*) was there. But I will not describe here neither the Rosh Hashanah nor the trip on the old boat. It is, therefore, that I was not the only Jew or human being. There were Jews and other human beings. Therefore, I am not an exception to write about. Until God helped, and we saw at night the lights of New York, how it looks to everyone, especially to the individual who was never in a big city. The heart was beating out of joy or much fear, for there is talk on the ship that the main thing after you come to the KESSLEGARDEN is to get out of it. It was natural that I was very scared. It turned out that also there, I was an exception, without any questions asked, and I didn't have to show the 10 dollars. I only showed an address, and they told me to go after my long journey, and they escorted me to my niece, my sister's daughter, in Brooklyn.

This is the end of my trip from my little SHTEL on the big sea, and came to the largest city in the world. And here begins for me a large (*in the sense of more embracing,* Wm. G.) life which requires to be a big man with health and with a big strong courage and to forget all minor things (*in text NARISHKAYTN,* Wm. G.) that I am sick and that I have donated years, to forget everything.

THE END OF MY VOYAGE!

The semi-printed words around the drawing say, from the top right to the left: MY MIDDLE YEARS—HOW I LIVED IN THE OLD HOME AND HERE IN THE NEW.

The narrative below the drawing says:

And so, I spent my middle years after I got married and had K'AYN HORE children and how beloved were to me my wife and children. My life, however, was full of hardship. I never had PARNOSE. I was always sick and poor in the old home. From the age of twenty-two till thirty-seven, I endured everything and tried various trades rather business and never had anything. But I had an understanding that God gave me a fine and decent wife and decent K'AYN HORE beautiful children and mainly that God gave me wisdom and hope, especially the courage to endure everything and with the thanks to God came to this land. Here I really began to suffer, as I describe everything which you will read, here in America, from thirty-seven until fifty-five what I have endured but everything with decency. I didn't do, God forbid, any harm to anybody. As in the old home, so here, too, I looked for my PARNOSE as the bird in the field and the little fish I the water. So, I learned.

Inside the drawing are birds and fish of different sizes with a lion in the middle and Stars of David in each corner.

Part Five
Becoming a Griner – Adjusting to Life in America

Now, thanks God, I am already in America in the golden land with my own, and it begins for me a new life. However, it was going to be an ongoing hard one but not only for me; for everyone who comes as a GRINER, but I was an exception-weak and a sufferer, as you already know from the previous writings. The day I came was September 22, 1906. It was SHABES T'SHUVE (*the SHABES between ROSH HASHANAH and YOM KIPPUR,* Wm. G.); the first couple of hours or the whole day, they were happy with me, and I was with them. But as soon as the mutual questioning came to an end, it began the talk of what I should begin to do. And here I want to bring out that I didn't come to those who were already well up. This wasn't my niece, who was already here long ago. This niece was not in the country long, only a couple of years. She married an old boy, very decent and honest. He (*her husband*) worked at a knives factory and earned fifteen dollars a week, and they lived in two rooms in Brooklyn.

    That first night I didn't have where to sleep. She was a very good soul (*person,* Wm. G.). They could not do anything for me and only encouraged me that I will adjust myself to the country. They liked how I came, not as a GRINER but like an American. After having slept over, they took me to my niece, who I traveled with until her ship sailed, and indeed thanks to her, I received the SHIFSKARTE and the ten dollars. As usual, they gave me a very warm welcome. They were happy to see me. But here, they certainly could not do anything for me. My nephew was five years in the land and worked all the time as a packer in the rags business and worked very hard. Maybe to be a sorter would be easier and maybe he earned 12 or 13 dollars a week for him, his wife and, K'AYN HORE, three children. Now I asked them what my uncle is doing. "He has a store of woolen goods. He is well up." So, I thought that my uncle will try.

And indeed, they brought me the same day to my uncle. He was not home, however, his wife and children displayed friendship to me, and they were happy that I already arrived. I asked about the uncle. I was told that he is in the store, and they gave me his address, 81 Canal Street. My nephew, who brought me to his home, then took me to his store and introduced me to him; that I was his sister's son-in-law. He kissed me very warmly, and he really looked different. Here I saw a store with good merchandise, and he himself was also a good-looking man. I was under the impression that with this uncle's help, I will come to something. He had a partner to whom he said that because of the guest, he is going home. We, indeed, were within fifteen minutes of his home on Madison Street. My heart was full of joy that with his help, I will do something. My nephew went immediately back to his work. He (*the Uncle,* Wm. G.) asked about everybody; especially about his only sister (*my mother-in-law*). He looked at me and says to everyone in the house, "Look how good he looks as if he would be a long time in America. Not to recognize that he is a GRINER. Very good that you are already here. Only a few days ago, I was talking about sending you a SHIFSKARTE. I did send ten dollars to the address you wrote to me." "But, Uncle, I didn't receive it. If you would have sent it earlier, it would sustain my life."

What complaints could I have about him? He sent it to me. Only that, such is my luck. It is not his fault. I also knew that a cousin of mine from Middletown, Connecticut, also sent me a couple of dollars. The man with whom I stayed in Antwerp would not take it for himself. He is a very honest Jew. He could not receive them anyway. All the money will be sent back, but in the meantime, I saw how all my roads were difficult to cross. Didn't I know my many efforts to improve my life? I didn't have the luck to sustain (*in text, to sustain my life,* Wm. G.) myself even when someone paid attention to me. I don't know why. I, God forbid, didn't do any evil to anybody. And this is the way it was going to be followed until this very day. In the meantime, they served me a good supper. We were sitting until late in the night. They asked about everything. I stayed overnight with them, although I was told that they don't have a place for me.

The night was for me, very long. After all, I am in the new land, I was full of hope, and now that I reached my destination, I became exhausted. Now I have to try to build a nest for myself and to earn in order to be able to support my wife and children, who I left in poverty. In the morning, when I got up, my uncle was already out and at the store. They gave me breakfast, and the aunt, in the meantime, complains to me how (*i.e., her husband,* Wm. G.) bad he is to her and how stingy he is. He has lots of money and earns a lot, and if not for her two children, girls, she would not know what she would do. In this way, her description introduced who he was to me.

Whether I had understood or not wanted to understand is not of my business. I knew that I needed his help. I want to work and have income. He knows better than anyone where I could find work. He is already a long time in the country. After having been a couple hours, I asked that a child should show me where the store is so that I could talk to my uncle that he should do something for me. He is the only one. For my nephew works very hard at dirt (*most likely rags,* Wm. G.) and the other one works at knives. "Yes, yes, he can try for you (*this is the talk of the Aunt,* Wm. G.). He knows people. You are right, go (*she says to her child,* Wm. G.) bring him there."

Thus, I came to him a second time. He greeted me with a good morning and was very appreciative, a gentleman. He asked me, "What kind of work is doing your nephew who brought you yesterday to me?" I answered him that he works at rags. "At rags," he looked at me, and he became very happy. "If so, it is good. If so, you will have employment immediately after the holiday and possibly already this week. Good, good, this is the best for you, for GRINEM. At such trades, one can get used quickly, quickly and become a businessman for himself. Furthermore, to continue to be a Jew (*i.e., to continue the Jewish way of life,* Wm. G.) and not work on Saturdays and holidays." I recognize in him that he is very satisfied. I looked at him and asked him, "Uncle, isn't there anything else in America?"

"No, no, this is the best for GRINEM. Not everybody can work at such business."

"How do you know?" I asked him, since I was already in his shop, where he works very hard and in dirt, if I couldn't stay and work for him.

His answer was, "I am more delicate than you, and yet I worked, and thanks God, I already achieved something." I saw that he knows what he is talking about.

At the beginning of our talk, he was angry with me; therefore, I kept quiet, for since he said yes, let it be yes. He told me that he has a landsman from his city of OLSHANY by the name of ZENIVETSKY, a very decent person who worked himself up here. He, my uncle, will tell him about me, that I am his sister's son-in-law, and then he will take me immediately to work for twelve dollars the first month. This was the price, three dollars weekly. I counted it as six rubles weekly. If I will be capable enough, then the next month, I will get sixteen dollars. So more and more. Over the winter until Passover, I can myself work up. Not bad, after all, it is not bad. But I did not have the desire to begin such work. My heart told me that this kind of work is not for me.

When I came to my nephew and told him about the plan, he got very disappointed. He knew very well the taste (*i.e., the kind of work,* Wm. G.) of rags, and he told me, "Uncle YISROEL, this kind of work is not for you. I warn you; you go around idle a couple of weeks rather than work at rags. I can't help myself. My brother-in-law recommended me to such work, and now I already have my family, and I can't help myself. But you just came, he can support you for a few weeks, you will look for something else. He should give you work which is clean. Even standing in the street, you will earn more and indeed preserve your heath."

It was on the eve of YOM KIPPUR, and soon it would be SUKKES, a good time to relax. When I came again to my Uncle, he told me that he already spoke to his landsman and with God's help, I can begin my work already, Sunday. I answered him, "Uncle, my nephew tells me that I, God forbid, should not go to this kind of work. It is not for me. You should try something better for me." So, he became really angry, and he disassociated himself from me. I didn't have anyone to whom to tell this.

I had an address of a cousin who lived in NEWARK and a sister in PHILADELPHIA whose husband died a year ago. If he would be living, I would go there, but I must stay here. I never, never, had in mind to find employment at such work. I came to work in America, not to make a fortune, but I never expected to be employed at such work for my wife and children. The work is like poison for me. Today is different than eighteen years ago. As usual, on Saturday, I went to synagogue. I went to the OLSHANER VOLINER SHUL. I met there people from all over VOLYNIA – OLSHANY, VISHNEVETS, KREMENETS from all SHTETLEKH. Everyone that I asked about the kind of work he is doing; the answer was almost identical – at rags or feathers. Some were distributing papers bags with a box. Also, a very hard work. Perhaps it is better, I thought, to be all day outside, and all of them deterred me to work at rags.

The main merchant in rags was in the synagogue, and I heard from all the GRINE, MR. ZENKIVETSKY is a very decent Jew. He was also the president. He already told me that my uncle spoke to him, asking him to take me to work. "But truly speaking, tell your uncle that he is not doing you any good. If he would want, he could do for you much better. I see that you are a weak person, you are not able to work. I employ Jews, whoever applies to me, but you can't work at rags. He can support you and do something better for you. You are young. I am telling you this because I understand who you are. If yes, I promise you that you will not work hard for me."

When I came to my uncle after DAVEN (*services,* Wm. G.), for he didn't pray in this synagogue, it wasn't any more suitable for him (*ironic remark,* Wm. G.) and told him what was said, he laughed and said, "Only such work is feasible for you." He figured out that I would have three dollars weekly, and I will have to pay for food and lodging, so nothing will be left to send home for my wife and children for a living. He then proposed for me such a plan that I should be able to retain the whole 3 dollars. There are shops where they pay for sleeping overnight, 4 dollars monthly or 6 dollars, so the lodging will not cost me. And also, for food. Yes, it is a good plan. I felt good this plan would work, but now so many years since that time when I write these words, I feel it in my body, even in my bones which I suffer from that time on. I am compelled to write and you will see everything.

But about a shop, it is entirely different. Not everybody can find it so soon, very hard. Work at rags is all over. If not in this place, then at another. The shops (*it means places to work where you also have lodging,* Wm. G.) are taken. But to my luck, he had a friend who had a shop at SUFFOLK Street and spoke to him on the phone and told him about me. The answer was that he himself does not need, but on the seventh floor, there is a tailor shop. The watchman there leaves for home, so I should come, and they will take me. And indeed, it was so. They employed me that very same day in this place for 4 dollars monthly and the dirt, pieces of textile, which I will brush together would belong to me and can earn for me another one or two dollars a month for the rubbish. So, with the job at rags and the job as a watchman, all together, I can earn eighteen dollars a month. How much do I have to spend? They figured out six to eight monthly.

I didn't even see New York one day, but immediately Sunday, went to work in the shop. I had to be there seven in the morning. So, I got up, and I prayed. For eating breakfast, it was still too early. On the street car, I already met standing a couple of people—young and old. My first entry into the place, I became very nervous, and I thought if it is worth it to come into this golden land, and my livelihood is to stay a whole day in this cellar, and dirt should penetrate into the heart, and also to be in the cold and damp. But there are other people working. I am not the only one, and they gave another man to show how to sort. The man asked me from where I come. He wanted to know everything. He regretted that I took on this kind of work, and he introduced himself to me. He works here a long time. Then I asked him how much he earns weekly. He tells me twelve dollars, even twenty is not good. Better to earn ten dollars weekly and less not to be at this kind of work.

I thought about my family, that I will, with God's help, send to them the first month twenty rubles that I earned for them, so I don't want anything... (*the very thought that he will be able to send to his family twenty rubles made him not to consider his working conditions,* Wm. G.). I worked until six in the evening. In winter is already dark. On the streets I walked through, I saw various people running. But I only thought about my family and not about anyone else. At that time, I was still saying KADISH for my father, so I used to go into the synagogue. The synagogues are open until late at night. I already had the address of the shop, rather my home as the watchman. To walk up seven floors was enough for me.

When I came, the owner of the shop greeted me friendly and spoke to my heart. "Don't worry, for you will be all right as all are. Only recently left the watchman with a sum of 3,000.00 dollars (*6,000 rubles*) to bring home to the old country. All together he was here four years. You will also have perhaps more, because I see in you a capable person. What kind of work are you doing young man?" I told him at rags. "Yes, yes, the rags people are doing very well." He explained to me how to conduct myself. "The first thing when we leave the shop, you have to bring everything in order. First sweep so that it should be clean in the morning when we are coming in at 4 or 5 in the morning. First, you should prepare it for the ironing board's men so that when we will come, we should have them ready for work and every day to take down the papers and the dirt into the street in the cans and see that all gas pipes should be closed. Do you hear? If you will keep everything in order, you will have six dollars a month and the rags (*i.e., the pieces of textile which are being cut off, the scraps,* Wm. G.) will belong to you so that you may have a sum of eight dollars a month. Also, for sleeping (*overnight*, Wm. G.), you will not have to pay. You will sleep with one who already made me a millionaire."

Downstairs in the big building was a restaurant where all the shop workers came down to eat. So, I went down too. I remember that I paid 12 cents for the supper, which was really good, an appetizer and also very good meat. I was satisfied that it was kosher and Jews with beards ate there. Almost all of them were LITVAKES. At that time, I didn't understand the difference. Now, I know. Looking at them as they, K'AYN HORE, ate, so I did too, almost like one of them. When I came back to the shop, I still met the owner, a very nice man, particularly wise. He comes from the big city BIALYSTOK, a born LITVAK. He gave me the key and told me again, and I was left alone. He closed the gas and warned me how dangerous it is if you don't close, and he left me without light, rather with the oil burner in order that I should see to prepare my sleeping place. I took some clothing from the table, which were not yet pressed, and the pillow which my wife gave me to put under my head. This pillow was a small one, but my pains were very strong beneath my head.

Whether I fell asleep that night, it is not necessary to know. I got up before it was needed. The days were already cold, and rains came and a new climate not too good for me, but every GRINER before, he gets accustomed. I attended everything in the shop, and I prayed. It was not a small thing, only recently from the old home. I made myself tea. I came to the shop almost naked and barefoot. I don't mean, God forbid, to say that I really was naked and barefoot, but dressed as if for summer, without a coat or a sweater. Who cared about himself, let alone others? Since I begin to work in the shop, I didn't see anybody, and they didn't see me. I only was watching the time, not to be late. To be in the morning at the right time at work. Equally in the evening to be in the shop as the watchman.

At dinner time came a Jew used to bring into the cellar everything. By this I mean; herring, liver, and other different foods: sardines, salami, apples. What could I afford to take? Either a piece of herring, a piece of liver with bread and a bottle of water. So, the time went by. I worked, sorting rags piece by piece, blue to blue, and black to black. My thoughts did not stop for a second and stimulated me. Only one thought what I hear from my wife and children that I will make them unhappy for their whole life if I will sit at this work. Thus, I was thinking for days and nights.

Sleeping alone in the shop, from my extensive thinking, nothing came out. Days and weeks were passing. I didn't want to spend anything for myself. I didn't see anybody. I only inhaled all day in the shop the dirt from the rags and at night to sweep out the dirt from the shop and make (*prepare,* Wm. G.) the ironing boards for work ready and carry down day by day the garbage to the street. The rags and the dirt all together got into me. I began to feel that I am not as well as I should be. I constantly had a headache, but to whom should I reveal this? I kept silent.

I find out that day by day, my hands and feet are being swollen. I already could not eat, let alone sleep. Yes, but here I want to call your attention, that I quickly became very accustomed to my work and felt sleeping in the shop, I considered very good for me. I used to read the paper when I left the first job at the end of the workday and also write letters home and meditate that in time, I will accumulate a few dollars and work in the streets for myself. These thoughts encouraged me as

I went to my job as the watchman. I forgot about everything, that the work is harmful for me, or that sleeping in the shop might not be good for me or eating in the restaurant is so lonely. I was earning money and already saved more than twenty dollars besides what I had sent home each month for them to live.

I know, my dears, that I don't need to describe everything as it happened, such details. For many had more important events and don't write, but for me, my writing is entirely something else, which will be seen and proven by the end. My life and what I lived through. The more I suffered, the more I wanted and made every effort to live and not to get depressed. And, thanks God, I endured everything until now. I hope that in the future, my life will be a better one and that my writing about it will be interesting to you to read.

I remember when a man was speaking to his landsman, and who constantly complained that he is sick and poor. So, the landsman replied, "Why do you sacrifice your health for the work that does not give you enough to live and your last dollar you are giving to the doctor, and you don't want to die? You are afraid of death." He was not a fool. I remember. What a brutal answer my landsman gave him, but it is worthy to live and want to live to see how our beloved God leads the world. His words remained in my memory. It pays to see everything. Out of all who I mention in my writing, many are already in the RIGHT WORLD (*i.e., deceased,* Wm. G.); many are still alive, but their situation is worse than being dead. My heart hurts me (*i.e., I regret,* Wm. G.) for those who died long ago, for they could still live and for those who are worse off than those who died. I don't have, God forbid, vengeance toward them, just to the contrary, I am sorry for them, they could still live. They didn't want to give away their health for money. I gave away money for life, which you will be able to see in my writing. I hope that my writing will be interesting. Even the little events. This will lead you to bigger events. My writing is only for myself. It gives me satisfaction. My writing is not for reading to others. Also, if my wife and children will not be able to read, then perhaps my oldest son will.

Yes, at that time, my wife gave birth to a boy, K'AYN HORE, the fifth child. Hence, I will send the twenty dollars. I didn't think about myself. I began to feel different. All of a sudden, I could not get up to go to work, let alone sleep in the shop. While I was working, I used to go to the home of my nephew. So, I thought about his wife and the children were in school, and he was at work. She greeted me very friendly. "How are you, Uncle? I didn't see you for a long time. We always talk about you, but this is America, Uncle, and I curse the day that I came here to my husband. My ZELIG works very hard. When you see him, you would not recognize him, and all this for twelve dollars a week. He makes me and the children unhappy. I had everything in the village, clean and nice. I was settled. They used to come to me to buy. I had a decent living. Here I live on the fifth floor, always going down and coming up. It would be better for him to come home with the couple of hundred dollars, he would be better off. Now it is too late. You will, with God's help, go through everything. What is the matter with you, Uncle?" I answered her, "I would already be satisfied, and I am satisfied, but I don't feel good." She said, "Yes, we spoke about it here. My ZELIG told me that he does not comprehend how you could work at rags. But that is not everything. What he does not understand at all is to sleep in a shop. How can you sleep? He slept a couple of nights when he was a GRINER, and he left, and you can do it for so long?" "I was satisfied, and now I am not satisfied because I am very sick. I must leave." "Were you to the doctor?" "No." And here I felt I am fainting, and I asked her for a place to lay down. She put a pillow under my head, and I was laying for a few minutes. Her husband came home for dinner. He asked who is laying, she answered Uncle YISROEL. "What happened? He does not feel good? What, so soon. What should I say? I who is working for such a long time but now you have a home, a bed to sleep, your meals. Yes, this is true. I knew that he will sleep in the shop and that he will become very sick. But give me to eat, now I don't have time to talk. Tell him that he should not go away. I will take him to a hospital or to a doctor." I heard all his talk for I didn't sleep.

From her complaints about America, I learned that their situation is worse than mine. Whatever it is, I am for myself. I will get stronger. I encouraged myself. I got up and went to the doctor, to a hospital, so they can tell me what is wrong. When I got to the hospital, they examined me. They asked me how long I am in the country and at what am I working. I told them everything. Then they told me that the first

The Inheritance (Yurusha)

thing is not to work at rags and not to sleep in the tailor shop. These two things are for me, worse than death. But these are things I can't give up. They gave me medicine, that's all. I was very worried by the information that I have to watch myself.

This is not like home. I went to America to do everything in order to help my family. And here it brought me much harm already the first twenty dollars, which I saved. I don't know what to spend first. Here comes Passover, and I must send home a couple of dollars more. I am walking around in shabby clothing; I have to buy something for myself. I really began to be worried, in the course of time more and more, until I became dangerously ill. I could not eat; I could nor sleep. My whole body became swollen, and I received the news that my wife gave birth to a son. This is not a small thing, K'AYN HORE, the fifth child, three girls and two boys. And here I became sick, and I can't work anymore. I could already earn five dollars weekly and a couple of more dollars from the tailor shop. The aggravation added to my sickness, but I did not give up. For days long, I used to go around undressed, and I caught a severe cold. I didn't have a place to sleep, so I slept in the shop. This time they took me to a private doctor who also was a watchman, a young man. The doctor told me if I want to survive, I should quit the work in the shop and not eat in a restaurant, and he gave me two medicines, one to take and the other to spread smoothly on my chest. I quit the work and decided not to attend the shop at night. But for the time being, I still slept in the shop, for no one wanted to take me in during the time of my sickness.

One Saturday at sunset, when it was still forbidden to turn on the gas, I took, in the darkness, the medicine, and I made a small mistake. Instead of taking the medicine, I took a spoon of the medicine to spread on my body. Actually, it was poison. It affected my breathing; I could not call for help. But with a terrible cry, I ran from Seventh to Fourth Street, where there lived my friend. I could not talk, but they understood that something happened to me. They carried me down and brought me to a druggist, and they saved me. I vomited the poison. I almost died, but I still was sick, especially nervous. For sick I was before this accident.

It is easy to write, but what I suffered; I don't understand until now how I could endure everything. It is even hard to describe what I went through. Perhaps I could describe it better if I could forget about everything, but regrettably enough, it is already the nineteenth year that I suffer until today because of the accident. It affects me once or twice a month and lasts all together a minute or just a few seconds. At such moments, I would rather die than to feel the taste, which I feel when it attacks me. Nobody knows it, only my family. Sometimes, they hear my cry, and many times not. But at night, when I am sleeping, it is impossible to describe. But as I said, I will write about everything. My misfortune is only because my whole life is only to suffer because of my health. My desire to live is great if only for my family. They are very dear to me. I didn't have yet one good day, but others don't know it. That is why I am writing about everything.

After the accident, I left the shop and stopped sleeping there. I rented a room and began to suffer from unemployment, and not being able to earn was a blow to me. What should I do, what will I be able to do for my wife and children? Who listens to me, here in America, where everyone is extremely busy? The one who would do something for me cannot, and the one who could do something for me, won't. He does not feel. He says that I don't want to work. This was said by my uncle, the rich one and the wise. I didn't go to him. It hurt me that I suffer because of him, for a man like him could do something for me. But he didn't listen to me. He was healthy and made money. He didn't even want to live (*i.e., to conduct a decent life,* Wm. G.), as I will describe further about his life. And his end that he is already in the TRUE WORLD (*deceased,* Wm. G.), it will be interesting to read and know. It is a good lesson for others what happened to this man, what kind of life he conducted. I don't want to illuminate about him too much, especially since he is already not among the living.

But I will keep my word, with God's help, to describe if God will give me good years and, God forbid, bad years (*here it is important to bring out that the author took the bad years also as ones from God and that nothing could be done against this,* Wm. G.). I will describe with whom I came in contact, everyone's door (*i.e., home,* Wm. G.) and their way of life and also my limited, weak and poor life, how I lived and how I live now and there is no hope for better. But even though I suffer, I thank God for what I have. For it could be, God forbid, worse.

A few of my landsman saw him and told him how sick I am, and that the doctor forbade me to work at rags and especially to sleep in the shop. And there is nobody except him who could do something for me. The whole situation angered him. "He does not want to work. He is lazy. He thinks that I will take him into my store. If not in the store, he can do more than others that he should earn something in the street where there is air to breathe. He left there a wife with 5 children and he himself also needs to make a living. If not (*if he will not get well and find work,* Wm. G.) so you know that he could be sent back home."

His answer was that this was the best plan, that I should go back home. That is what my landsman told me that my uncle had said. It hurt me very much. I was convinced that if I would have work in the street, I would feel much better. The aunt, his wife, was a very good person. As he was bad for everybody, including himself, she to the contrary, was good to everybody and for herself. They had a girl of the age of twenty years, a very good person. I used to come over during the day at the time when he was not home. Sometimes they gave me something to eat. They wanted to give me a couple of dollars, rather cents, but unfortunately, she never had it in her hands. Even for herself, so stingy he was. When he used to come home, he was told how sick I was. So, he came to me where I lived and told me that I should go with him to a hospital so that he should know what is wrong with me. I was delighted. He spoke there, telling them about everything. I didn't understand. Going back, he said to me, "The best thing for you would be that you should return home."

When I heard his words, I said, "What are you saying, Uncle? Home to whom and for what?" He answered me, "You are sick, and you should not be in America." "No, no, Uncle. Even if I knew that I will die, I would not go home. Here if I die, I want for myself, and before I will go home, all of them will die. I want to live, and I feel, thanks God, to live. I am not so sick. I am very nervous because I don't have any work. They forbade me to work at rags and to sleep in the shop. This has affected me. Now if I would have some work and that somebody should try for me, I would be well with God's help, and I have hope in him. How could I possibly go home sick and without a cent? One needs, first of all, to have for a SHIFSKARTE." "Don't worry about a SHIFSKARTE. If it is within a year, they send you home without cost. This I will do for you." "But, Uncle, I don't want to go. I will be, with God's help, well. I came to America not for me but for my family. And die, I would rather in America, not at home." He didn't answer me anymore. I came back to where I was sleeping and had boarding. When he came home, he warned the aunt and the children to disassociate themselves from me because I had the real sickness, which is called... I don't know.

Time was not at a standstill. The first Passover season in America arrived. I don't remember anymore today all of the details. I had to give seven dollars for Passover since he didn't want to have me in his home. Perhaps he was told so, but I don't believe it. This is what he is saying to others as to why he is not taking me to him for Passover. He gave me five dollars, and I paid for Passover with a stranger. At the first SEDER, I have YARTSAYT (*Hebrew date of the anniversary of death,* Wm. G.) after my mother, blessed it be her memory. Everything happened together. I became ill; thus, I didn't observe Passover. I couldn't eat, I couldn't sleep, and I was the two days (*of Passover,* Wm. G.) in bed.

The doctor told me that it is nothing wrong with me, that I am only nervous. This I understood myself. I was very depressed because of everything, longing very much for my family. I could not send money home, that's all which strongly affected my nerves, especially the words I was told that my uncle said. I didn't enjoy the holiday. I didn't know anything, and no one came to me. On HOL-HAMOEYD (*the intermediate days of the holiday,* Wm. G.) I began to think what to do with myself. To go back home, I didn't let come to my mind. I should begin to think how to improve my conditions. I didn't want to show up to my nephews. First, because they get aggravation because of me, and secondly, they could not do anything for me. As you already know, one is working at rags and the second one at knives. They are poor people and will only have aggravation because of me. That's all.

So, I recalled that I have an address of a cousin of mine who is already a long time in America. He lives not far, altogether an hour's journey by ferry to Newark. I didn't think long. If you have an address, you can reach the place. In about an hour, I was already at my cousin Mr. SAM LESSER. There I saw something different, a beautiful house, a very fine woman and fine children and everything in the best conditions. It was during the daytime, and he was at work at a big place. They had a lot of eggs because of Passover, and I knew he must have a good income and not just to earn a livelihood. His children were already studying, one law, the other pharmacy and the girls likewise. This is what I like to see with my good friends and relatives, especially at her home, who knew me from the old home. She didn't recognize me. I told her who I am. Then she recognized me and asked me when I came, "You are such a long time here, and you came to us only today? You didn't even let us know that you are here…"

She immediately gave me to eat all the best as usual on Passover; wine, gefilte fish, latkes (*Passover pancakes,* Wm. G.). I look at this, but I can't eat anything. "What is the matter with you? You most likely fixed yourself up as GRINER who doesn't know how to go on with your life in this country." I told her something, not everything, for I was afraid that she would not let me stay with her even one day. I saw that she and the children have a lot of pity. The day passes. In the evening came Mr. Lesser, a gentleman dressed like a prince. We kissed each other, really as cousins. But before I could tell him anything, she already told him that I was already here the whole winter.

"Now that he is already fixed (*i.e., settled,* Wm. G.) and is sick, he came to us." He understood everything in a different way and, with devotion (*in text love,* Wm. G.), asked about everything about what is with me. I told him. He put his hand on his head, he raised his voice, "How could such a weak young man as you go to work at rags in addition to this, to sleep in a shop? Who sleeps in a shop? A healthy, a healthy person or just healthy and strong or beggars. You want to sleep in a shop? Who told you about a shop? With whom you got in touch?"

I told him that I came to an uncle by the name of BERL LIEBERMAN from TSHAN.

"Oh, this beggar, this rascal, this nothing, why didn't you come to me first? Didn't you have my address?"

"Yes, I had your address, your father gave it to me. But since I came to one and then to another and realized that they can't do anything for me, especially since I came to an uncle about whom I was told that he is very rich and he told me to work at rags and sleep in the shop for he did the same thing as a GRINER and he has succeeded, I took his bad advice. I have asked about you and was told that you are also a worker."

"Yes," he interrupted me, "a worker is nothing to be ashamed of. But a person with feelings (*noble,* Wm. G.) and a heart (*i.e., good hearted,* Wm. G.) should fail? I say no, you are a young man, you will, with God's help, not fail. Don't worry, you just didn't reach the right way yet. FRAYDL give supper, we will eat."

I answered him, "I already ate."

"You should not ask how he ate" (*these are apparently FRAYDL'S words,* Wm. G.).

"Well, he will eat with me."

His words encouraged me. I may say that this was the first supper that I really enjoyed.

The conversation was around the old home, about everyone, about his father who was still alive at that time, about his whole family. He told me that his brother-in-law came also not long ago. He visited him, he wanted to try something for him, but he does not like America, and he will go back home. He is now with his sister in St. Louis. From there, he will come back and will go straight home. I answered him that "he (*the brother-in-law,* Wm. G.), should not have come to America because at home he has a nice house and had PARNOSE (*livelihood,* Wm. G.), he has a rich mother who wanted to give him a couple of thousand rubles so that he shouldn't leave. On the other hand, I had to leave because of poverty. I became a debtor and didn't have any work, and not even one ruble, and the children, K'AYN HORE, were growing up. What is going to come out from them in the small SHTETL? It will be the same way my father, blessed be his memory, made for me. Therefore, I went, but such is my luck that I became so sick and to be unable to work." "You are not, God forbid, sick. You are healthier than the strongest, that you can still live. Who can eat as much as you did?

I didn't tell him about taking the poison, but he heard my cry at night. "What is this?" So, I answered him that this comes from my stomach. When he got up in the morning, I heard that he ordered his wife and the older son that they should take me to their family doctor and that he should examine me very carefully. And so, it was after breakfast, his boy, who studied pharmacy, told me to go with him. Coming to the doctor, I told him everything but not about taking the poison. He said that I will be, with God's help, well but that better care should be taken of me. In other words, that I should not work in a shop. Work will not be harmful to me, even the hardest work but only in the street and fresh air. He said that I am only worn out and tired from aggravation but that I am strong. I should eat sufficiently and drink and sleep in a good room, everything that I could not afford to do.

When I came back from the doctor, he (*the son,* Wm. G.) told his mother. He prepared for me the medicine. When my cousin came home, he was informed about everything. He consoled me and encouraged me to have good hopes. I was very careful these days. At the end of Passover, on the holy days, we went to the synagogue. He introduced me to everybody as his cousin, a GRINER. Yes, I didn't have any clothing, so he gave me his boy's and he was walking around with me during the whole Passover. He was a respectable person, in friendship with the Rabbi, in close friendship. So, he took me to the Rabbi, and this gave me a lot of satisfaction. This, by itself, made me feel better.

After Passover, he told me that the best thing for me would be to go to Philadelphia. "Since your sister lives in Philadelphia, you should go there and look for something. But only in the street, but before that, you should go in the country a couple of weeks, to have fresh air, to drink milk and eat fresh meals." But since I myself don't have anything for this, and I alone can't do much, he suggests that I should go to his brother, an older one in Middletown, Connecticut, YISROEL LESSER. "Stay there for a while. From there, you can go to Philadelphia." He took out 10 dollars and said that's all what he can do for me. For me, it was a great thing, not so much about the 10 dollars, rather his talk to me with such kind words. He maybe could take me to his work, but he knew that I needed to be in the street, outside where there is air. Because of his friendship shown to me, indeed, my mood improved. I went to Middletown.

There, life was entirely different. There I didn't care about anything, only that I should rest and enjoy fresh air and eat in time and sleep. I was a good guest, but he could not do anything for me because his wife was not entirely with a clear mind. He himself didn't have where to be. I was there a couple of weeks, and I felt much better. He also gave me 10 dollars.

Part Six
Settling in Philadelphia – A Griner No More

From there, I went straight to Philadelphia and had with me 25 dollars. It was natural to come to my sister. I could not have there any satisfaction, for as I have already mentioned several times, that I am always coming too late, after the good (*the good that prevailed before,* Wm. G.). So, it was with my coming to my sister. As soon as she came to her husband, all together a year before me, her husband died and left her with little children. Now one can understand what their situation was. Two girls were already working, and she had a couple of boarders, so I also stayed temporarily with her, but not for long. She didn't have a place for me, and even if she would have, I myself didn't want because I wanted to sleep in a good airy room. Also, the food should be good for I understand it differently. The main thing is health. If I will be healthy, God will certainly add to my health.

I began to peddle in the street with everything possible; rags, old clothing, whatever I could get or find. Sometimes I made seventy-five cents a day, sometimes a dollar. It was the year of the crisis, 1908 or 1909, I don't remember. People who used to earn before, a lot, didn't earn anything during those years. They used to collect bread from the stalls, as a GRINER, and many as I, were most lucky. Others envied us for we were not ashamed, carrying a package of bread from the stalls. I began to feel every day better, but not completely. I took the medicine, but it was the street that brought back my health. It was a very bad time for everybody.

I moved out from my sister. She had as boarders a few LANDSLAYT (*people from back home,* Wm. G.), both men and a girl. I, thanks God, already understood better, how to live in America for my general health. So, I took a room for 6 dollars monthly. Then, years back, I was careful with my food. I was complaining one time at supper that I don't feel good, that the soup was very sweet. So, the landlady said that she put in some sugar for the meat was very lean and without taste. Don't ask, I stopped eating there and moved out. I looked for something better for a little more money, not to live only for money. This I understood already very well.

And so, little by little, I got accustomed (*in the text AYNGETRAYET*, Wm. G.) to America. In the meantime, a year passed, and soon will be two years, and I am not thinking about my family. I think mainly and pray to God to be well first of all. If I will be well, the situation will improve anyway. It will not be so always. And it really got better, and I became less of a GRINER (*in text OSGEGRINT*, Wm. G.), and I got acquainted with many people and came among societies so that I may see something and learn during the time I am not employed. Time was not at a standstill. It was close to the period of two years (*since the author came to America*, Wm. G.), and I didn't yet save one dollar. I was still much in debt. For I earned very little. It was a very bad two years with my sickness together with the crises.

I didn't want to live as I lived the few months during my stay in New York. I paid more for everything for I wanted to have the best room to sleep and also the same with the meals, so that every detail, especially with the clothing. I looked upon everything with open eyes on America. Each time I loved it more and more. That I am suffering this way is not America's fault. Whoever comes as a boy, not to leave a wife and child, he could really work himself up. Whose fault is it that I gave away my youth and strength in the old home for nothing? And here, as a GRINER, without language, without education, without business, without qualifications, should I already have everything? Ah... I understood it very well, and I tried in the beginning, even though the work was hard for me, so I tried with a partner who was, K'AYN HORE, a landsman not far from my SHETL, R' MOSHE BARENBLUT, from VIZERODEK, VOLYNER GUBERNYE (*i.e., like a state in the USA*, Wm. G.). I got acquainted with him here. A very fine man. So, we concluded a partnership together.

He came a few years before me and was a boarder at my sister. Thus, we became acquainted. He already saved a few hundred dollars.

In order that you should know everything, so I ought to describe everything. He also left at home a wife and children. But it was entirely different. He did not leave because of needing money for he made a nice living from his store. He went because he was afraid that he will be drafted into the army. He had in mind to return home a healthy man, but he lived differently. He saved as much as he earned. For me, it was not enough. I had to send home. I, therefore, had to borrow, and he on the other hand, had something saved, and I became a debtor.

We did business for a couple of years, and I tell you everything in order for you to know that my mind was working. But, the more I wanted to do better, nothing worked out. I don't know why until this very day; it is for me a question without an answer. At that time, business came to a standstill. It was impossible to sell, and yet we wanted to buy. So, we bought new merchandise. I had no money, only the partner did. He invested his couple of hundred dollars, and he rented a place to store the merchandise and hoped that in time the situation will improve, and we will make a profit, but I needed, for the time being, to make a living and send money home so that they will have bread to eat. If it would begin to improve, we hoped to be able to sell the merchandise.

We decided that the next day I should bring a merchant, but here something else happened. As soon as my partner came to the place, he became lost, the lock was broken down, and all the merchandise was gone. Nothing was left. The partner came to me and told me everything that happened. I could not believe it. Not so much I, but as a stranger said, "It can't be maybe that he sold the merchandise by himself. The money is his." I really didn't want to believe, but they began to talk to me so much that I began to believe it and then I changed my thoughts and made this young man as the thief.

This is the luck of a poor Jew. In addition to being persecuted by poverty and having no luck, he is also punished that someone is committing a crime to an innocent and honest man. This was the case with me. We got separated (*in text divided,* Wm. G.). Later, we were reconciled. We used to get together but not anymore, a partner. I paid him out little by little my part of the debt. I didn't want to go around for these goods. It was hard for me to deal with such goods. I used to buy better goods-remnants, silken, all kinds of trimmings. I worked easier and earned more doing that. I used to receive letters from home that it is almost three years since I left and what will be the end. When are you coming home? You promised me that you will not stay more than two years and here it is close to three years, and you don't think about coming. This one brought home 500 dollars, the other one 600, the third one 1,000 dollars and most likely are doing business and you, if you would come home with some money, who could be equal to you? What could I answer her? My writings were only to her and only that I will bring her to America and establish a home. For I was convinced that America is for children, even for the older one, but one must know how to conduct himself. How bad I felt but the land was very dear to me, that God brought me here so that I should save my wife and children that they should experience a better world. I liked very much, America. That I am in a bad situation is not America's fault.

But to me, they only wrote to come home, that they don't want to go to America. To bring my whole family was impossible for me. I wanted to bring first my oldest boy, thirteen years old. At that time, I already belonged to a lodge together with LANDSLAYT (*countryman*, Wm. G.), founded by people from the same SHTETL where my first wife lived, who I divorced. At that time came from there a young man, a GRINER, who knew me very well from the time I was in his SHTETL. He gave me regards from my girl she had from me when I got separated from my first wife. He brought out loudly that the girl belongs to me when she will get older. The mother got remarried to someone from the same city. She took the oldest SHOYHET (*ritual slaughter,* Wm. G.) with a couple of children. He told me that she doesn't want to have any children from him. Then I asked, is my child with her?

The man answered, "If you could bring the child here to you, you would do a good deed. For she is not satisfied with being with her stepfather. She goes around naked and barefoot." I got cramps in my heart, she is now sixteen or seventeen. I brought her into this sinful world, let it be, not from love, but why does she have to suffer, it is not her fault. It is my fault. True, I don't know her and I don't have the love for her as to my other children, but when I will bring her into this country and she will eat full and will be dressed nice, she could also earn, and she could study and learn the language and write, and this will be good for such a child, and she may achieve a lot. This is my debt to this innocent child, and at the same time, nothing wrong can happen to me. My figuring was very good for me, let alone for her, but only one thing bothered me and made me suffer. Perhaps she resembles her mother in looks or especially in her character. Furthermore, there passed many years that my former wife was by herself and not remarried, and she probably cursed me not just one time and instilled in the girl a hate. Whether I wanted or not, it didn't let me anymore to be at ease.

The young man immediately wrote to my first wife that he saw me and spoke to me and that I promised that I will send for the girl in the near future. A few weeks passed, and I received a letter from her written with such a plea that I can't describe it, that I should have mercy on her and especially on the child and bring her to America. Since I planned to send a SHIFSKARTE for my oldest boy, I answered her letter, if she wants to go, I will send for both her and for my boy that they should go together, a sister and a brother. I wrote to my wife that I want to bring my girl to America. I am sending SHIFSKARTN for both of them that she (*his wife,* Wm. G.) should write to the girl that she should come and that they will go together. Yes, it can't be better. I requested from my girl that she send me her picture because I don't know her, and when she comes to the KESSLEGARDEN, I should be able to recognize her.

With this hope, I waited for an answer. It was natural that I made plans that first of all, I am going to do a good thing, which I must do out of the duty of humanism, especially the obligation of a father to his child to bring her to me. How happy she will be, being near her father who will try (*i.e., to do something,* Wm. G.) for her future and she will enjoy life. But regrettably, it turned out different. A man thinks (*plans*) and God laughs (*a Yiddish proverb A MENTSH TRACHT UN GOT LACHT,* Wm. G.). So, it was with me, with my thoughts, that I am going to do a good thing. But the road was very hard for me to accomplish even for a bigger person (*i.e., better situated,* Wm. G.). The first letter I received from my wife that I should not, for heaven's sake, do such a thing, that I will make myself unhappy. Think what you want to do. Don't forget that you have, K'AYN HORE, five children and myself, and she has one child, and she will not have any more. And you don't know her as a child, and she does not know you as a father. If she sends her away from herself (*i.e., the mother will send away the daughter,* Wm. G.), you should not take her to you. But I know very well that you will not listen to me. Remember and remember what I am writing to you. I am afraid that you will not listen to me. I know you.

Reading her writing then, I did not know what to do, YES-NO? I could not find a place for myself. Here to the LANDSLAYT I said that I already wrote to my daughter. I also understood that my wife positively did not want me to bring her because I will suffer. She is probably 100 percent right. But this is not the girl's fault. I must send for her. With this I will obliterate much which will be forgotten. Her mother hates her and me. God will help me for this, and I will be healthy, and I will have more luck, and I will live to bring my whole family. I am going to do a good thing for them and for me. After a few days, I received a letter from her with a picture, and she wished me good. But when I looked at the picture, I became very much depressed. This did not keep me back from sending, I must send, it can't be otherwise, and I spoke to myself that I have hope in God that in America, everything with God's help will be good. In order that I should not delay, I went to the office to get the SHIFSKARTN, and I took a couple of dollars for the cost of the trip and wrote two letters, one to my wife and the other one to the girl that she should immediately leave her mother and go to my wife and she should be there until they will depart to America.

A great stone got off my heart (*a Yiddish saying when somebody is relieved from a burden,* Wm. G.). I felt very good after that and cheered up, and I became in a better mood because I did a good thing, the obligation of a father. I used to think that God punished me because in my life, it was hard for me to go on, but perhaps it was for this. I didn't feel, God forbid, as a sinner. I committed no crime. I also took everything for good in the way it was. It is indeed the donated years. This was indoctrinated in me, but the stay here a couple of years and to go through everything that I did, helped me to forget about this fully, and I laughed at this (*i.e., about donated years,* Wm. G.). But the thought that I brought a child (*i.e., the daughter,* Wm. G.) always followed me and plagued my conscience. But now my heart became clear (*i.e., absolved in his mind,* Wm. G.).

Nobody has to be grateful to me. She will be, with God's help, all right in this land, and I continued my work. I worked very hard but with much hope. I didn't have much strength, as you already know from my writing. I worked with much exertion, even at the smallest thing that I attempted to do. I wanted to improve my life. So many obstacles were always in my way, which I find it very hard to properly describe so that you will know and feel what really happened. It is unbelievable, and there was nobody I could tell, and there is nobody who will give me credit for this. So, I suffered and kept silent. I didn't want to tell this to strangers. Of my own people, I didn't have anybody here in Philadelphia except my sister, the widow, but what could she do for me? She also was very depressed.

So, were passing the weeks and the months and years. It is easier to describe than to go on from day to day. I used to receive letters from my wife every week that she will not send our boy, especially with this girl, and that the best thing is for me to come home. It would be better than to bring them all over for the money that I will have to spend. I used to answer her that this will never happen (*i.e., to bring the boy and to leave the others,* Wm. G.). I didn't go for my own sake, only for the sake of the children. I will save you all. It can't be otherwise. I want to bring the girl, it is also because I, the little man, believe that I must do this. Possibly, God will help me because of her, and I begged her (*his wife,* Wm. G.) that she, God forbid, should not hold back sending them to me. After their arrival, I will, with God's help, begin to try for you, everything with God's help, to establish a decent life. One does not lose money on children in America. I want to contribute the couple of hundred dollars that they will cost (*i.e., their education,* Wm. G.), and with God's help, it will be profitable. For children is America, a good world and parents have pleasure (*in text NACHES,* Wm. G.) from them. If, God forbid, they don't listen to the parents, it is also better than in the old home. You should not delay and see to it to send out the children, not to keep them back and quick (*i.e., to send them,* Wm. G.).

And so, it was a couple of weeks later that I received a letter that they already left. I counted the days and the weeks that I should live to see them. I committed myself strongly that I should do everything possible in the world that the girl should love me and I her. If one is alive, he lives to see. One day I received a letter that they are already on the ship and that they will travel for days. I was most happy that in a couple of days I will see my children, especially such a child that I don't know and she doesn't know me. The days went by, and on a certain day, I was informed by the office that my children are already here and that I should come to take them. The ship was the Haverford, and it arrived from Liverpool on July 6, 1910. My joy was very great. I told them in the place where I was a boarder that I am going to get my children. They (*my landlords*) were pleased at my news and prepared everything for them. I was flying, not walking. I came to the KESSLEGARDEN, and I was looking for them. I didn't see them, even if I would, maybe I would not recognize them. God helped me, and I found them, and they were questioned whether everything was in order, and they gave me the children...

Coming home with them, I breathed easier for the first time, and I saw very fine children (*Chane and Mordche on the passenger list who became Anna and Max*, ER), the girl sixteen (*maybe seventeen*), and the boy thirteen (*maybe fourteen*), K'AYN HORE, grown up. LANDSLAYT came to visit us. How the girl was, I need not to write. I took upon myself to show to the girl more love, even if I would not feel it to apply yet. To do everything in order that she should be happy with me and satisfied with America. The same day or the next one, I shopped for her—dresses and shoes. I dressed her up that nobody should recognize that she is a GRINE. For my boy, I didn't spend even one dollar. The first week and the next one everything was good. But it didn't take long, the girl began to take account from me what I can't describe. I tried to win her over by good ways. I saw that it is not her fault. Her mother planted into her a hate of me... I explained to her that I will be for her a faithful father. I tried to bring her into this land where she can achieve a lot (*the author used a Russian term USPEYN for achieve,* Wm. G.), to learn the language and go to school, night school and work during the day. She will earn for all her needs and expenses. She will, with God's help, have everything. We went to see a picture, but the more I showed to her my love, the more she hated me. I saw it, and I wanted to improve the relationship. Regrettably enough, it didn't help. Later on, she showed it (*her hate,* Wm. G.) in a different way that I am ashamed to describe. I got sick again from all these troubles (*in text TSORES,* Wm. G.). The boy was still too young to go to work, even if he would, they would not allow him. He didn't want to go to school either.

They both began to act against me in such ways that I almost lost my mind, which is something that I didn't have for a long time. I cursed myself for what I had done in bringing them here. But it happened, I will see what I have to do. In the meantime, I received a letter from my wife why I forget to send money. My wife was hoping to receive more, and now that I brought the children, I don't send her anything. Don't ask, how bitter was my situation, how bad I felt? I was ashamed to tell it. I kept everything in myself. I hoped, in the course of time, it will change, but to my bad luck, it became every year worse. The weeks and months and years were passing without any achievements, only with great pains. I wanted to do the best, but I did for myself, the worst. But this was nobody's fault. I did it to myself. I, therefore, must suffer, and I really suffered very much and kept quiet.

I realized that we can't live together. I told her, perhaps it would be better for you not to stay with me.

Her answer was with joy. "Yes, yes, this is what I want."

"If so, my child, why do you have to cause me pains, you can go. But only there where I will tell you, and you are to behave in a good way and to be decent and comfortable that everybody should love you, for it is America."

The next day she moved out from me, not where I wanted but only where she wanted. She already had acquaintances. I was ashamed to face people. People were wondering that a child does not want to stay with the father, especially a girl. My answer was that you can't blame her, she didn't know me.

About the girl herself, I could write a book. So far, I want to leave her as it is. I will still mention her many times in a good way and not, God forbid, in a bad one. I went through a lot with her (*because of her,* Wm. G.), and with the boy, nothing. With him was entirely different. He didn't work because he was too young. He didn't want to go to school either, don't ask. I realized that it will not be enough, the four years of my stay in America, but it will take another four years until I will be able to bring my family. They (*the girl and the boy,* Wm. G.) affected me so much that I didn't know what to do. To go back to my old home is definitely excluded. But, then what? I used to think that I should go away from Philadelphia because of my girl. She made miserable my years because she didn't conduct herself as I wanted. The pain was very great (*it was very painful,* Wm. G.). Something urged me to go far away, far away, but I was kept by the city where everybody already knew me. I would be better that I should send her home because she does not listen to me and does not behave as I want. I didn't want this (*he could not make a final decision,* Wm. G.), maybe everything will pass over. It is impossible to write about them and what I went through because of them. The boy annoyed me that he wanted to go to the uncle in New York, the same one I wrote about earlier, my mother-in-law's brother, the rich one. "What has he done, so much for me...my child, what are you going to do at your uncle? Your father does for you little? I want you to eat and drink and be a MENTSH (*a Yiddish expression that describes a person's well-being,* Wm. G.) and to go to school and learn and help me a little."

I could not take from him anymore either. I dressed him up as it was fitting for him. "Go in good health, but I will not send for you." My sweet dream evaporated. The girl with strangers, makes money and has a good time. It is not like I hoped, the boy also left. After all, what is the matter with me? Maybe it is my fault. I wanted only good for them. It can't be that it is my fault. My fate as indicated, donated me, therefore, these years. This way it should be, and you can't have any complaints to God. Also, that I am not worthy. This was the way I made confessions to myself, and I cried very much at nights and all days. Nobody should notice it. This is the way God leads. I have only to thank him and to go ahead and try.

Why has my wife and children to suffer there? Perhaps if we would be all together, it would be different. This encouraged me. I didn't let myself down because of such a thing, such misfortune. I should leave Philadelphia. She was not, God forbid, debauched, it is plain that she understood very little, a person from a small SHTETL.

For what do you need your father who divorced your mother? Now he wants your earnings. Not for you (*the author reports his thoughts about his presumption of the girl's thoughts,* Wm. G.). And the same people (*it does not say who were the same people. I assume that these were his acquaintances or people from his society,* Wm. G.), are coming to me to tell me that her conduct is not decent.

In time, I became accustomed to the thought, let us say, that I didn't bring her. I felt bad when I met her in the street, she used to avoid me. Then I suffered very much. I think that I can be understood that everything that I write is from the depth from my heart, so deep-rooted (*i.e., the whole problem with the girl,* Wm. G.) that sometimes I felt like fainting, but I restrained myself. Actually, I blamed myself and tried to maintain my demeanor. She already earned money, and she didn't listen to me. The boy was in New York a couple of weeks. He was a guest a week or two at the good uncle or another one, his shoes got torn. They asked him why he is not with me. So, he began to write me letters, father send me a few dollars so I will come home. I will be a good boy. I let him know that I have not sent you away, you can come home at any time. I will not send you a cent. Furthermore, I want you to know that after you will come home to me, you should go to work since you don't want to go to school. I am a sick man, you are, K'AYN HORE, young. I must, one time, be strict. I received the second and the third letter, he will throw himself into the water (*a Yiddish saying if one is desperate,* Wm. G.). You can do whatever you want. A week passed, and I received a letter that he works, and that he will earn a few dollars, then he will come home all right.

In the meantime, I went on with my business. Time was going on. Before PURIM, I went peddling by horse and wagon and was meditating. I made my account; it is almost five years since I am here, and what are my achievements during this time? I brought over two children. It cost me a lot of health and money. Now the girl is for herself and laughs at me. She is even an enemy to me. The boy is in New York, and here I have to send all the time money home. I am already overworked. So, riding and filled with these thoughts, I completely forgot that I am riding on 6th Street toward the car (*trolley car*). At that moment, the car came and began to ring so that the horse got scared and turned me over and the four wheels ran over my weak body and I became unconscious. When I regained my conscious and opened my eyes, I saw that I am in Mount Sinai Hospital. There they had saved me. They brought me back to my conscious.

Through the papers, people found out that I had an accident. Those who knew me, also my sister and the children found out. Here is also a lot to write. Everything came to me with great difficulties, with thorns on my way. I don't know why. I was not, God forbid, a criminal at the old home, let alone here in my new country. Didn't I make every effort for my family and wanted the best, and I got the worst. Very hard was my life. But the more I suffered, the more I received the mood to strive further. I was in the hospital from before PURIM until two days before Passover. They did everything for me in the hospital. They gave me X-rays, treatment, therapy and medicine, and I slowly recovered. They came from the car company and interrogated me. They found out that the horse was a wild one and that it was my fault; that I drove against the car.

My only worry was that it was before Passover and that I didn't send money home. The years before, when I was worse off, I did not miss to send money for Passover. Now, when I have here the children, I didn't send, not only because I didn't have any, I was sick and in the hospital. For almost two weeks, I didn't know what was going on with me. I was very worried. I had a few best friends who used to help me always with a loan whenever I needed. They came to me eight days before Passover to the hospital. I felt much better physically, but I was very much depressed by the fact that I didn't send money for my family for Passover. They sent fifteen dollars, but I knew that they will not receive it for Passover. I received a couple of letters full with tears, why I forgot them? She thought that I will have the children with me and that this will be good for them and especially for me. But what could I do? To write to her the truth, I could not and didn't want to do for it was too painful for me. She warned me not to take them out, therefore, I didn't write. Either she knew that I had an accident or not. Regardless of the realities, she was all right there and I here (*it sounds more ironic than the reality,* Wm. G.). Two days before Passover, I came home from the hospital.

I decided to prepare Passover for me and the children. My boy came home from New York, I got scared—bleak and dark, in shabby, torn clothes and without a haircut. I almost didn't recognize him. He cried and begged me to forgive him. Of course, I forgot about everything and dressed him up in a suit and shoes, a good-looking boy he was. I almost could not recognize him that he was the same boy who came home from New York. Only the girl was not sincere with me. She was my greatest enemy. I understood it very well. I could not help myself. I made an effort (*in text tried* Wm. G.) that Passover should be in the best way, although I was very weak after about a month in the hospital. I needed a real home. What could I do? I thanked God that I stayed alive and that I am now together with my children. Passover went by. The Mr. and Mrs., where I lived, spoke to my girl that she should remain, and we should be together. She didn't want to hear, she only wanted to be free.

She earned, she had permanent work. I can't deny it. She didn't have understanding. Perhaps it was not so much her fault as it was others who told her to be so. Thus, was everything as I describe. In the meantime, I suffered from both of them. The boy didn't even start to work. In the house where I lived was also a man of twenty-five years of age, a very fine man who worked at neckties. After Passover, he took my boy to his work for five dollars weekly. I was very satisfied. Let him work for the time being rather than to go around idle in the street. He will, with God's help, become less a GRINER. When he will get older, he will understand the world better, and so, also his father.

So was it with the girl. She left after the holiday, and I didn't see her anymore. From home, I continued to receive letters, what happened to you since you have the children with you, you forget entirely about me? You didn't send me money for Passover. This hurt me very much. I was for a time in the hospital so I didn't send her, I couldn't. I sent her a few days before Passover. I knew that she already has now the few dollars. But she had Passover. What should I write her now? In fact, I didn't want, but I had to write the whole truth about the children as well as about myself, how I am suffering because of them, then she would write that I didn't listen to her. But I can't hide it any more from her, and I write to her about everything. I didn't suffer so much about my boy, he worked during the day, and at night he went to school. He became different later on and began to work at a store and earned more than the girl. But I suffered much from what was on the bottom of my heart. Perhaps I would forget it, but again, I can't; not, God forbid, that she is debauched or for some reason to have arguments with her.

My years were running in America, and I could not achieve anything, just alone by myself. To go back home never came to my mind, although I was well convinced that with my older children, especially when I will bring my wife with the little children, and I am already so worn out that it will be very hard. These thoughts I let go away from me, and I wrote to her that she should prepare herself for the trip, for I am going to send her SHIFSKARTN, and she and her parents used to answer me that I should not think about her coming to America. She can't go. She is sick, and the children are sick, in one word, NO! NO! A couple of young men came home from America and told her that I am always sick. My answer to her was everything is true, but America is very dear to me, even to die, God forbid, is better here for a poor man.

I already belonged to a lodge and corporation, and I wanted to console and encourage her. I wrote her that even to die in this land is better, let alone to live. I saw that the years are passing by in vain and that I didn't accomplish anything; not for the family, not for myself. I gave up my hard work, I didn't have anything anyway, and to bring my wife and children, and that they see me dragging a pushcart, I didn't want very much, so I peddled with trimmings—it is easier and more dignified. I will try to earn and as soon as possible to send for them, and God will have to help me. They should not suffer there. Perhaps everything will get better. I was already six years in the land, and I already had my first papers for two years, and, thanks God, I made a better living. I saved a few dollars to send for them. I needed a lot to have everything. I didn't have anybody to help me. I thanked God that they didn't exploit me. I could already have something from the boy, let alone from the girl. She didn't want to have anything to do with me, as you already know. I applied my strength; my only helper was my mood.

I got the tickets in the office of ROSENBLUM. I paid cash, not to go with a small boat as I was traveling, also not to travel for twenty days as I traveled only two weeks. From Hamburg direct to Philadelphia, everything should be in the best order, and I sent away and wrote two or three times weekly and warned them that they should go and when is the best time to travel and money for the trip so that they should have everything that there should not be a lack of anything. I lived with the hope that soon I will be helped out and have here my wife and children and convince them that America is a good land, but it is always like this, that the foolish man thinks (*plans*), and our dear God laughs. He really laughed at me and constantly was breaking me. Why, until this very day, why do all my undertakings that I think that they were good and not bad come with such hardship and with prickly thorns? Before anything else, it cost me a lot of health, and especially money. The road with thorns is already too much. From my sending until their coming took time. It was already seven years since I was in America. Here it is very difficult for me to write. The worst, the worst I overcame. I don't know if it happened to any other person what happened to me. Then after waiting so long, a long year to wait and to write constantly letters as to when and how they should go, and it didn't help. The terrible fate misled her and the children. They left in March and had to take the boat, which goes straight to Philadelphia from Hamburg. They came when the ship was gone. It was too long to wait for this ship, so they were told that they should take the boat NECKAR that goes to Baltimore. What knew GRINES? And truly speaking, what does it matter? From Baltimore to Philadelphia is altogether 2 hours by train. I received a postcard. In fact, I was angry why they didn't go directly, but it was too late. Let them travel in good health and come in peace.

My joy is not to describe. My love for my wife and children didn't fade away, as was the case with others who were seven years in America. I can say that I was truly honest and faithful to my family, therefore, I suffered so much and hoped, and my imagination was such that I can't describe. I rented a house a few weeks before; almost the nicest. All my LANDSLAYT had much more, but such a house, they didn't have. I felt that since I suffered so many years, at home I should prepare for her at least a nice home. Let my family have pleasure. But not only for them alone. I like to live in a nice house, that there should be everything. Money is not the main thing. I always like to give away money for charity in order to live, not to live for money. I wanted very much to live and try for my family that they should live in the same way as my true friends. I made every effort to live in a way I will undertake to please them, and so God will help me.

I furnished it very nice, even with carpet in the whole house, even the steps. It was a three-story house. One floor, I rented out. I had rooms; for almost everyone a room and a room for my goods, woolens and trimmings, all the best, especially the trimmings. I enjoyed it very much, and I saw that I am gaining health. I took a look; I had my own a couple of hundred dollars, and I was a debtor of a few hundred dollars. I did good and nice business. My joy was great, and I counted the days and the hours. Soon, soon I will have a telegram from the office that I should go and accept my wife and children, who I didn't see almost seven years since I left the home. At home, when I went one week without seeing my beloved wife and children, it was difficult, and now, I have been so long without them. In the same way, they without me. But soon I will have them.

Part Seven
My Nightmare and Finally Gaining My Family

Exactly April 1, 1913, came a telegram from ROSENBLUM that my family arrived in Baltimore and that I should wait for them at the station at 22nd and Chestnut Street at 8 in the evening. One can well understand my joy. I and my boy and good friends which I had here, they came to my house and everyone was happy. For they had pity for me. They saw how I suffered and how I was faithful, and since we lived to see this day, so everyone wanted to come and take interest in my joy. Every minute was too big (*i.e., too long,* Wm. G.) for myself and for my boy. Suddenly a second telegram came, but not from ROSENBLUM, only from Baltimore, that my family was detained in KESSLEGARDEN (*used here generically to mean immigration,* Wm. G.) for a minor reason, a child is not entirely well. What and why, I don't know.

    You have to excuse me, I missed what I needed to write before I came to this. Even now, after so many years passed that they give me a lot of comfort. I had plenty TSURES, so I am nervous, especially because of what I went through. It can't really be described; it is too hard. But I took upon myself to write about my life, what I lived through and what I am going through now. And with God's help, I will continue to live and will have everything. But with God's help, I will still be able to write a lot of good things, and everything will be good.

    I spoke in the office to Mr. ROSENBLUM, who assured me that it is nothing. Instead that they were to come at eight in the evening, they will come at ten. Also, all my friends tried to persuade me that everything will be all right. We prepared ourselves, but we didn't eat supper. We all went to the station, also my friends, men women, girls and boys. The minutes were for all of us dear (*i.e. that we were patient,*

Wm. G.)...my heart told me something is wrong, I almost fainted. God helped; the train arrived with many immigrants for whom their relatives were waiting. Everyone met his own, embraced and kissed. I directed my eyes all over, and I didn't see anyone, not my wife and none of my children. A dark cloud descended upon my face and my soul. I was like in the darkness, everyone was running toward me, "What is the matter with you? Why are you so distressed? If they didn't come with this train, they will come with the next train, at eleven o'clock."

I didn't let to be consoled by anybody. My heart told me that something happened. Apparently, my happiness and my joy are not about to come to me so quick after all I went through. But whatever the reason would be, the main thing is that they are alive and in America. If I could know for sure, I would take everything without complaints. But, after all, what happened there with my wife and children? Who will come to tell me something about them? I could not take it. All my good friends were standing near me, also my boy, who was also depressed, who asked, "What can it be?" While speaking, came over to me a woman, a GRINE, who just arrived from Baltimore, who waited for her friends. She was asked, "Do you know, didn't you travel with a woman, her name is LEAH ROSEN with four children?"

She didn't answer immediately, she does not know.

After a few minutes, the same woman said, "Yes, I know about a woman and children, they were detained, a little girl is sick. I don't know whether it is her eyes, her head or something else. I just recalled, I saw them, yes, yes."

I didn't like her words. Why this should happen to me, but thanks God that I, at least I know that they all came well.

I got a little bit relaxed, so what will come with God's help tomorrow, will be better, although the hours were for me very long and dearer to me than all the years of waiting. But one has to be strong and to thank God for as it is. My heart was trembling in me that something terrible happened to them. We all left the station and came home to my house where many friends were waiting, and a supper was prepared. Instead of a nice supper, I was ashamed like a real fool. It was indeed the first of April that I was a fool so deceived and ashamed. Everyone talked to me and wanted to comfort me, but I felt I should expect something that I will be satisfied. I could not help myself; I could not sleep the whole night. I thanked God that I lived to see the early morning in order to hear something new.

In the morning came a telegram again that I should come to Baltimore, that I am needed there. My heart told me that it was not good. I, with my boy, went immediately. Coming to the KESSLEGARDEN we didn't see my wife and children. They took us to the doctor. The children looked out through the bars like from a prison and screamed, father and brother, they recognized us. These were the older children. They didn't let us in. I was talking to the older girl; she didn't know anything. And so, waiting outside, after a while, I knew would pass by my wife with the child who have come back from the doctor. I can't describe how I felt each minute. I was unable to stand or to sit. I felt that my strength goes away from me. It took almost two hours of waiting until finally we lived to see them.

If I would not know that she has to come, I would positively not recognize her, so deserted, depressed and upset from her trip, especially the last two days. We fell, each other, into our arms and the rest you can imagine for yourself. This can't be described, but only with tears. She, my wife, screamed strongly, "My beloved husband, is this America? I waited so long, went illegally through the border and traveled on the sea so long and now here we are detained. Why, I don't know. Tell me, perhaps you know better, you are already here longer in America." I wanted to answer her, but they separated her from me-us and were confined, that's all. I didn't have anyone with whom to talk. The children were screaming there and cried that they wanted to see their father and older brother. My wife was crying and screaming that she wants to see her husband, who she didn't see for so many years. It can be understood that I and my boy were also not silent…it is not easy to write and is impossible to witness it. To live and go through everything is still a great ache in my heart.

The supervisors who observed us pitied us, and they permitted us to enter the circle with them for not more than fifteen minutes. I already knew while we were outside, so I stuck in a few cents (*most likely to a supervisor,* Wm. G.), and we were already more than an hour together. I spoke to them and comforted them that soon they will be released. She told me that "They found on HAYKE something (*it could have been ringworm,* Wm. G.) that does not allow her to be let in. She has to be cured first; otherwise, it can't be. Therefore, we were detained. She has to be examined by a few doctors." What could I do in a strange city where nobody knows me? I spoke to them that a day later or two that they will be released and that we will go together home to Philadelphia, where I already prepared a nice home for them in the best conditions.

They would not let us stay any longer. The hour or more was for us only like a few minutes. It was very hard to get separated after so many years not seeing each other. I could not help myself. I and my boy went to town to find LANDSLAYT, who would advise me to whom to talk and, indeed, where to stay the few days. I found out. I really found a few and, indeed, true friends who went with me all over. They could not help me and not advise me, for they themselves didn't know anything. We stayed there a day and a night. On the second day, as soon as the day began, for I could not sleep, I immediately went to them. It was the time when they permitted me to go in, before not but the few cents helped. They let us in, and we were there as long as we wanted to be. They told my wife that they have to take her with the child to the doctor. I felt at my heart, easier, that they will not detain her. It never came to my mind that I will have trouble with them. A clerk came over to me and said that he is sorry that he has to take them to the doctor. I and my boy waited until they will come back.

We waited for perhaps two hours until I saw them. My wife was crying very much, and she embarrassed me.

"The doctor said that the girl has to be sent back, and because of the child, we all will be sent back. Is this true, my husband? This is America, the free land, which you love so much?"

I looked at her and didn't know what to answer her. After a while, I regained my composure. "No, no, my wife, not so quick they will, God forbid, send you back. It can't be. Perhaps our sufferings were not enough yet. My dear wife, we will get away with a lawsuit. We don't deserve this from God. I worked for many years in America in honesty, and you and the children suffered at home, now when God brought us together; no, no, it can't be, and it will not be." I comforted them and stayed with them a couple of hours, and I again went in town to find out what I should do. Nobody could give me the right answer, they didn't know. I went to an official in charge of immigrants. One said that this is nothing, that in a few days they will let them go. Many Jews and Christians were detained. Another one said that it is going a fight between Democrats and Republicans, the first year when President Wilson had to occupy the chair in the White House to become President. They told us different things, but in the meantime, it happened to us. And here, in Baltimore, I am a stranger. If this would happen to me in Philadelphia, where I am acquainted with many people who could do for me everything, it could all work out. I already had the first papers. I stayed with my son a few days in Baltimore and saw that I will not accomplish anything. I am asked, but I keep quiet. What will come out from such a silence and not to rely on bad people?

So, we went back to Philadelphia. I told it to everybody, but nobody could help me only with a groan. The answer was if you would have the case here, we would be able to do something for you. And, in fact, it was so. Nobody could help me. I was running around like insane asking what I should do. But there was one answer from all that here we could do something but not outside Philadelphia. I was a few days in Philadelphia when I received a telegram that I should come soon, that I am needed. I took the train. When I came, they already knew me, they opened and let me in. My wife and children are crying. I almost didn't recognize them since the last few days, so they changed.

"A misfortune happened to us. The child, HERSHELE, became very sick. He has high fever."

"Where is he?"

"They don't let any approach him. In the last few days, three children already died."

I forgot about everything and asked the clerks who supervise to let me see my child, that I am the father who brought them. They let me see him, but I was told he is dangerously sick. One hope is for the child that he should be taken from here to the hospital, and perhaps he could be saved there. Here I am a stranger, and to whom can I complain that it has to be done very soon. If not, God forbid, the child will be lost. I already forget about my wife and other children and prayed to God that

I don't want anything, only that my child should be well. I went in town and cried and begged to save my child from the KESSLEGARDEN for a fire is burning, children die day by day. I will pay as much it will be requested.

My landsman went to other well-known people, and God helped. They took my child out from there, rather from the fire, to the greatest hospital, but there was little hope. I forget already about my wife and children. Even if not, what could I do? Perhaps we would know their fate, but the fact that my child is now in the hospital changed everything. I again stayed a few days with them, together. I rented a room where to sleep. A Jew lived near the KESSLEGARDEN; he was a watchmaker. I rented a room from him and also to cook food for my family, for they could not eat there. Thus, they were carrying food to them day by day.

I again went to Philadelphia. I was very busy with my business. In fact, they were not on my mind. I needed the money. I was not a rich man. I had a couple of hundred dollars, so I sent for them and prepared a nice house in the best conditions. I had in my business some dollars. Money was not my main concern. I tried and obtained as much as I wanted. Thus, I disregarded the question of money for me, only to save them. When I was in Baltimore, they looked for me in Philadelphia, and when I was in Philadelphia, they looked for me in Baltimore. It was two days in Philadelphia and two days in Baltimore.

In the meantime, came Passover, so I and my boy came to them and boarded over Passover at a landsman, also to carry food for my family, although the city supervised that the immigrants should have everything. I didn't want it, and I didn't need it. The first two days of Passover, I went to the synagogue so I should be able to see people and ask them what I should do. I was told that they can't be released until our little child will be well and will leave the hospital. On HOL-HAMOYED of Passover, I went to Philadelphia for a few days, and my older boy went with me. I received a telegram that I should come immediately to say goodbye to my child since he is near death. It is easy to write now, but how I felt reading the telegram, I can't describe and not to tell. I applied all my nerves and strength, the last ounce, in order to describe everything; not everything, because it is not possible to portray what I went through. I said to my boy, "We are going. God knows if we will still see him alive." I had tickets because I was constantly traveling. The two hours on the train were for me two years.

My strength left me; my feet didn't want to serve me to walk. I got dismayed during the time we traveled from Philadelphia to Baltimore. My boy understood it very well and felt it. He already, K'AYN HORE, was a young man and understood.

So, he said to me, "Pop, we only have to pray to God that we should still see him, especially talk to him."

I can't describe the ride from the station to the hospital. They let us in immediately. He was by himself in a room for I paid for him a private room. I didn't see anybody. I didn't ask anybody; we went straight to his room. We saw him crying and screaming and calling, "MAMEH." When we heard this, we thanked God for the great mercy he showed to us and hoped that God will soon help us. And so it was; from hour to hour, it became better. I stayed a few hours with him and saw the chief doctor, who said now he will already live. The boy had been so sick, the doctor said that they had already put the feather to his nose. At the night of the crisis of his sickness, he had double pneumonia. As he recovered, it became easier for us. We went from him to my wife and children to tell them that the child feels, thanks God, better. He is saved, and they trust that he will live. They didn't let her go to see the child, only when they saw that the situation gets worse and they were putting the feather to his nose did they bring her like a prisoner to him.

Coming to my wife and children in the KESSLEGARDEN, one can understand how I met them (*in what conditions,* Wm. G.). They already forget about themselves and only pray to God for the child that he should recover.

When they saw us, "What is the news about HERSHEL, were you already there?" "Yes, we were."

"How is he?"

"He is alive, thanks God. He will, with God's help, live. The crisis, which broke out last night, maybe is over."

One can well understand what was going on with my wife and children and how they forget about everything and only prayed to God for the child's sake. That they should be sent home and that the child should live was my only prayers to God, blessed be his NAME (*in Hebrew HASHEM,* Wm. G.).

Out of joy, we all cried together. We expressed each to the other our feelings that God will help us soon. One has not to lose his mood. They were cared for by my older daughter of about fifteen, who helped everybody for every day came new immigrants. They (*i.e., the author's family,* Wm. G.) were already…they got used to this life. Furthermore, they had hope that soon they will go home with me to Philadelphia. I told them everything, how I prepared a nice house, how children have it good in America. I also felt different because they let me stay with my family as long as I wanted. I don't know whether this was because they liked me or the reason was the very often few cents which it always cost me. Anyway, we didn't suffer so much, but to be there and to see everything that was happening, one can't be satisfied and to forget so quickly.

The second days of Passover (*the last two days, seven and eight, which are Holy Days,* Wm. G.) I spent in a better mood. I went to the synagogue, and I heard a good Cantor. I wanted to forget and meditate in my prayers. Furthermore, I didn't think that they will be sent back home from America. It is enough to be terrified, but now when my child will get well, with God's help, they will be sent to Philadelphia. Whenever I asked, I was told that as soon as my boy will leave the hospital, they will be released. I, therefore, didn't try to do anything more.

After Passover, I and my boy went home and waited for good news. Since I needed to have a lot, I had to be in Philadelphia and collect a few dollars. I phoned, and every time they answered me that everything is all right. That one of these days, they will take the child out of the hospital, and that all will be sent home to me. I waited every day for a good telegram that I should come to take them or that they will send. But the telegram was not good, for it told me that my child is already out from the hospital and that in a few days they all will be sent back to Europe. As soon as I finished reading, a darkness overtook my eyes. I fell to the floor and fainted. My boy and all in the house began to scream, people from the street began to run in and stayed with me until I regained my conscious. I didn't expect such a blow.

It took time until I regained my composure, I mean my senses. Yes, here I want to call your attention that already six weeks passed since they came. You may well understand how much strength and money I lost. Only one thing was left with me, mood and hope. For these two, I fought very strongly all the years, particularly now, and I always thanked God for this, and I thank him ever since. I see that he helps us, as you will see in my further writings, with God's help. But now, when I read the telegram that they are being sent back, I got lost and felt that I was abandoned by God. When I regained my composure, I saw so many people around me, those who knew me, everybody, and I felt my heart was very heavy, my boy was crying, "Father, don't let yourself down." God helped me, I came back to my thoughts, and I said to myself that if I will let myself down, it will be my fault and also their murderer. I must live, if only for my wife and children. If I will let myself down, they, God forbid, will also be forlorn.

Furthermore, it came to my mind, didn't I ask God that he should give back the life to my child even if it meant the family must be sent back; he listened to my commandment rather my request. Now it is possible that it is my destiny to be another year homeless, that I take it with indulgence only that nobody should, God forbid, fail. Now when God helped us that he is alive, so they are sending them back. Better into the land than into the sand, and I armed myself with fresh mood. Not that I took it, only that I thank Him (*i.e., God,* Wm. G.) that he gave the fresh mood to me and not, God forbid, took away from me. This was my weapon, to always have a war with my life, especially now.

I needed fresh money. The old one was exhausted. I didn't have and became a heavy debtor but it should not be recognizable to others. Yes, I almost forgot, when I fainted, a few teeth fell out. I let it be fixed so that I should look good, and I continued to go to them. Coming to them, they all cried. "We will not endure this. We don't have anymore, the strength to go back. The child can hardly move with his legs in the same way as I with the other children." I came out with a scream to the authorities, which gnawed me all the time and gave me faint hopes that when my child will be out of the hospital, my wife and children will also be freed. The answer was that they can be released now, but we must send back the girl. If not, we have to keep her in the hospital not less than a year time, and I have to give for her 3,000-dollar bond and pay fifty dollars weekly. They put these difficulties in order to scare me. My answer was that I will fulfill everything. They inquired in Philadelphia to find out whether I am a well-to-do person. It turned out that, no, I wasn't.

The truth was that to take her to the hospital, nothing could be done. At home, everyone wanted to help me, but here it was entirely different, a conspiracy of the officials was going on both from the Democrats and Republicans. As I said before, there was great confusion, not necessarily only for me. There was at this time, young and old, Christians and Jews, everybody who were disregarded and no mercy was shown to anyone and they were being sent back. It really came out that we became victims, it is impossible to explain. One should not be forced to remember this, but I have to as I am now, it should be known what such a little man went through. They wanted earlier to release my wife and the other children to me, but my wife refused. She will not let the child go back home by herself. Not so quick were they sent, I didn't let it and fought them. I kept the family back from two ships on which they were to be sent back. I operated with other's money because I didn't have any of my own, having already spent, long ago, the work of all my years.

I borrowed money, I tried above my possibilities, and I went to Washington with my older boy. I engaged a big lawyer. When I saw that I lost so much, I took away from the family, including what I did for my older daughter. I realized that I lost my few dollars as well as from others, and especially my health. After two months, I gave up my struggle against them (*i.e., the officials,* Wm. G.), and on a certain day, I was notified that they are being sent back. I expected that this is the way it will be. It even came to my mind that I should go with them, but I recalled that I went to America only because of the children, that I am not even allowed to make such a dangerous step.

I bought everything for the children, for the girls, nice American dresses and shoes and hats, and for the boy (ZVI HERSH), the one she gave birth to shortly after my departure, all the best for their trip. In the last days, I brought my sister to say goodbye to my family. She hadn't seen them. She stayed there a day and went back to Philadelphia, taking with her the older girl (RIFKA) to be, in case of necessity, the lady of the house. I remained with them and comforted them when I was able to see them. This is the way it had to happen. "You are not the only one who saw it with your own eyes that many mothers remained without a child and that two died here. I tried everything and did everything for you. But God wanted it this way, and indeed, he did good to us that our child remained alive. We have to thank him that we have our child. I only pray to Him, blessed be his name, that he should give me further mood and strength and, with His help, I will continue to try for you, and I will have you soon back in America. We got used to this that it has to be this way."

The last days we were joking with the officials there. On a beautiful day, the last days of May, meant only for pleasure, the greatest (*i.e., rich,* Wm. G.) Americans were going on the same ship. I didn't want any more to hold them back, for I kept them back from two ships, and every time it cost more money and health. Now I realized that I don't have to hold back, and I waited for the hour when the ship has to depart. The hour came; I walked them all to the ship. This is hard for me to tell, particularly what I went through and felt. So, my beloved wife and my children understand it very well. The crew was very big. The greatest intelligent men and women and their children traveled on this boat. All went, and I with my wife and children between them. I had, at that time, 33 dollars in my pocket. I gave it to my wife, and I promised her to send her more money that I shouldn't eat and drink and give to the children everything that all of them should guard their health and to go, for heaven's sake, to a big doctor, and with God's will, in a year and in good health, I will bring them back.

I have the desire to describe everything, although it is very hard and it can't bring back any health, but it is worthy to tell. As we were walking between all the people, I saw an envelope laying on the floor. I picked it up and took a look. I saw three single dollars, so I thought, should I give them also to my wife. Then I realized that I didn't have a cent in my pocket. I have to return two dollars to the watchmaker, and how is it possible to be left without a dollar? A ticket back to Philadelphia I had, and so the three dollars were left with me.

There were a lot of people traveling on the ship at the end of May. The beautiful sun was shining, everything had a good smell, the fresh air of the month of May. People kissed each other and bid farewell. They all were shining from happiness. The only ones we were, I, my wife and children, upon whom a black darkness descended. As soon as my wife and children boarded the ship, the music began to play, and they forgot about themselves (*their situation,* Wm. G.). Only I, myself, was left forlorn at the edge of the ocean and saw that the big and beautiful ship begins to depart from the shore and disappears more and more before my eyes. Everyone with his white handkerchief waves goodbye to his friend. But not for me, no, for me, they disappeared immediately as soon as they came on the deck of the ship they were swallowed and locked up as in a prison, isolated. I was standing long, long and looked at the sea until the ship completely disappeared from before my eyes. But I still remained there thinking. When I got away from my thoughts, I didn't see anybody around me. All people, big and small went away. Only I and my thoughts remained long, long absorbed and thought about the whole time of my years here in America. All that I went through.

Everything was like a dream. I felt that everything was true. I became so desperate about everything that I went through, and I got completely lost. It came to my mind, I should rather say that I lost my mind, almost that the best thing for me would be as I stand here by myself alone at the coast that I should throw myself into the water. Let it take an end to my life, if this can be called life. That God could do something like this to a family? But in a second, I regained my thoughts; my mood was awakened. Why am I thinking of such silly things? It is true, I was very hurt. I lost my health and I—in hardship and sweat—saved a couple of dollars for what I worked so many years. And now, when I was already standing at the edge my happiness, the waves of the ocean, in anger, took back my family to the same shores from which they came. But if I get lost, God forbid, everything will be lost. I will bring misfortune upon my wife and children. Also, others will suffer because of me. No, no, it should not be and will not be. Only because of them, I must be strong and remain alive and continue swimming along in the great and deep ocean (*i.e., the world,* Wm. G.) and, with the help of The Master of The World, achieve what my heart desires all the years. It is true that everything comes to me very hard, all my roads are full of thorny obstacles. But I hope in Him that everything will be, with His help, good.

So, I was wrestling with my nerves. Nobody disturbed me, for I alone was standing there. A thought was molesting me. What am I going to do being sick, poor and in debt, what will I do? But I reversed my thoughts that I am still a rich man. I remembered that I have in my pocket the three dollars, that it was good that I found, and that I have a ticket to go back to Philadelphia. I left the shore, and after I cried very much, it became easier for me to leave. I said to myself that I have to thank God, who bestowed upon us such great mercy that they were sent home healthy. I recalled my boy when he was in the hospital, so very sick, when they gave up his life. Furthermore, I recalled the children, which I have with me, and first of all, the girl that should be the mistress of my tiny house, because it had to be this way. I began to regain my strength. The three dollars that I had in my pocket; I gave two dollars to the watchmaker for sleeping a few nights. So, I was left with one dollar. I went into a saloon, and I ordered a glass of beer and for a bite, a slice of bread. Truly, I never went into a saloon, and I never drank, but this time, I only wanted to get drunk.

I went back to the city to say goodbye to the good friends who tried for us. To my deep regret, it didn't help. It was not their fault. They pitied me very much. We bid farewell to each other, and I came home to Philadelphia, ashamed. I suffered for almost two months, not eating, not sleeping. I lost my health and money and, in the end, they had been sent back. It was natural that I was comforted and helped also because I didn't lose my credit. My children, my boy and my girl, they also encouraged my mood. The older girl (CHANA), from my first wife, was already dating a boy. I continued my business. At that time, I lost a few teeth, they hurt me. I should rather say, they were pulled out. So, they put in dentures. It was something new, and I could show up before people so that I didn't let myself down, that nobody, God forbid, recognize that they weren't my teeth. Although my heart was full of pains, nobody should know what was going on with me. I only said that I will soon send tickets for them and that within the year, I must have them, with God's help, back with me.

What could strangers tell me? What did they know? Their answer was God should help you. I knew that I am very much in debt and I can't undertake to bring them. I felt that I will not be able to hold out so much. I was longing for them and especially pity for them. Here from a child, I didn't have any help. The older girl was estranged, as I described before. I suffered because of her. The boy worked and earned a few dollars weekly and this not always. The GRINE girl I had to have in the house. It was very bad for me (*i.e., I was in a precarious situation,* Wm. G.) wherever I wanted to turn. I was always independent. I never complained, God forbid, to anybody. I carried the burden by myself. I only thought to obtain money and to help myself, not to take away, God forbid, from anybody. Only to help myself, to bring, with God's help, my family here. I will overcome everything, when we will be together it will be different. With children in America, everything, with God's help, will be different. It is not only for me such a difficult undertaking, but with the help of the almighty and of my children, we will be helped. Regardless to what my situation was, I was not adjusted, but to get out money from another person, I had the skill. I paid very well with high interest, including with my health, which I never had, but mood and confidence I always had even until now. I wish this could be for all my future years. This (*i.e., courage and confidence,* Wm. G.) helped me all my years, and I hope to God that he will never it take away from me.

Before I took from someone, I suffered much (*in text, my life came to an end,* Wm. G.), particularly that I had to pay it back in time—I never had it. Hence, I had to take from another one, and thus, I was manipulating. Now you can understand how one feels and looks like and lives with such pressure. But nobody knew it, only myself. With my honesty, mood and belief, that I, with God's help, will overcome everything, and that in the end, everything will be good. I used to confide a little bit, do you know to who, to my sister and to her children and for her children to help me. Not in the form of a donation, only to help me out. It will be better than to ask favors and borrow from others and pay a high interest. Regrettably enough, instead of help, my sister berated me. Not because of maliciousness toward me, but because of devotion. She knew that I am a weak person and that I further insist on bringing my family and will get more and more in debt and that I will bring upon myself misfortune. She knew that my wife and children are not like others. "They will be dissatisfied regardless what you do for

The Inheritance (Yurusha) 121

them." She, therefore, was against me, not about sending for them but that I should wait. I also knew this and understood that it was right. For I already had a sample from my first two children. I felt that I can't live this way, to suffer further for years. Whatever, it should not be this way. I must play, like in cards, with my fortune; to make a strong effort and try to bring them exactly to the year. I should do all I can to have them. Money was not, for me, a hindrance, as you already know, no matter how much I should pay. It had to be.

One thing kept me back from sending for them. The fear that the children might be sick, then they will not be permitted to enter, and then I will be forlorn beyond repair. But to this I found an answer. Here in Philadelphia, I was already acquainted with the politicians from the time I had to do with the problems of my family in Baltimore. I belonged to a lodge, and I was acquainted with many people, people of influence. I must to mention, for the good, Mr. MOSKOVITSH from the HEVRE KEDISHE (*a voluntary burial society that existed in almost every Jewish community in Eastern Europe,* Wm. G.). He helped me a lot, not with money but as a good fellow brother. He was the president of the lodge, and he was a big politician. If this would happen with my wife and children here in Philadelphia, they would not be sent back. There in Baltimore, he could not do anything for me, but here, yes. He had his best friend, Mr. COOPER, an employee in the immigration office, and he sold passenger tickets from a company. His office was on Washington Avenue. So, this Mr. MOSKOVITSH went with me to him, and he told him everything, the truth, and he undertook to sell me tickets and to bring them to me, with God's help, without fear—SHOLEM. He told me that if I would have obtained tickets from him, it would not have been so… (*It means that they would not have been sent back,* Wm. G.). But this was the way of God, perhaps it is better so, what knows the sinful human being: good that I am a Jew, and one has to thank God for this. No matter, God forbid, it would not be, it could, God forbid, be worse.

The fact that all of them, thanks God, will be here is already good for me. I should not sin, and I told him the whole truth, and he undertook to sell me tickets, SHIFSKARTN, and to bring them to me without any fear. And it really was so. How much he told me to pay, I paid. Everything was done in the right way, and I sent money so that they should have to live on and for travel expenses, and I wrote them that they should be further ready to go. She answered me a couple of letters that she is still afraid to go, that the girl must still be under the doctor's care (*in text ZIKH LETSHN—a Slavic term also used in Eastern Europe Yiddish,* Wm. G.). When the doctor will permit, then we will go. I tried to send as much as possible, for they needed to pay the doctor. While here, I and my boy were contemplating how to make a living, and God helped us. We were earning, and we were able to keep the house. All was in the best order because I knew that with God's will, I will have my family back. I wrote to them always in the letters how they should go. They already knew a little bit and had experience to travel.

Yes, I forgot, I didn't write about myself, what I went through or about my wife. I didn't write anything and nothing about the children. I will, therefore, write and mention about their journey back home. They went on the best ship. Yes, a pleasure and they were accorded in the best way. But only on the ship. As soon as they arrived on the land, they began to feel how unhappy they are. Was it not enough for them the journey to America, to stay almost two months detained, not to see the bright light, not the bright world of life and to enjoy something? And to be so many years and to toil with little children in poverty and to wait always for a couple of dollars which I used to send to her to sustain their life and to live with hope that God will bring them to be together with me. Sometimes they received the few dollars in time and sometimes not in time, and they suffered from hunger and cold, especially in the first few years. She and the children went through plenty. Their luck was that she and the children were with her parents.

And here, in Baltimore, she had the hope that we would finally be together after so many years apart, and that hope was destroyed, and they were sent back. But this was not yet the end, what they went through coming to the border, a woman with little children, obtained by fraud for a couple of dollars the necessary papers, and the end was that they were caught; driven in a procession of convicts from town to town, and from village to village. Now one can understand how much they went through. I suffered in America, but at the same time, I could enjoy other things. But they continued to be in the same bleak life. One can understand how she felt. I am writing about her, not about the children. What do little children know? They are back in their home, but my wife felt very bad. It is impossible for me to describe the voyage that my wife went through during those years.

When she, thanks God, got out from the old home with great pains and here went through so much, I cannot imagine how I can properly describe it in my writings. Her story is much more than I tell about myself and my life. They brought my wife and children to my native SHTETL, VISHNEVETS, there where I have brothers and were detained like prisoners. My brothers were notified, also acquaintances who knew me. They brought them food and tried to make their road shorter, to send them home to LONIVITS to be with her parents. But the authorities didn't let them go, as they would have robbed the whole of Russia, until God helped them, and they came home in peace. Incidentally, at that week was the wedding of her sister. The father and the mother were very happy with their oldest daughter and with the grandchildren being there. It was not a small thing to have them at the HUPEH (*marriage ceremony,* Wm. G.). They were happy together and danced. This is the way God, blessed be His name, leads and truly they thanked God…This is the way it has to be.

Now, back to my writing. I sent money as always and for SHIFSKARTN. She didn't write me such letters as she used to write, that she will not go and only that I should come home. Now she wrote entirely different. She would like to live to this good minute to go back to America. She got the feeling through the walls, American life, LADIES FIRST! But to our deep regret, she could not catch it yet and still had to wait a little longer. The girl still needed help from the doctor. I could not blame all on America, but it could be dealt differently. It depended on politics, not on private persons. So, you could not have any anger. I sent money above my possibilities. It took ten months' time, after which I received a letter that they are leaving. My heart was very much trembling, but here I knew that they are going direct to Philadelphia. As soon as I received the first letter, I went to Mr. COOPER, and I showed to him what she writes to me. He told me to be quiet (*i.e., not to worry and stay calm,* Wm. G.), that everything will be all right.

"You go, do business and earn money." This all was his answer. He is a very fine man. He further told me that "If you would have bought (*in text taken,* Wm. G.) before the SHIFSKARTN from me, this would not happen. But now the past was in vain. Don't worry, everything will be all right. God should help that they all should come in good health. Go, go."

He encouraged me greatly and added strength. I was already satisfied. I received again a letter from HAMBURG that they were going to LIVERPOOL to take the boat. My wife was there, very frightened, and she wrote me to be assured that everything should be all right; he even had promised me that as soon as the boat arrives, he himself will be on the boat, and it really was so.

Before PURIM, I received a telegram that I should come to take down from the ship, HAVERFORD, my wife and children. How happy we all felt. The first time they came on April 1, 1913, and the second time on February 21, 1914. I, with the children living with me and many good friends went to the port where the ship has to arrive on Washington Ave. We waited almost a whole day, and the ship didn't arrive. The hour was like a year. She arrived at seven o'clock in the evening. I didn't meet Mr. COOPER (*in the text COOPERMAN. Apparently, it is the same person who shortened his name from COOPERMAN to COOPER,* Wm. G.) in his office. He kept his promise. He was already on the boat. All immigrants were kept overnight. Only I am the most happiest from all. They handed me over my wife and children in the evening, a few minutes after the arrival of the ship, without any difficulties.

They only asked a few words. "Is she your wife and are the children yours? Take them and go with them in good health." The joy of all of us is not to describe. All together, it was a short distance of several blocks from my house. I lived at 1226 MOYAMENSING Avenue. There was bright light, clean and beautiful in the house for good friends were waiting and many came to share our joy. Everything was good. But I myself felt at that time very much (*i.e., he had much to think,* Wm. G.). First of all, my health, secondly, PARNOSE (*living subsistence, livelihood.* Wm. G.). My money was exhausted and also from others, and now, here much was needed. I kept myself strong, not to say a word. I watched that nothing, God forbid, should be lacking, and with good health and God's help, everything will improve. I will earn a little bit, a little from the children and everything will be, with God's will, all right.

Part Eight
Trials and Tribulations – My Real Life in America

My love for my wife during those eight years didn't cool off. To the contrary, it warmed up. I loved her in the old home, let alone here. Why not? She was pretty and a good housewife and wise. Most important, she was good to everybody, with a pure soul. K'AYN HORE she had many virtues, only one fault, she was never satisfied. So, I suffered much because of her. She immediately made this known in the old home and here, and about this I knew before. So, I tried the best above my strength (*i.e., possibilities,* Wm. G.) to have a nice house with everything in order that she should be satisfied. To my deep regret, no. If an outsider would not know this, everything would be all right. But it came out from her, herself. I showed that I rented the nicest house and furnished it beautifully, even the steps with carpets, for I came among rich homes (*in text between,* Wm. G.), so I learned from them how it should be. Let it be as it is, there was everything. The house had a cellar where one could live. That is where I kept the merchandise; the best clips, pieces and trimmings. There were three rooms where others could live. I used to always have a full cellar with remnants and trimmings, the best clips and rags, everything. I sold the merchandise to New York, and I made a nice living.

But now, I remained without money. In the last couple of weeks, I didn't have anything on my mind but their arrival. The business was neglected, but I didn't tell this to my wife. Thanks God that we all are already together. I beg you (*i.e., the wife,* Wm. G.) give me mood and be satisfied. If you will be satisfied, everything will be, with God's help, good. If, God forbid, no, it will ruin me. What happened, you will have in my further writing. She didn't speak to me, but she looked dissatisfied. I showed her some merchandise of trimmings and took her down to the cellar, where outsiders lived before. Here I used to keep the woolen merchandise. I showed it to her and also explained my business dealings. "Do you see? The commerce here is not like it was for us in the old home—grain. At home, I used to carry, and I had support, about 200 pounds and earned a half ruble (*in colloquial Yiddish a ruble was called A KERBAL, in text KERBAL,* Wm. G.). Here, if I buy 100 pounds, I earn two or three dollars and sometimes five dollars. But one thing is not good for now. I don't have, now, customers, no money. But don't worry. God will help us. We will have everything."

But instead of giving me a word of consolation—don't worry, my husband, God will help us, you will continue to have, and our only concern is health. We will all try, don't worry, God will help, she raised her hands and began to scream and cry in a loud voice. I became scared. I thought that something had happened to her.

She yelled immediately in a painful tone, "Woe to me, for what did you bring me to America, to a bundle of rags? This is your trade of seven or eight years' time?"

I thought that the woman lost her mind. I answered her, "Why are you screaming, and why are you crying? I will explain everything to you, have patience, don't be wild, and listen to my few words. God should help that I will be able to continue trading in these rags and have merchandise as before. Then you will see how happy we will be and will make, with God's help, a nice living. I will take you to my acquaintances and landsmen who are in America before me and have the families here for a long time and didn't bring them twice as I brought you. Their wives brought money to their husbands, sold the business at home, and traveled on their own money and didn't need to have sent as I did for you. Nor did they have such a misfortune as I had with your deportation back to home and to bring you back within the year. Nevertheless, I prepared for you the best and nicest house with everything. Their wives have boarders until today, and washing their laundry, and I don't want this for you. Finally, you didn't see yet, anything. You were not in anybody's home; you didn't see what they are doing and what their husbands are doing and you already make noise. What is it with you? I don't request from you a thank you, but don't degrade me, and don't take away my mood. With your words, you are killing me."

But my words didn't help. She cursed herself. I answered her, "I am afraid, my wife, that you will condemn, so that the rags that you see here I will, God forbid, not have either. For you are not satisfied. It hurts me too much, my heart."

First of all, this is impossible, secondly, I don't want to insult her, and after all, she is very dear to me. She has a greater percentage of virtues. Therefore, I must forgive her. I will rather insult myself, for everything is my fault from the very first minute. I should not have written this, but as I pointed out in the beginning of my writing that I will not omit anything. The truth has to be written, everything as it was. Perhaps my own wife will read it as well as my children. They will see it, how they are also guilty, how badly they treated me the whole time, almost from the first minutes until now when I am so weak that I can't hold the pen in my hand. I can't walk with my feet. I can't do anything, and my mind wanders, and I can't concentrate about something, and I certainly don't remember what I was told minutes before. Therefore, my writing is so broken (*i.e., no sequence of action and thought,* Wm. G.). I can't spell, and nothing comes easy. From such a life, one can't feel good. I am strong enough that I can write as much as I do.

I stopped soon so not to get aggravated. I feel that I did a lot, which another one would positively not be able to accomplish. For her, it is nothing what I went through and accomplished. I lost my mood. All the places where I owed 100 dollars, I could not go to borrow even ten dollars, and where I was not in debt, I could not go to borrow a hundred. The poverty in the house began to be felt. Furthermore, that the children should go to work, she was also opposed with the same words that I already wrote. "This is America that my children should go to work in the shops." I wanted to convince her with quiet words... "Listen to me, America is different. Even at the greatest richest men, at the millionaires, their children are working. Usually, not everyone in a shop but everybody has his work according to his profession." She doesn't know about this, and she doesn't want to know otherwise. Everything remained the same.

The good friends who used to come to me spoke many times how dissatisfied she is. They felt hurt. Both men and women who envied me so much about the nice house and especially about my business could not understand that she is not satisfied. She only wants and wants. It usually came to conversations, and I usually tried to explain to her that "everyone must work himself up but that this has to be slowly. At first, on the first step, next the second until it comes higher and higher. But from the very beginning to jump very high, this is impossible. Then you must fall back and break your head and hands and feet and remain lying, not to be able to do anything." I thought my words will have an effect and could make her happy. It is true that we were in a bad situation after she arrived. I, certainly, was not happy either. I begged her to "come with me, we will go to visit a friend. There you will have an opportunity to see."

I used to give her all examples in looking (*around about others,* Wm. G.). To my deep regret, I could not talk to her as you should talk to a wife. She, little by little, took out from me my vital strength. You may think that she hated me, just the opposite, she loved me too much and was also very jealous. If I spoke with a woman, it is dangerous for me. I was not happy about this, so I suffered. I was already and American eight years and she a GRINE, but she loved me very much, and I hoped that in time she will look around and it will be different. But she is not different until this very day. In the meantime, my landsmen and friends learned that my wife is not happy in America, especially with me. I belonged with them to our corporation and sometimes connected in business, and I would get from there a couple of dollars. So, they stopped it and many times refused to give to me. They were angry, not at me, only at her. In the meantime, I suffered. I objected to her, "See what you are doing?" My one word to her, and she came back screaming. I could not endure it any more.

Usually, children lean toward the mother, more devoted particularly a GRINE. My wife was miserable. I didn't tell it to my sister, for she told me before not to bring her. I didn't want that people should know that much. But people recognized in me my pain. It is summer, long days and great heat and to go around daily depressed and to borrow further, I didn't want. I could not, indeed, receive as it was before. It could be recognized (*i.e., his precarious situation,* Wm. G.) by my face. At the same time, some people knew that in my house is different than in others. Nothing is being tried, nothing was undertaken by the family. The end was that I got sick again because of my worries, and I didn't even have what was needed for medicine. To all this luck (*ironical used in Yiddish when actually there was not any happy event,* Wm. G.), my wife was pregnant, K'AYN HORE, A HASENE (*a wedding*) without KLEZMORIM (*musicians*) as it is fitting (*the bittersweet irony that comes when something comes at the worst time,* Wm. G.).

I went several times to the hospital. The doctor concludes that I am only run down and very nervous. Something has to be done for me. The best would be that I should be for a couple of months separated, it means to get away from my family. Soon they arrived and handed me over a card to come to the place that I didn't like. I felt that I am all right. I suffer because of the terrible attitude that my family portrays to me. If my wife and children would say a good word and, indeed, to help with something, I would feel well. I felt much pain in my heart because of them, for they didn't understand my situation. I refused to go where they wanted to send me, and I continued to go on with my work and continued to try. This is the way it was going for a short time, and I hoped to God that, with his will, it would get better.

The birth went through B'SHOLEM (*i.e., in peace, with luck, etc.,* Wm. G.), and she had a boy who shined in the house with his beauty. I kept them at home. People didn't know about my poverty. I didn't have money to celebrate the BRIS (*the circumcision ceremony,* Wm. G.), but everything was in the best order. I already was a member of the beautiful synagogue and sat on the third row. Many noted people came and observed a decent BRIS. It was not a little thing, an American boy! Even though I didn't have what the BRIS cost, I got a fresh mood and hoped that, now, everything will be, with God's will, good. But it didn't come so soon, for such was my destiny, it couldn't be otherwise.

My words were never adequate. There was a war going on. She wanted to accomplish what she wanted, and in the same way, I. The children were always on her side. Finally, I realized in my heart that I could not pay back what I owed from before, neither could I do anything, and so I suffered very much. I was always thinking and looked for ways how to improve our situation. But from all this thinking, I came to the conclusion that without money, I would not be able to accomplish anything. I was only capable for business. I was a debtor to a couple of good friends, and I could not earn any more. At the same time, I stopped paying the corporation, I could not any more. In short, it was very bad for me. All roads seem to be blocked with thorns. I didn't even have merchandise. To go and take again, I could not because I didn't pay the bills. What to do with my family, about this we could never put things straight. They didn't understand me. In fact, they didn't want to understand me. I continued to be worried, and so it remained.

At that time, my rich uncle from New York married off his older daughter. He invited us to come to the wedding. I didn't have the ten dollars for travel expenses, nor did she have a dress to put on. I thought that since he didn't see for twenty-five years, after all his sister's child, I will try that she should go and not so much for the sake of the wedding but for the sake of all of us, perhaps she will influence him that he should help us in this terrible situation in which we are now. I knew that it is very hard to get out from him something. I thought that when he will see her, and she will tell him everything, for her sake and for the children's sake, he will help her. I figured that the wedding will cost him more than 200 dollars.

I sent her eight days before in order that they should be able to make for her something or to buy and so that she should be able to talk to him. I, myself, could not go. But on the day of the wedding, I thought it over, that I should go and also talk to him. Perhaps he will lend me, if not donate, what I need. I was only lacking in the couple of dollars to pay the bills for merchandise. I went.

They celebrated a very beautiful wedding. The bride is very beautiful and with all virtues. She took for a groom a lawyer, also very capable. He, my uncle, gave a few thousand dollars dowry. It was natural that everyone enjoyed him, but not me and not my wife. For we knew that we borrowed the few dollars for travel expenses. After the HUPEH, my wife and I went home. Before we left, I asked her whether she spoke to him. "Yes, I spoke much. I don't see that he will help us with anything. I sufficiently rested all these eight days. He was satisfied. I told him that I don't have anything to go to the HUPEH. It didn't bother him, as if to say, you can stay home. So was with help for us. He told me that I should not worry that a husband should make a living for a wife and children in America. Even to stand with a box with pennies in the street, a man can make a living."

"What did you answer him?"

"Yes, uncle, it is true, but for this, you also need money. Furthermore, why should he stand with pennies, they know him, thanks God, as a businessman and able to earn, only that he spent too much for us to bring twice to America. Now if he gets help, he could, with God's will, make business equally to others. God would help us, we could have PARNOSE (*livelihood,* Wm. G.), Uncle, save us. This way I told him."

"What did he answer?"

"He kept quiet."

I knew him very well. It was very painful for me that I am so unhappy and desperate that I have to ask him and above all, not to be helped. With whom should I speak? I looked to see who I could speak to, but all were strangers. We only knew my aunt's sister with her husband, who were at the wedding. They came from the country near Boston, SOMERVILLE, Mass., their name was ZAYDMAN. The taste is still in me. I can never forget it. It is worthy to write about it now, although it will not be so interesting, but with God's will, in my further writing, it will be very interesting; a picture of life that I went through while looking to improve my situation. I looked for people. Unfortunately, I didn't find, God forbid, I didn't look for myself, only for my family.

Since they were receptive and friendly, we opened our hearts to them that they (*the ZAYDMANS,* Wm. G.) should talk with him (*their brother-in-law, the uncle,* Wm. G.). Perhaps, he will be ashamed, and it may evoke in him pity, and send us home with some help in order that we should be able to maintain our lives. But, instead, to talk to him, they told us how in a bad situation they were a few years ago. They were broke in business and remained without a cent. They turned to him, not to her, their sister, for she never had a cent herself. Their talk, as well as with others, didn't help much. They knew that our talk will not help much. Only God helped them through a stranger, and as it is now that they have it good. It can't be better. They persuaded us that we should not be desperate. "You are young, the world is a world, not merely in Philadelphia. It is even in the smallest community in America that one can make a living, if only you are in good health."

"It is true," I answered. "I can, thanks God, make a living also in Philadelphia if I would only be strong and healthy and if I could pull a pushcart or to work. You know about my health, how much I suffered. But since I reached to establish myself in business, I can, with God's help, make a living. If I could have some money, I would positively continue to make a good living. I won't have to go around and look, but you can't help me." It is a lot to write and I wanted to remind these people that it would look, God forbid, that I always relied on people that they should help me and not The Master of the World. So, I am telling you that if I would only have the interest that people received from me, I would not be in such a bad situation as I am now.

We only remained talking, and all we got was aggravation with the good and the bad. On the second day, after the HUPEH, we went home ashamed. What should we do? Thinking does not give anything. It is getting worse every day much more and more. This does not add health. If I would totally collapse, certainly, nobody would help me. I experienced it all my years, that I should not let myself down. Thus, it came to my mind that I will go look for my luck somewhere else. Maybe someone of us has worked himself up or will just be a good brother. If I will not try, nothing will be and indeed why not? I heard that my oldest brother's son is already long in America, and that he is also near Boston or further than Boston, in the country or maybe in Boston itself. Nothing will come to me; I must go to it.

My uncle's brother-in-law also told me that he would try for me if I would come to him in the country (*Somerville, Mass.*). Perhaps it would be better for my health and also for my family, and we will need less than in the city. Yes, yes, the human thinks (*plans*), and God laughs. But I have the right to think, especially that I have here difficult PARNOSE, and that I should think of something better. Maybe it would not be right for me, but would it be so bad for me between the two options? My thoughts were interrupted. Why should I leave Philadelphia? Why, is it Philadelphia's fault? Didn't I earn good before? Can't I earn again? My problem is that I, for my family, got into debt. It can still be good for me, if I would only have money to do business and my older children should find work.

For so many years, I got used to the people I met. I know them and they know me. My heart was crying in me (*a Yiddish expression DOS HARTS HOT GEVEYNT IN MIR if one had much aggravation and hardship,* Wm. G.). I could not take it anymore, this bad time. We were in such need, but nobody wanted to know. I also had much chagrin. On a certain day, I left Philadelphia without a cent, only a ticket for New York and planned to go to the uncle with strength and conviction that he is the only one who can help us. If not, I will have to leave my family. But I was only thinking this way.

Arriving in New York, I cooled off, and I spoke to myself, to whom I am going to talk. Only a few weeks ago, we were there and spoke to him, and it helped nothing. I continued thinking about who I should be looking to talk to. If I would have the courage to speak to strange landsmen, all of them would help me. But in my whole life, I am too weak for this. I could never decide this. This way, the day passed in New York. I saw many acquaintances with who I used to do business. "You can afford to travel around these days?" What could they know what is going on in my heart? I was well dressed; I didn't want to say anything. One thought was on my mind; that I still want to see my uncle. He must help me.

I spoke to him with courage in a good and in a bad way. But to my regret, I had to leave him with the words that because of him, I have to leave my family, which is so beloved to me and for which I waited so long to have them here with me. When I left him, I thought about where I should go, and here, I don't even have a cent in my pocket for carfare. I came to my niece's daughter, and I told her everything, but I only brought her worries. Regrettably, she could not help me. She gave me five dollars, and she gave me the address of her acquaintance in Boston so that I might have where to stay overnight, for I didn't have the address of my nephew. I only hear that he is in Boston or near Boston. I had many landsmen in Boston, but I didn't want them to know before I find my nephew. Perhaps through him, I will accomplish something, and maybe I will need the help from others. I am not a beggar just to travel around and ask for money, but that is what I am doing. I am looking for a way to accomplish something for business or work. Maybe, he is wealthy and can help with some dollars as a loan that I should be able to come home. After all, it was very painful for me. I devoted much health to my family. You can well understand how I felt when I went by boat to Boston, for the train was more expensive. I didn't spend for myself a cent.

The trip was very interesting, more than my whole writing until now. While I am writing these lines, I am very nervous, for I went through a lot. I saw and especially felt at each step that neither I nor anybody felt it, only The Master of the World. If I could write like a writer and would be able to bring out everything and if I was able to describe it all, it would be important to be read by people. But, since I am little, weak and a poor human being, I can't bring out everything. The writing is only for myself. I will try, and I will make an effort that everything should come out the way it happened. I will not fail to write only the truth of what happened during my traveling the land these few weeks to look for help.

At first, when I came to Boston, I came to an entirely strange landsman. Usually, the ship goes all night from New York to Boston. Coming to Boston, it was still very early in the morning. I had with me a handbook, a satchel. I looked like a businessman. They were unable to recognize, as you already know, I was always a clean and good-looking person. Even now, when I am older and exhausted, when my hands are shaking because I am weak, nevertheless I am going around clean and nice. But the face and the body are showing already a lot. But at that time, I looked like a big businessman, I would rather say, like an American "ALRIGHTNIK."

Since I had the address, I went there and met only the woman. The husband had already left for work. The time was eight o'clock. She didn't know me; neither I her. I gave her regards from my niece. I told her that I want to find my nephew in the Boston area. He is from ZASLAV, VOLNER GUBERNYE (*VOLYN was a territory in GUBERNYE which is like a state in the USA and ZASLAV is a very well-known city,* Wm. G.). She didn't know, neither had she heard about there, but she told me that maybe I could find out in the synagogue. I didn't stay there long. I thought much and went into the street to find out where the VOLYNER synagogue is located.

Here I had some luck. As I walked up a few blocks, an old man came toward me, a very good-looking Jew with a nice gray beard. I realized that he is coming from the synagogue and from him I will find out. My heart didn't mislead me. I stopped him and greeted him with a good morning, and he very warmly answered me with a good year.

I asked him, "My dear Jew, could you tell me how to find VOLYNER landsman, born in VOLYN?"

The Jew answered, "Yes, VOLYNER, but from which city?"

"From VISHNEVETS, from KREMENITS, from LONIVITS."

"I heard about them, but whom do you need?"

"I need a ZASLAVER, who's from ZASLAV, YANKL LEDERMAN, and his father's name is FAYVL."

"I know him very well, from before at home and especially here. Only last week I saw him."

"That is good news for me, could you tell me his address?"

"Of course, I will tell you, but young man, who are you? For what do you need him?"

"I am his uncle, his father's brother. Since I am in Boston, I would like to see him. I didn't see him for a long time, many years ago."

"And you, yourself, where are you dwelling?"

"In Philadelphia," and he looks at me and is happy that such an uncle will see him. He thought that he (*the nephew,* Wm. G.) will get some help from me.

He began to tell me that only last week he was visiting his daughter, she lives in the countryside an hour traveling from Boston, the fare is seventy-five cents, and there also lives my nephew. He works in a shoe factory now, and that it is, thanks God, for this. A year ago, he had to be sent home to Boston to his father, so sick he was. Everything was told to me by the old man in the street.

"Go, go ,young man, they will be very delighted with you. He is so lonesome. He has nobody except from his wife's family, but they are also poor. A lot was done for him, but thanks God for this...the main thing is that he feels better and makes a poor living. He has a very respectable wife. She helps him."

He, the old man, informed me more than I wanted and everything as an indication that perhaps, I could do something for my nephew.

I completely forgot about myself, my sufferings became double greater. The old man almost didn't let me go, and he told me much more about my nephew, and he wants that I go with him to the synagogue, and he will tell me more. But I felt that I can't stand any more on my feet, to make the trip, to get away from home, to leave the family without a cent, was all too much. Today or tomorrow, the rent has to be paid and here I am away from home, and I went looking for what, I myself don't know. I felt that the earth is opening before me, and I am falling in. Darkness was before my eyes.

I waked up immediately as from the sleep and see that I am standing before the same man, a gray beard, most likely of seventy-five or eighty years of age. I became ashamed in front of him and straightened with pride, and I didn't want to talk. He should excuse me; I don't have time. I have to attend to business, and I asked the name of the town in the country. He told me, Everett Mass., and where I should take the train. I didn't ask anything more. He told me his name and that I should give his regards to his daughter and to my nephew, and I said goodbye to him. I went back to the place where I left my satchel. The street on the way was, for me, like a darkness. I didn't see anything, so deep I was absorbed in pains and in my thoughts that I asked myself, what should I do now? Why should I go there, and with what could they help me there? I will not be able to reveal my heart and my true circumstances and troubles. He will have pains because of me, and I because of him. I can't help him, and he can't help me.

My thoughts were absorbed, and I wanted to free myself from them. Should I not go, then the old man would say that he saw me and spoke to me. However, since I heard of his bad situation, I didn't want, out of pity, to look at his face. Should I go, then I have altogether one dollar plus fifty cents, and to go to the countryside to him will cost me seventy-five cents, and I will have for the fare back. Well, whatever will be, I will go. I want to see him and know his wife and children. He will not be able to help me. But to able to be a week or two, after all, in the country in the middle of the summer with such heat in the city, will be like a blessing. I was very much run down, I needed very much a rest. Yes, yes, I will go. At least I will have where to be. I don't have to tell them the truth, only that I want to see them. Since I am already here, I will go there. So, I went back and took my satchel. I don't remember whether or not I had a bite. I said goodbye to the woman, and I went to the train. In about an hour, I was in my nephew's house.

Before me was standing a very beautiful woman. This I could see immediately. Her beautiful face showed it, as well as her eyes and especially her figure. Next, I could see that she is a good housekeeper, clean and nice is the house and in every corner, equally a little child that she was holding with her. This I could also depict.

"Who do you need, young man?"

I only asked her, "Are you YANKL LEDERMAN'S wife?"

"Yes," she answered me.

"And who are you?"

"I am your husband's landsman."

She didn't let me talk too much and recognized in me that I am a new venture, more than a landsman. She knew that I must be her father-in law's brother. Therefore, she told me immediately, "It looks that you are my father-in-law's brother."

"Yes," I answered her. I saw that she was so very much delighted that I can't describe it.

I was also very much delighted to see that my nephew has such a fine wife and such fine children. But my heart was filled with sorrow, why should he be so poor and especially sick and that I should be like him, but what could be done. While we were speaking, a boy came home from school or from the HEYDER (*the traditional Jewish school in Europe*, Wm. G.). He was about twelve years old.

"See what a dear guest we have. Your father does not know anything. Go to the shop and tell him to come home."

I kept her back. "It is not needed. He will come home a couple of hours later. America works, it is very great."

"But an uncle, who we have not seen for such a long time, not just one time have we spoken about you that you have to be in America, but where, we didn't know. Now, thanks God, I wish to live to the minute that LEDERMAN (*this is a way of speaking, wives called their husbands by the family name,* Wm. G.) will see you for the whole time." Yes, it is already time, to see each other and talk about ourselves and our family.

It was time to eat. I armed myself with strength, my heart was beating very strong. The house was poor, but the cleanliness made a good impression. A strange person was at that time in the house, he was eating. She introduced him to me, that he is her boarder and that I am her uncle. "See, Uncle," she said to me, "now I am keeping only one boarder, but a year ago, I had two. One has to make a living. Lederman was at his father's. There he was helped. My father-in-law wrote to me that I, with the children, should also come, but Lederman didn't want. He (*the father-in-law,* Wm. G.) wanted to give us his whole wealth. Why not, perhaps it would be better. Uncle, it is this way, and the husband should be heard (*i.e., listen to his opinion,* Wm. G.). He came back with a couple of hundred dollars that the father-in-law gave him and went with a partner in business and lost every cent. He still owes to people. Now I thank God that he at least feels better and can work. Only health and everything will be all right."

The couple of hours I spoke to her and spent with her, I gained a lot of pleasure. I ate a little and thought that to be sick and poor is the worst, but a wicked wife is worse than death. But such a woman (*as his nephew's wife,* Wm. G.) could help her husband to get well and worked up again. From her talk, I learned, and I thought, if my wife would be so, I would have not to run and look like a madman. I can't, God forbid, say anything bad about my wife, but it is bad until today. She already told me everything. Nothing was almost left for him to tell. From the old man on the street and from her, I knew how to adjust myself, not to make myself a big man, and not to let myself down, either.

"Now, Uncle, I would like to know where you live and how you came just to us."

Naturally, I said a lie that I went to Boston for business, but I also knew that Lederman lives near Boston. "It so happened that I met an old man from ZASLAV. I already forget his name. He gave me the address, so I came here."

"You did very well, my dear Uncle. I should already live that Lederman should come home from work and should see, some surprise he will have. Such a dear guest."

The more she was happy with me, the more I felt worse.

"But, Uncle, do you know what I am going to tell you, the children and to the man (*her husband,* Wm. G.), should not be said that you are a landsman. Then we will see whether they will recognize you. Let it be this way."

We were talking, spent time, she asked about my family. I, in the same way, asked her about her family until the time came that my nephew came home from the shop.

She greeted him with joy. This I could see. Everyone would be able to see her decency. "Look, Lederman, a landsman of yours came to see you."

"No, no, my dear wife, this is not a landsman, only my Uncle YISROEL," and he fell into my arms. We kissed each other and cried more. He had a reason to cry, in the same way as me. I cried more about my present situation and in what conditions I met him. I could already see that he will not be able to do anything for me, let alone me for him, and here I have all together seventy-five cents in my pocket. We ate supper together and spent time together. He told me what he went through during his stay of a few years in America, what a time he had, and what he is going through now.

I understood that I can't be helped here. I can only bring them sorrow. I kept everything in myself. I could not imagine this, and I thought to spend here only a couple of days to talk over and to look for some way out.

He asked me, "Why do you look so bad?"

I answered him, "I don't feel good for a long time since I came to America. However, since the air is better here and the heat is not as great here in the country, I would like to spend some time and stay."

"With the greatest pleasure," she answered, "why not?"

The first night I slept with him, for there was not an extra bed. I almost didn't sleep, so nervous I was then. Only in the morning, when he went to work, I fell asleep, and I really slept late. To get out from the bed, I couldn't, so weak I was. But to go to the hospital, I didn't want.

I tried very hard and finally was able to come down. I met my niece in the best order. She looked good, smiled, and was singing cheerfully. She was informal and was friendly to me. On the table, everything was set to eat, and she was especially kind to me. I really ate with an appetite. All together, I was there a couple of days. I felt completely better. But here, my luck didn't last long. I intended to be there ten days or a couple of weeks. But the news was given to me that I should be happy, that next week, with God's will, on the SHABES, her sister's bridegroom will be called upon for an UFRUF (*it is a custom that a bridegroom is called to the Torah to read or say the blessings on the SHABES before the HUPEH,* Wm. G.) and that Sunday will be the HUPEH.

When I heard this news, nothing was left for me to do except to look for an excuse and get out from here as quick as possible. To be here for the HUPEH, you have to go to the synagogue with the bridegroom, and this costs a couple of dollars, and there will be wedding expenses. I also need to have things for myself. I can't show up like this. And here, I only have seventy-five cents to go back to Boston. I am getting more nervous. To tell them, I didn't want to bring them more sorrow. Furthermore, my mind could not absorb a wedding. What should I do? I didn't say anything. In the meantime, the bride and the bridegroom came to me.

"Yes, Uncle, you will already stay with us for the wedding."

I answered them, "To my deep regret, I can't stay. First of all, I am already a long time away from home, and I must be back at home at the fixed time. Furthermore, it is a wedding, and one needs to get dressed in other clothing. One can't appear like I am amongst strangers." They answered me that I will be welcomed by everyone. "No, my dears, I can't."

I said to my nephew, "I am leaving tomorrow morning back to Boston. I must be there to see some people and to go home."

"When will you go? Tomorrow is already Friday. Stay here over Saturday and Sunday. You will go Monday." But I can't, they understood it. I said goodbye before I went to sleep, for he goes to the shop very early. How could I leave in the morning when the boy is still home? I have to give him something. My heart is being torn to pieces. God, why should it be this way? What did I do that I am suffering so much, that I was driven into such a terrible situation? I felt that I am losing my mind.

I could not sleep the whole night. I hardly could wait for the morning. I heard how he left the house, and the children got up and went to school. Then I went out from the bed. I prayed and took a bite, and said goodbye to her, and I left as if I had done the worst thing. To take the car, I figured that I can't. I would not have enough for the ticket. I only remember how I must have looked, at that time, to others; how I felt, I can't describe. I left this street and went through another street, took a deep breath, and kept walking. As soon as I came to the train and got inside, I thanked God. Now, I can remain myself with my thoughts.

But as soon as I sat down, the bride showed up before me. She went to Boston to buy something and sat down next to me and began to talk to me. "I am asking you, Uncle, is it right for you to go away while you are already here and I go with MAZL to get married? You would have a good time."

"It is true, dear bride, but business is before pleasure (*the last four words are in English but written in Yiddish. Wm. G.*). She thought for herself that I am a big beggar (*in text, a Yiddish expression SHNORER, Wm. G.*). Maybe she thought that since I learned about the wedding, I don't want to stay. Perhaps it would have to cost me a couple of dollars. She was entitled to think it.

Now you can well understand my trip and what I went through, and how I was traveling together with her. I was thinking how to get away from her while leaving the train and not to meet her anymore. It was so, I said goodbye to her, and I wished her good luck. As soon as I found myself on the strange streets of Boston where nobody knows me, I began to continue to think about what to do, where to go now, at dawn? It was still long until daytime. If I would have a couple of dollars, it would be different. I think that I had in my pocket ten or five cents, that's all. So it was, God should be my witness, that I am not saying a lie. I hope that he will help me in my older years, although I lost at that time my whole health and also my mood. I write the whole truth. If I would be a writer, it would come out different, but this is my way and my story, and I undertook to describe everything. You should know what I went through during my life on behalf of my wife and children.

But it didn't pay off in my present circumstances. You will see the most important in my last chapters that I hope to God that I will be able to properly tell even though my mind is very weak, especially my spelling and writing, which, I know, is very hard to read. But it has to be this way because I am the littlest. What could I do with five or ten cents? If I would have more, I could enjoy myself greatly (*i.e., to eat something,* Wm. G.). It came to my mind that I should go to a pawn shop and pawn my watch. Perhaps they will give me five dollars. I paid fifteen dollars. I could enjoy myself to go somewhere to eat, and I would be able to go back to New York. There I could accomplish more than here. Now, how do you like my writing? I know that only an insane person can write this way but not to endure it.

Yes, yes, my dears, the nerves worked like the wires of the telegraph or other instruments. Better to say than the turbulent waves of the seas. Such was working day and night my distorted mind. It came again to my mind to go to a landsman for SHABES. I knew my best friend, good friend who was in Boston still without the family. He only had with him a son of twenty years of age. Most likely, he accepts me as a good guest. I had his address, but I didn't want to go. I was not eager. I wanted to omit people known to me because of my shame. I only wanted to be with a stranger. I will go to the pawn shop, and indeed, I went into one and then a second but more than two dollars they didn't want to give to me.

So, it came to my mind, I am a stranger here. Nobody knows me. I will go to HAKHNOSES-ORKHIM (*a shelter for poor wanderers, a community institution for guests and travelers to show hospitality. It was part of a Jewish Communities welfare activities. See more about this in my book,* Social & Welfare Institutions in Poland, Wm. G.). There, I will eat something and stay over SHABES, and I will have where to sleep, and no one will know me. What can I do? God knows the truth, that I am not a beggar (*in text SHNORER,* Wm. G.). After all, I am away from home. I met a Jew and asked him where this institution is located. He told me that I have to take a car and told me how to go.

I didn't have the money for the car, so I walked. The sooner you want to be the road, the farther away, especially for me. Something is wrong with me. Until now, I can't find out. Perhaps, God will explain it to me in my older years. So, I hope in him, and this keeps my mood up. It is summertime. The heat was high, and I carried my satchel as a businessman. This was not easy for me. My heart told me how hard it was. I didn't have courage, especially because of my distorted thoughts. This gave me great pains not only to my mind and body but especially my soul hurt me very much. If it would be another half hour, I would collapse in the street, and maybe that would be better for me. But I didn't want this and, thanks God, I understood it very well. What would that mean for me in a strange city and especially for my family if they had to be informed?

Finally, I came to the place and immediately reported to the supervisor of the institution. He looked at me and asked, "What are you, young man, a Cantor, a Rabbi or a Sexton, or a preacher or speaker?"

My answer was, "I am none of them. Only a little man who needs to eat and have a place to sleep and help with a couple of dollars. I am away from home with no money, and I want you to do something for me. I don't have enough to go back to New York."

"Young man, we don't help here with money. But if you want, you can be here a day or two, and we will give you a place to sleep and food to eat."

I took a look around where I am and what kind of people are there. I realized then that I will not be able to drink and eat here and especially to sleep. I rested for a while and continued to think what to do.

A thought hit my mind that I have the address of my uncle's brother-in-law, who spoke to me very friendly at the wedding. He is in Boston, maybe fifteen minutes by car. Why shouldn't I go to them for SHABES and tell them everything because they already know a little bit from the conversation before. He, himself, told me about a plan. Yes, yes, I will go there immediately. Either I will be peddling there, or I will get work. It does not cost any more than five cents car fare, and I thought this is the way God leads. I don't have to be here to belittle myself. I asked which car. It is like to go to West Philadelphia. They showed it to me, and I went.

Here it will be different. Here I will tell everything about my trip and about all my plans. First God and next all that they should help me to find a solution to my problems. If you go in good health and come in good health, is very good in America. The car or train went very fast, and, in a few minutes, I was already there in SOMERVILLE. If you have the address, you will find it. They showed me the house. When I came to it, I didn't believe that here lives a Jew. Another thing I looked to see if the number is the same. I rang the bell and immediately stood before me Mrs. ZAYDMAN. I recognized her, so she me. Only a few months ago we saw each other. Maybe she will simulate that she does not know me since she saw standing before her, an ashamed hapless person. I have mentioned many times in my writing how I felt about myself, but to feel belittled, never.

She didn't let me outside too long, and she invited me into the house. "How are you, and what are you doing, and how is your wife and children?" She asked about everything all at once, so to speak, make it short, she was in a hurry to leave.

I asked her where her husband is. Her answer was that she does not know why he didn't come home yet. Always on Fridays, he is already home at that time, now not.

She continued, "I have to go away, and he is not here yet." While talking, she asked me when I am leaving and from where I am coming?

I encouraged myself and said, "You want to know. I have time."

"You would like to stay over SHABES?"

"Certainly yes, only what, even if you would not want, I must because I don't even have five cents carfare to go back in town."

"And so, we will have time to talk. I am expecting a friend, since we have to go to certain people about help for a poor family. So, it is very good, one person should live for the other as for himself. Yes, yes, I don't forget God helped us a lot. Therefore, I don't forget about others."

"This way it should be," I answered her, "only that like my uncle lives, your brother-in-law, he does not live even for himself."

I looked around the house. Everything was in rich taste and placed exactly where it should be. As I was talking to her, she suddenly said to me, "here comes my husband." He arrived with a good team, a good horse, and cart with goods. I went out to him as soon as he drove in, and we began to kiss each other. He left the merchandise on the cart, went into the house, and he began to ask me various questions. I told him that

I want to stay with him for SHABES. He was pleased.

"If so," he said to me, "I will go outside and take down the goods, and then I will be free to talk with you."

It seemed to me from his words that I will be helped here with something. I went with him and helped him to take down the goods, although he didn't want to accept my help. In the meantime, I would be able to answer all his questions and bring out to him and tell him my true situation and that he must do something for me. He still remembered everything from our talk in New York. "I am young, and I want to work. Perhaps God blessed me, and he leads me this way to you and especially that I don't have a cent in my pocket."

He listened to everything I said. I told him that I already was at my nephew Lederman. He knew him from the same town. "I can't go home; I owe a lot of people, and that I don't have anything to help myself. You know it very well, as I told you at the wedding. It is not getting better; it gets always worse. Now you can understand the trip I made. Maybe, God leads it this way. I see that the country is very big. I am not anymore a GRINER. During the time I was a GRINER, I peddled in Philadelphia with rags, clippings and trimmings. So, I want to peddle here."

So, he answered me, "Why not, the country is big enough. Even if you go around with a pack, a bag with merchandise, you will make a nice living. You don't have any other way out. You can't go home. You may peddle. If not, you can work here, but I would prefer peddling."

"I used to work, but for me, is better to be outside."

"We will see to it. Don't worry."

I felt that he gave me a new soul. I helped him very much to take off the merchandise from the cart. When everything was finished, we went into the house where on the table was prepared the best food. Everything was fresh. His wife was dressed as the biggest lady. She really was tall. We began to eat, but I could not eat. I was swallowing in me my tears. My heart was telling me to calm down. As soon as we finished the meal, they went into another room, where most likely he told her everything. And so, it was that she left with another lady who had come, and she didn't say anything to me. I was left alone with him. Then he told me that he completely forgot that a GRINER is not permitted to peddle here without citizen papers. I let him know that in about a month, I will receive my papers. Then he told me that even with papers, I can't peddle here for a year. "So, I will work for the time being." He called on the telephone a man and a second one, and he tells me that they don't need anybody.

I understood that they, he and his wife, spoke about me. At least if I would not be away from home, and if I would have a couple of dollars in my pocket, I could go away from him, and I wouldn't say anything. But I am supposed to stay overnight, and it is the eve of the SHABES. SHABES, for me, was not a small thing, and about this you will learn from my further chapters where I describe the SHABES. I have, thanks God, what to write, not for anybody, only for myself. I am proud of myself. Not for anyone with my mood and self-restraint. I am satisfied until today, whatever I should not have endured.

If I could say it better, if I would have a strong disposition, I would not make myself to be recognized that I am in such a position. I considered to stay overnight in the street than to stay here. I understand everything very well and kept silent, even though God leads me this way, and that I should be strong and mainly watch my present situation and to see the further positive outcome from my trip. It must come, and with God's help, will come. So, I, the lonely man, thought and hoped to God, blessed be His name, that good will come without any excuses. First, I have to go through everything in order that I should know that there is a beloved God in this sinful world.

I didn't think long, and I said to him, for nobody was in the house, "Listen to me, Mr. ZAYDMAN, I see that you can't do anything for me," and I also wanted to tell him that his wife does not want it, and for her activities for the poor is everything in secrecy, and to do something for me, you refuse. But I saw that it is not the time, particularly the place, and I want to get sooner out from here before she comes back home. But what should I do if I don't even have five cents to get back into the city, and what would I do there? I will have to go to my landsman to stay over SHABES. I can't help myself. If so, should I stay here? I will go to Boston, and on Sunday, with God's will, I will go to New York. I had the last five cents when I came here. "Give me or lend me for the trip expenses from Boston by boat to New York." What he gave me I remember. I will remember it all my life, two dollars and seventy-five cents, and I said goodbye.

I took the car and went back to Boston. Now, please understand what I went through during one long summer day. It is easy to write but to describe my troubles from that time is very difficult, especially during this time. If you think that everyone could do this, then I say to you, NO! It is so difficult to tell you how I felt, but in my further chapters, you will see how many years this trip gave me, which I benefit from until this very day. The best proof is that I am able to bring out everything and that I continue to have to endure much, still gives me courage in my life. I am not discouraged, despite the fact that I suffer more, and the more I suffer, the more I feel love for the world and to those few who I met and who knew me.

But everybody, they didn't understand me. I am happy when I am writing, although I am full of pains, in sickness and poverty, but my love grows every time greater and greater. I thanked him for the two dollars and seventy-five cents, and I went back to Boston and straight to my landsman and stayed over the SHABES, not exposing anything with my remarks to his "What are you doing here?"

"I came from my nephew. I wanted to see him, so also you. On Sunday, I want to go back by boat to New York." We spent the time very well. On Saturdays, his boy was working. On Sundays, the father was working. If I would say that I am in need of a few dollars, he would have given me. I didn't want that he should know anything. I was already in America for a long time. He was still without the family a couple of years in the country. But since I have arranged that his boy will take me early Sunday morning to the boat, I will ask the boy. He will certainly give to me or lend a few dollars.

I needed a haircut—my hair was too long—and a clean collar and a shoeshine. I hated to walk around dirty and shabby, and here I have only money to pay for a ticket, nothing more. Even five cents will not remain in my pocket. If he would have given me at least three dollars, it would have been good. But Mr. ZAYDMAN figured out exactly the cost of the ticket by boat, not by train, and so it was. I don't write even one word that is not the truth. When the boy took me, I said to him, "I completely forgot that I will be short two dollars cash for I only have checks. I should have said it to your father, but I think that you have money with you. Give me two dollars. You will tell your father that I borrowed from you. I will send it back to you as soon as I will come home.

Yes, you will laugh about all the silly things that I write here, but for me, they were not silly, especially now. Hence, not all the silly things encountered during my lifetime give me still now life, but some do.

The more I saw the depravity and indecency led my eyes so that I could see better and learn more about the other's wickedness in order that I should understand better and better for myself. I wanted it, but to my deep regret, I could not. But now, listen to his answer to my request for help with a few dollars.

"I am afraid of my father. I'm still a GRINER."

"Don't be afraid. You remember at home how much money I used to borrow from your father."

"I will not give you. I must give back the whole lump."

"Don't be a fool. Your father would say yes."

I saw that he does not understand anything, so I asked for one dollar. His hands were trembling when I took the dollar from him, and I went back to New York. I took an account of my whole trip, and I felt that I came out strong and satisfied even though I did not yet solve my problems. I was able to travel and to see people and know where many thorny roads are so that I can find another path with not as many thorns. Something was glowing in my pure soul even though my body was suffering.

When I came to New York, I had the dollar. I took a shave and a shoeshine and bought a few collars. When I came to my niece, she handed me over a few letters from home where good friends ask about me, including one who I owed 200 dollars. It was all very encouraging, but I could not go to him to ask him again for money. He wrote me to tell me to come home immediately, and they will lend me and help me, for they know me well and why I had to go away, to look from others where I am not known, for help. He added that they know that Philadelphia is good for me, and even though I am in debt, I will, with the help of The Master of the World, pay back; that God will help me.

When I told my niece what he wrote, she said, "Write to him, for heaven's sake. You should return as soon as possible after he receives your letter."

They were angry that in such a time of trouble, I should travel around. I saw my merchant, who I used to sell goods to before, but during the time I was indisposed, I didn't do any business. He told me to buy good merchandise for him. About money, he will write to his cousin in Philadelphia, and he will help me with money. To return home, I didn't have for a ticket. I wrote my wife to ask if they came from AMERICAN TRADE COTTON to ask for money from whom I used to take merchandise for ten days with a discount and for thirty days net. I had to give them 120 dollars, and I didn't have any hope to answer them with payment. Their goods I already sold long ago. They are the greatest firm, a Christian one, and I made from their product half of my living. If I would not owe them, I could get more goods from them. I was so nervous and was scared of this company and worried about our relationship.

So, I wrote if they asked for money, and the answer was no. I asked for three dollars for a ticket home, and it was sent immediately. I left New York and came back home. My family was very happy and certainly me too. Everything is good if you have PARNOSE. They found out that I am here. Some of my best friends came to me and encouraged me. "Don't worry, Mr. Rosen, only be well, then you will, with God's help, give us back. We know you very well. You try, and God will help you." They took out 200 dollars if I want to continue to do business with them. Also, to pay rent for two months for a store so that nothing will be left for me to worry about being out on the street. I will be able to continue to get merchandise and sell, and so I will be able to try again and to receive new credit.

First, I took the bill for 120 dollars and saw it is written down that if it was paid in ten days, I will get a discount, and for thirty days or sixty days, not. If so, why did I become so afraid, I still have eight days' time to pay within the sixty days. It came to my mind that I will write to them that I need merchandise. If they will send me, then it will be very good. I will sell the goods with a small percentage in order that I should be able to pay them the bill and have again time, sixty days.

Before, I used to pay every order in ten days and deduct the discount. So blind, upset, and nervous, I used to be about paying the bill only for the discount that I didn't pay attention that I have sixty days.

I didn't think long and wrote to the company that I need such a kind of goods that I can sell immediately. On the next day, I saw the goods. I was ashamed of myself. What is the matter with me? Is this not a dream, or is it a reality? I was traveling over a month, but for what, I don't know myself. I spent time and health, and I humiliated myself for nothing when right here at home, I could have done everything. But I knew very well that because I am exactly a little man with weak nerves and always afraid of the fear that could come one day, for I was too decent, and for this, I don't deserve any thanks, only to realize that it all comes from something else.

But again, I must give deep thanks for my deep belief in The Master of the World and that my sufferings had to be this way. Now I hope to God that everything, with God's will, will be good. I immediately sold the goods with a lesser profit only to get the cash in order to pay the bill and further to be able to take more goods. Also, I now have money to go out into the street as I was doing before. And as wrong as it was before, now it was entirely different. Wherever I went, the cash register was open for me. I was asked to take money and goods which I needed. The years of war (*i.e., WWI,* Wm. G.) were approaching. I didn't listen and didn't look at anyone else to see that people were before making a lot of money, to the right and to left. I was involved in my work, running around, buying and selling, and working hard to make a living for my family and to give back to everybody every cent.

I didn't listen to what people are talking and only occupied with myself. I was thanking God that I am back home, and I make, thanks God, a living and that my wife and children don't need, God forbid, to beg for help from others and that they don't suffer anymore. At my first undertaking, I purchased a couple of thousand pounds of the best clips. It was a few cents more expensive on the pound. When I saw that I had a nice profit, I sold and bought more. I was satisfied, although at that time, others made hundreds of dollars. But I was satisfied and so the time, thanks God, was running good for me. I had a nice PARNOSE, and I could save a dollar, and I began to pay my debts little by little.

You know well that with our Jews, they should be in good health, if God forbid as one should be not in the best way, then out of pity which one renders to the other, things are going the way that the one is soon being "killed" because of too much pity, and not to see any more his face. Whatever can be done, it should be done. The first thing is they give him too much credit, and so on. When it is seen that some business is being done and that they are coming, and when you don't show a poor face, then you hear the same that they are losing money and at the same time, they make a profit of 100 dollars, and they say that they made a thousand. So, it was with me. As soon as I sold my first load and then the second and made a profit, so people said that I made twenty-five times more (*This paragraph is a critical and satirical description of the social relations of Jew to Jew at that time, especially in the economic life.* Wm. G.).

My mind was not any more able to figure out (*i.e., in business,* Wm. G.). My whole body was weak. I told my friends, "You know it very well. Yet if you will take upon yourself to understand and if you will help me, I will make a comeback, and I will throw myself anew into the great waves and repair the holes, which I destroyed and to be again at the helm in order to go forward. But you all have to watch my success," that, yes, was my answer. I had again come home, what could strangers know? They saw that I am weak, and I have a big store, most likely I am a wholesaler. But my people knew the truth very well, but to my deep regret, they didn't fully understand.

I came home entirely different, although I suffered there much, and I thought that usually they were very happy with my homecoming, and so was I. I loved my wife and children, and why not. If everything would be as it should be, we would be the most happy. I didn't believe mainly in money for the sake to have money. I wanted to live like a human being and also to let live the other person. I was afraid more than of death to waste, God forbid, the other's money. I don't know why. I can't explain it.

However, I blamed my family that they caused it that I should always suffer and work hard and never to regain my positive attitude. Everyone had a different opinion in life. I, however, when left to myself, I used to do good business, but many, K'AYN HORE, were divided and not together in opinion. I constantly saw that this is not good, so I protested and fought a war at home. They didn't listen to me, only betrayed. The end was that I always had to give up the store which I had. It became not good and fresh money was needed again and again. I had to support the other with more goods. I lost a lot of money. I trusted everybody. I thought that everybody is like me. I paid my bills much over my strength (*i.e., capabilities,* Wm. G.).

I really paid up a lot, but the banks and similar places with whom I was connected saw that my face looks very bad. Further, they noticed it in my deposits and also in my purchase of goods. It is usual for them to conduct everybody's business when is not, only many owners and bookkeepers. A working man can conduct himself, and I, as a small businessman, also needed their help. But since I was only one, there were some who carried away goods (*it seems they were simply stolen,* Wm. G.). Then you can imagine that I needed to go bankrupt. That is what should have come out from it, but I wanted to be an exception, not to give up when my ship was already sunk.

Another in my place, when he sees that it is not good, lets sink everything. I began the business by myself, was in the store by myself, and kept my head a little bit above the water. I worked above my strength, paid up little by little, and indeed to everybody, I paid back as much as I could, but for myself, nothing as you will see in my final writings. From day to day, I became full (*i.e., equipped with goods,* Wm. G.). I had in the cellar ten thousand clips rags, which was there for maybe three years' time. I did it with my own hands. Nobody helped me. Whose fault is it, you can understand. I was weak and sick. I was in the cellar to pick up the rotten rags and the fresh rags, the clips, and I sold them, and I received altogether seven cents a pound which had cost thirty-two cents a pound.

After the work, I became exhausted. I fell, and I didn't believe that I would be able to get up, especially to do something. From the money I took in, not even a cent was left for me, so that I should be able to go away for a few weeks to rest from this hard work to recuperate. In addition to the pains of the labor at such work from which I had to lose for each pound, twenty-five cents. I had 10,000 pounds, and in addition to this hard work, the store was filled with merchandise. I didn't let up.

I also want to mention here that the store was rented for fifty dollars monthly, and before I would move, he wanted to sell it to me, but I would rather give him more at a later time. He is now a SHOYHET (*a ritual slaughterer,* Wm. G.) What does he know, although I told him that I am ruined here, but what can I do? Perhaps the next year would be better. He thought that I am a complainer, a beggar. He always came exactly when customers were there; one for a package of cotton or for a package of needles. He raised the rent from fifty dollars a month to sixty dollars, and ten dollars a month was a lot to me. But I kept quiet, and the end of all, I had to lose money, and the goods I had were worth maybe 25 percent and I could not sell them. So, I really got sick, and I was in bed.

I had a lot of acquaintances; everyone knew me. If not, I made myself acquaintances as a little man, like a bird, I used to fly in between people where they also listened to me. I want to call attention that I write so like a bird because my confidence in myself during my life is indeed indicating a bird. Not one time I came between such people, but it didn't bring me anything wrong. Everyone was wondering, they could not imagine, that not long ago, he was in such a bad situation, and he became ill, and now he delivers so much merchandise, from where did he take money? Most likely, his friends gave him as it was the case. Whatever was the talk, but I was satisfied. I, myself, didn't mind much. Thus, thanks God, I was well off for a short time. I paid up many of my debts. I didn't feel a shortage of money. Everyone offered me (*i.e., goods,* Wm. G.).

During the years of the war, people worked themselves up, even the individual who never could earn something, particularly I, who was very skilled all the time in business. I was only busy with myself. I was satisfied, even if I was sick, I was already used to this as always. But, if you make a living, you listen more careful. It didn't mean as much anymore, for I already had something to save myself. At that time, people worked themselves up. I didn't even notice it. How come? I was so involved in my life, which gave me an opportunity that I should not have the need to leave the home and to face everybody face to face with a full heart. Thank God, I returned to everyone to the cent. I was already known, for my hand was not closed to help.

At that time, I became active in all useful societies, whatever I could do for the people. I was not, God forbid, a big spender of money. I was watching every cent. I didn't play cards. I only devoted my time to important things. I liked the synagogue, and indeed to go regularly to daily services, and especially on SHABES and holidays, not only for the reason of piety but for the pleasure to my soul. In the synagogue, I got acquainted with many good friends from whom I got the best favors with money (*i.e., private loans,* Wm. G.). They used to ask me if I need money. As usual, I was always short. For my own money, I didn't have yet. I was still a big debtor, and I gave back, needed much for business, and didn't have left for me and my family. So, I was helped much by synagogue Jews. If I gave someone interest, it was a very small one, and thanks to these monies, I could do good business. But honestly, it is very difficult what I experienced later, especially now when I write these lines.

During the time of the war, I kept my eyes closed, not looking (*i.e., not paying attention,* Wm. G.) at anyone, as I already wrote many times. I was satisfied with myself, with my family and good friends, and I strove to help the one about whom I knew that he needs help regardless if one turned to me or I to the other, and, with God's help, I helped. With my dollars, I influenced the other. I lived happily but only for a short time until the war intensified very much, which ruined everybody and his family. There were also those who were fortunate. I had a son of twenty years. He also had to be taken into the army, but thanks God, they didn't take him. Also, close friends from who we could not be separated, and they also were satisfied.

At that time, I used to do business to buy and sell all kinds of men's trimmings. I had customers from all over. When I came to one of my customers to sell my goods, he told me that he has for sale dresses.

"How come you have dresses?" So he answered that he has a cousin who became ill, so he sent to him to sell. This was not my line of expertise, so I took a dress or two to show it to my nephew, who is in this business, and I showed to him to find out the value of a dozen. Perhaps he will sell them or tell me to whom to sell.

He looked at the dresses and said to me, "Uncle, you can make with these dresses 300 and perhaps more, but I regret to say that I will not buy them, and I think that you should also not buy them. Furthermore, as you want, the goods are stolen."

My answer to him was, "What are you saying about this man?"

"Yes, yes, Uncle, you are as a GRINER. Today is such a time that the one who has a grocery store has for sale drugs, woolens, everything. So, it is many things are stolen goods."

I came home and told my wife what my nephew told me. She was laughing at me.

"You are a dupe, my husband. If you will not buy it, who else would buy it? He will sell it and will make a profit, and you will miss out," according to my wife, but even if there would be a profit in the thousands, I would not buy. I came back to the man that he should show me a bill.

He said, "A bill I should give you at the present time? See, I already have other merchandise. If you will buy one time, I will sell you again and again."

I left, and I didn't buy. I thought many times how people worked themselves up. If such an opportunity already occurred to me, so I go frightened. I found out how many people made money and are making money. Many succeeded and many, at that time, went to prison.

Not one time I came to this man in his store, for he had as a disguise some trimmings and other things to cover for all the merchandise that was stolen which was brought to him. I used to come to him almost twice a week. He was a tailor. I used to sell him trimmings. He used to tell me, "If you would buy the first time, you would always buy, for I have goods of all kind that they bring to me. I wanted, very much, to do business with you for I know you as a decent man."

"Exactly because of this, that I am such a person, I can't buy such merchandise. I buy merchandise that I know that I can sell, that the other (*i.e., the seller,* Wm. G.) gives me a bill. When I am selling, I give the other a bill. Even if I make less, I am satisfied. Such goods that are stolen, I never bought, and I will never buy."

He screamed at me, "You are a nothing. You don't know how to make money. You are only for work, to buy rags, haul and pack, and earn cents, not dollars. Look only at the ferries that carry the goods, all businessmen make money only from such business—goods."

He really said the truth, but I was too weak to get away from home where I was in debt of money and where it was known how unhappy I became. I already saw how people make money. My eyes looked openly, and I could do the same, but I didn't do this, and I didn't regret it. It didn't take long, and this young man was caught, and he gave away his earnings and dividends and went broke from his own business, and he thanked God that he didn't go to prison. Maybe you would like to know from where he took all the goods? A Christian who used to carry goods from the depot, and from there, they brought all kinds of crates with various goods, woolen and silk and cotton and shirts and stockings and dresses, almost everything to be sold. If I didn't want to buy, they laughed at me. This is the way little people worked themselves up, but later some died just because of fear. Some are, until today, still in prison, and some who were lucky are free and considered "ALLRIGHTNIKS" and got away with it.

I was the luckiest of all, if only I was in good health. Once the war came to an end, my quiet, peaceful life came also to an end because of the flu that broke out in Philadelphia as elsewhere. I, my family, was almost the first to be affected by what nobody wanted. The first victim was my girl of fifteen years, very gifted with everything. The most beautiful and the healthiest of all the children, and we brought the family doctor. He said that it is nothing that she should stay a few days in bed. There were the first days of SUKES (*Tabernacles,* Wm. G.), and on the other days, guests from New York came to us. We were playing and dancing. It was already that there will be peace after the war. She was now feeling all right. She went out from bed and spent also another day, and then she became very sick. We again called the doctor. He already knew what disease is going around in the city, so he knew the way to treat her. But the danger of the sickness could already be seen. The other children also had to go to bed. The house became a hospital. In the meantime, news came about many similar cases, also my wife got sick, only I was the hero not to get sick. The doctor came and saw what was going on. The first girl was in danger, so they took her to Mount Sinai Hospital in order to save the other children from a danger, and she was suffering until the eighth day of the SUKKOTH holiday (*SHEMINI ATZERETH,* Wm. G.).

On SIMCHES-TORAH (*a Jewish holiday on the day following SUKES, celebrating the completion of the year's reading cycle of the Torah,* Wm. G.), she was already home, dead. You can understand that while everyone was in bed, I was the only one who was healthy. It did happen to many others, but for me, the weak, who hardly managed to be satisfied, now it is again the worst, even if one does not have PARNOSE. If one does not have today, he can hope to God for later. But, God forbid, if it happens that a child dies, you can never get it back; there is no later. I continued to pray to God. I still have more children; they should be in good health, and so many months were lost from this illness. We could not do anything. We were exhausted from the flu. It cost a lot of money. I could not earn anything. The war stopped. Business became very bad. I didn't save any capital, as you already know about my life.

**Family portrait shortly before the death of Bluma, ca. 1917.
Left standing: Harry (Hershl), Irene (Chayke), Reba (Rivka),
Max (Mordechai), and Bluma. Seated: Leah, David, and Israel.**

I had about a few hundred dollars but not in cash-in goods, and I was much in debt to the banks and to private persons. I didn't have my own house. I lived in a rented house all the time since I brought my family. We had a very good home. It cost me twenty-five dollars rent a month. Since I was left with much goods that cost me a lot and there was nobody to whom to sell, so it came to my mind a plan that I should rent a house with a store on a main street. I had a lot of trimmings and woolen goods. I knew that I will open a store. I had a lot of friends and also credit, and, with God's will, I will be helped, and I will be able to make a living.

I didn't feel much strength in me from so much suffering. Next, I wanted to try this since I was too late during the war. I was selling my merchandise to everyone who had a store. I made a little profit, but the owner of the store made more. And now when the prices for goods went down and the times were very bad, I want to open a store. They tried to talk me out from it, but I understood it differently, that now is the time that I must do it. I also had left over many clips and rags, the best, which cost me thirty-two cents, 10 thousand packs, 10,000. I wanted to sell them for twenty cents, and I could not sell, and the price fell day by day. I could not buy, and I could not sell. I saw that I am losing my saved dollars. It didn't bother me so much for my own people as for strangers. I want to hold on and keep on my feet and not to lose my mood. I had to open a store, and so it was. If you look for it, you will find it. So, it is with everything. If it is destined something good, it will come and if so, God forbid, something bad. I found a house and a store at 1522 South Fifth Street before TASKER. The owner, a very nice man, a Jew and coincidently a SHOYHET, by the name of RABINOWITCH. He spoke to me very nice. He didn't want to sell, but he said that I can rent. After that, I will see that God will help me that I will make a living.

I was afraid to invest 1,000 dollars of others' money and goods. I will need a lot. I didn't want to get into trouble, ERLEKH IZ ZER SHVERLEKH (*a Yiddish proverb, that the honest way is a difficult way,* Wm. G.). The more I was afraid, the more I see now that it came. In short, it is too much to describe. I rented the store with the house above for a year. If God will help me, and I will see that I make a living there, then I will buy it. I don't care that I will pay 200 dollars more. He gave me his word, as a decent Jew, and especially as a SHOYHET, that later in a year, if I would like to buy the house, he will sell it to me for 200 dollars less. He wanted fifty-eight hundred. I moved into a broken and dilapidated store, and I installed beautiful lamps. There was no electricity, so I made it. I did paper hanging and painting and fixtures. I made it look bright. Whoever passed by, stopped, looked at the window and admired. I tried to have the best goods. I had a lot from before, and I tried to bring in more, and I really hoped that God will help me, and I will make a living, and so it was, indeed, my success. A new light was shining on us, and a better life with a lot of new hopes.

The business I used to do before mainly stopped. I had 10,000 pounds of clips and rags for what nobody asked, and nobody wanted to buy for even ten cents a pound. It was natural that I was very much worried. How much health I gave while I collected so much merchandise by myself with my own hands. I packed it. Nobody helped me. I did it all myself. Now the clips are laying, the best woolen rags, it is so long, that the rats have eaten some of it. I again was thinking, thanks God for this, that I can still do something else. My credit was still very good all over, and they considered me as a gentleman. Indeed, why not? I repaid to everyone from before, and I let myself be known to everybody and thanked God. But what should I do if my luck doesn't last long?

I began to think again that I am not worthy of much success since I am such a little man. I was considered by everybody that I have a lot, since I paid in time and kept my word. Yes, this I can say, that during my life, I didn't do anything wrong to anybody, like to buy out or to spoil or to take away (*without paying,* Wm. G.) from anybody. Moreover, they considered me as a decent man. What's more, I felt humiliated and was afraid of the other's cents (*i.e., he was afraid that he will not be able to repay,* Wm. G.). At that time, I used to go more often to New York for merchandise. The store required it. It became usual almost every two weeks or every month to go to New York.

I recalled my uncle, the rich one, and certainly the wicked one. You most likely forgot, but regrettably, not I, and I think that I never will. One can't forget it. I heard that before the war, he sold his business, took all his money, and gave it away with loans on interest, and since some took from him a few thousand dollars (*i.e., they didn't repay the loans,* Wm. G.), he took it to his heart and became very sick. So, I was told. Further, he was worried that he sold his store with the goods before the war, while after it, each yard was worth two to three dollars more. Whatever it was or not, he became sick. After all, I am his nephew, so I wanted to see him and talk to him that it does not pay to get sick because of money.

Furthermore, I want to tell you the truth. I wanted to see and listen what he had to tell me. He is a bad man, anyway. I went to see him. He lived private in the Bronx, in a very rich section. When I came to the house and rang, the aunt came toward me. She recognized me and was very delighted with my coming. For truly she was a good woman to him and to everybody. But she could not do anything by herself. She was happy with me because she didn't see me for a long time. She asked me and told me about her misfortune that the uncle is dangerously sick. He lost his mind, everything because of the money, and she brought me to him.

He was sitting in a rocking chair, pale, looked older, and he didn't recognize me. The aunt told him, "BERL, do you recognize this young man?"

His answer was, "No. Who is he?"

"YISROEL, CHAVE'S son-in-law."

"I didn't recognize you. How are you? How are things with PARNOSE?" and he talks to me as it should be, not to recognize in him that anything is wrong other than he is very weak. "Do you have any business?"

I answered him, "Yes, Uncle."

"What kind of business?"

"A trimmings and woolens store."

"You dealt in clips and remnants. You most likely made a lot of money during the war?"

My answer was, "How could I make money since I didn't have money to buy something and hold out? I, thanks God, made a living and repaid to everybody to whom I was in debt. Perhaps if I would have had enough money, and I was not in debt from before, I would have made" …I asked myself am I a man?

He answered me, "You know that I am so sick and have money. Could not you have come to me? I would give you money, as much you would have needed. You would have so I would.

I wanted to answer his words, but his daughter interfered and said, "Stop talking enough about money. The money made you and brought you to insanity, and it will bring you into the end."

I really wanted to remind him that when I came with my wife and told him that we didn't have money to pay the rent, and I don't have anything to go out in the street to earn a living, and begged for his help, that he turned us away. But I didn't want to hurt the aunt. He wouldn't understand and knew nothing. He came in soon with different words, he murmured and mumbled; only about money, ten dollars a yard for goods. My heart was very painful about him. After all, a learned man and a wise man should be so misled and miserable while he could be happy and make his wife and children happy and help many people. I can't say that I was just a little bit angry at him, but I wanted him to be well and live and to understand life; that money is not the main thing. If God helps and one has money, it also needs to be understood what to do with it. But regrettably, I could not help him, also not his wife and children and not even any doctors, not even professors. It was too late.

He suffered for a long time and spent many thousands of dollars. The end was that he died. He only lived to marry off one child and still left two unmarried girls. This man could still live; he, himself, didn't do anything to help. Not one time when I suffer and worry, I always recall my uncle and many others like him. But my worries were different. My worries were for PARNOSE and that I am always a debtor. I want to live peacefully and want that my family should also enjoy life and good friends. With him, it was different. He didn't live and not his family and he didn't help anybody. My constant worries ruined me so much and destroyed my health all those years that I had to stay in bed, very sick. Not, God forbid, I lost my thoughts because of money, only I labored hard and had too much strain in life. At the end, it came out so much of my problems that I was afraid, was scared because of the money which I always owed to others. You know from before that when I was in debt to a great firm, The American Trade Company, 120 dollars, I could not endure it, especially now when I owe the same company 1,500 dollars and to the banks 2,000 and still more to good friends.

I invested the money in the store, and the prices of the goods went down. They don't let you get relief; bills have to be paid, and the clips are still in the cellar, 10,000 pounds, which cost thirty-two cents a pound. Because of this anguish, I became very sick, and I could not get up. I was in great danger. I understood my situation. No one knew it, only myself; not even my wife and the children I don't want, God forbid, to know. I don't want to calumniate my wife and children. They are very fine for everyone, but regrettably, not for me. They didn't understand the American way of life, and they didn't take any interest in my business. They didn't know anything and indeed didn't want to know, even then, when I told them. It was very painful for me. But I kept it in myself. This was my greatest mistake.

I had good friends. They came to visit me, but what could the other one know, and indeed he was not about to know. I had a beautiful store with goods. I wanted to live very much, not so much for myself, but for the others, in order that I should be able to repay what I owed. I was a young man and didn't yet enjoy the world. The only thing I enjoyed was to suffer. I am always behind. It was suggested to me to go away from home. I went, but I came back soon because the place was not good for me if I would not be so sick. If I would not take everything so seriously (*in text to my heart,* Wm. G.). If only I would have to whom to speak, to tell the truth. Thanks God, my mind was always working. Of this, I always took care, rather saying, The Master of the World, he guarded me. I knew that I should be silent. Life and death is in the tongue (*the author used a Hebrew saying HAHAYIM V'HAMOVES B'YAD HALASHOHN,* Wm. G.). Nobody should know my condition. I suffered before when I was in debt with a small sum and spent it, so I lost my credit, and now when I owe thousands, I suffered even more and kept silent. Every day got worse and worse, and I was very nervous.

You can understand from all these years how I was worn out. The more I understood my situation, the more I suffered and kept silent. I could not stand it anymore, and I fell back again. I paid at that time to the banks and corporations, also at that time, I took also from the good friends and paid the other, took goods here and paid the other, I mean the first one; so, I was maneuvering and manipulating everything by myself. My wife did not understand me and especially my children. When I got angry, excited and when I used to talk to them and speak that everyone should help me and take care of the business with me, and in that way, I would not suffer so much, and I would not be so sick. But as an answer, they objected that I am not good for business, that I am too honest.

These talks hurt me very much. I could never bring them to my side, that they should understand me. Because of this, I suffered very much. I was sure for myself that I did everything for them, above my strength, everything for them. At the end, now, when it came out in such a way, they blame me for that. I could not reveal to strangers my unfaithful family life. As you know from my earlier writings, that I had to leave Philadelphia after they found out about my life, and out of pity, I could not get a couple of dollars. I remembered this very well, and I was afraid of the best good friend to discover my pains about my family life; how not supportive they are to me, even to my sister, I didn't tell anything, especially to her children, for they used to help me out with a couple of hundred dollars. In telling it good and right, it means that here comes out how little I was. I may say that it was my fault because I kept silent. My children were already, K'AYN HORE, adults. I thought that with God's help, it would soon come to an end.

I wanted to avoid that nobody should know how not supportive they are of me; how incorrect is their conduct. I must say that I did not lead right, that I didn't see that I don't have loving helpers. It was not their fault, they didn't understand. I should not have to give up (*i.e., the store,* Wm. G.). I can sell and to pay to everybody and the children should rather go to work, everyone. I didn't do this. I only continued to get into this great ocean and continued to swim (*an allegory of his situation,* Wm. G.), and broader and larger were the waves.

My shop was loaded with more merchandise. It had to be enough not only for me, but I had my boy as a storekeeper, and I was thinking for him. I took money from the banks and borrowed privately, and why all this happened because I was too faithful and also because I wanted the best for them.

My oldest boy worked at a building as a glazier. He fell down. They brought him home hardly alive. I was afraid for him to continue working. He already had some saved dollars. So as a father, I tried to give him the store, such as I cared about the school and also in business college for the girl. She could already earn, but when I saw that he can't stand by himself, and at the same time that my daughter was very weak to go to work, I figured out that they both should stand in the store and work together. My thought was always good, but unfortunately, it was of no avail. It was not their fault. So, I kept my store and needed to manage them. It does not mean with my work only to manage the money problems but to get it (*the money,* Wm. G.).

I was already weak and exhausted. When they needed money, when I was talking in a good way, it didn't help, let alone in an angry way. I felt then when I will give out, I will be helped, but they, God forbid, will have to close. I felt that I am the captain of my own ship, and I have strangers' money and also goods from strangers and that I will go down. It will be my fault. I was always at the helm and never lost the sight, although I encountered many storms and not one time my ship was damaged, and I paid for it with much of my health and especially with money. In other words, plainly talking, I saw that holes are coming in my daily balance. I am getting deeper in debt every day.

I used to talk it over with them, "Have pity, I am always exhausted from my constant leading such a heavy ship where I always get hit from side to side. It takes a long time until I will be able to regain my bearings, and you are standing aside. Help me pull it and repair it. Maybe God will help that we, all together, will be able to bring it to the shore unharmed and save ourselves, but understand with me and be devoted to me. Consider me as your captain, but you have to be devoted servants and see to it that, God forbid, there should not occur more holes, and we should repair the holes that we already made. If you will do so, then you will see that in the end, we will land at the shore; and also, there to be very careful to climb up. You have to put your feet on the first step, not to jump, then you will see that everything will be different."

They laughed at me. "Who listens to you? You are a fine man. You are showing that you are decent and hard-working. America laughs at you without any pity."

I used to get always very upset and aggravated, why should it be so? I haven't accomplished anything. I saw that I am again going down. I was too weak to get free. I had only one way for me to feel better, and that was to get away from the home for a couple of weeks. Then I would see that I am a perfect person, that I am healthy, but only for a few weeks, during which I could forget. But when I continued to think that I left them in the middle of the ocean, that they could not travel forward and not back, then my heart became ill. What should I do?

I used to write letters to them and warned them. Dear wife and dear children, as you can see, you need me to be your leader, so indeed, let me. I am begging you, since nobody knows what the trouble is with me, only you, you can help me. You should be faithful and support me. Everyone should follow his work in which he is skilled to do and to help me. Then you will see, with God's will, that God will help us that we will make a success in the store. If, God forbid, it continues to go as it has until now, it will be impossible for me. I am too much exhausted. My eyes can't see so good My hands have not enough strength to work and carry such heavy loads as before as you have seen.

I want to point out that I am writing like a bird. Not one time I was among such people who tore up all my feathers, and I could hardly save my life, and it took a long time until it grew back, and you understand what I mean (*allegory,* Wm. G.). If you don't understand it yet, then you will understand everything later. Not one time will I still mention the bird and say that it is equal to me, my friend in life. Yes, I had a lot of acquaintances. I belonged all over to many societies and organizations, and it didn't pay much.

A book treasurer at the synagogue, he thought that he fools me. I thought that I fool him. So is the world. So, they are cheating. But this is only in saying. You can't cheat. Only time is the best bluff. I was appointed as the treasurer because I was considered as an honest man. I was well known from all circumstances. They also considered me as a person who worked himself up, and I took the job because I needed money such that I would not have to pay interest. I must tell everything, although I would like to omit it. It looks as I would run for prestige, but with God's will, you will learn something different.

Being a treasurer had a different meaning for me. I used to get favors from synagogue brothers; they used to lend me money from the synagogue (*GMILES HESED a loan without interest,* Wm. G.), which helped me in my bad times when I could not help myself. The checking account was in my own name, and because of this, the banks looked at me as the biggest. I considered myself as the most little man, for I was indeed in a very bad situation. We got together each Saturday and each holiday in the synagogue. Everyone was happy, and I was upset. I saw many people to whom I owed money, and I didn't have the ability to pay back. I was also in debt to the synagogue treasury. My life was very bitter. They didn't know of my bad situation. They should not know about this. To quit, I didn't have the opportunity. I was connected not only as treasurer but also as a private person in the synagogue. I was very active there. I had many people to whom I owed 500 dollars each, which I paid as I did the banks. I was tied up.

When I became very sick, they wanted to hear, after all, I was a treasurer. So, I had many visitors. What could they know? I had a very nice house, not mine, but many thought that it is mine. The store was full of trimmings and woolen goods. Everyone knows that such goods are very expensive. They had a lot of pity because of my lying in bed. I really had friends.

When I got better, the doctors advised that I should go away, for I was very exhausted and run down. A few of my good friends heard it. After that, while I didn't go away, they wanted me to go. I pronounced some disguised words that while I have a lot, I can't do anything to go away because I don't have at hand the few hundred dollars that it will cost. They suggested at that time to go to MONTCLAIR for six weeks. Then, two good friends requested from me that I should not refuse them. They will lend me 200 dollars for a time in order that I should be able to go away for a time. Since I knew and believed that this will be good for me if I go away, although I was further thinking what it will be after I come home and it will continue to be so, and I will have to work to repay the few hundred dollars for they are only lending to me.

Perhaps I will get better, and my family will consider that I am suffering. I must also say that not only I suffered, they all suffered and mainly my wife. She is different from everyone by her good nature, a very good pure soul. This was not good for her (*i.e., the author's sickness,* Wm. G.) and not for me. I could not suffer, but she could, and this was not good. But with my friends was something contrary and I went away very sick. I could not stand on my feet, and I was very nervous. Coming to MONTCLAIR, I found out that I am well, for there I saw real cripples who could not walk and not use any more their hands. By comparison, I was, thanks God, well, and only my body hurt.

Since I have to write the truth, I must bring out what I could easily omit, but I understand it as a fish is taken out from the water. So simply, I was told by the man who gives me the MAZAZEN (*in Yiddish, the transliteration of massages,* Wm. G.), "Young man, you are not, God forbid, a cripple. You are well. Your rheumatism is in your bones, and you will, with God's will, get well and soon will be helped. Like those who have a lot of meat on their bodies, what you have to do is eat more and sleep and mainly not to worry that you will see that I said the right words."

I agreed with him, in short, I also asked there a doctor about things that could help me. He told me not to take a bath every day and instead of three weeks, I should be there for six weeks. I obeyed everything and began to feel very good the first couple of weeks, and I felt that, thanks God, I will be a complete healthy person, if only I would not have in my mind the notes with the checks and the business, especially the anger of my family, I would be able to recuperate very soon. But another thought came to me about myself and my wife and children. I don't live just for myself, but what can I do if they don't understand me and don't consider their mistake? What can come out from such a life? I will write them how I feel here and how I will feel when I, with God's will, will come home. It remains in my thoughts to remain and not to come home for it will be better for you and for me, and I wrote to them, BETTER IN THE LAND, THAN IN THE SAND.

Her answer was that I must come home. I again am writing, you can't live without me, not to be without me, but when I am with you, why don't you listen to me, why do you leave everything to me? In the meantime, they are sending me notes received from the banks, although I advised what to do, and I left a signed note. Everything was not good. The banks learned that I am not home, so they canceled my credit as much as they could. This was also because of the negligence of my grown children and because I was not at home.

My heart was ailing. Why am I so unhappy? Other people who can't even write their names, shoemakers and tailors, plain folks, and God helped them. Their children grew up and supported their fathers. With me, it is entirely different. As long as the children were little, I worked hard and bitter, driving a pushcart. I went through everything. I was alone for seven years. I brought them to America twice. I did everything and had mood. Perhaps, in the end, God will help me. I should live to see bigger (*in the sense economically better-established,* Wm. G.) than me, especially that I alone am the person who tries and established, thanks God, a store with merchandise; myself the buyer and the seller and the accountant and at the end should it turn out this way. I was worried being there away from home, and after all, I knew that it will not be good. But the letters from them brought me back home.

I came home before ROSH-HASHONE. I felt good, and I was an important guest at my family, also from my friends. There was no business at that time. It was the same time to do synagogue business. Since it was known that I resigned as treasurer, for I had thought it over and was concerned about others' money, especially about the synagogue's money, that what would I do if I put the money into the banks where I was in debt 2,000 dollars and they will take it back, for banks are sensing when businesses are not good. They are the first owners of the money. I, thanks God, understood it and felt it good. I, therefore, resigned at that time when a few thousand dollars came in. As a decent and considerate person, I had to do it this way, but it turned out not good. The 200 dollars that my friends gave me to go away ... this was certainly not good. I didn't know about it at all. I only knew that I am not completely well and I don't have to do anything with the synagogue business and with God's will, after SUKES continue to do and collect what my customers owe me and to go ahead and repair my broken ship so that I should be able to continue traveling (*to do business,* Wm. G.) in my great ocean of life.

Things were not easy, and I always saw more danger. I didn't lose my hope and mood. My store could mislead people, especially me. On this, I was the greatest misleader; not to take away, God forbid, from anyone. I may say that during my life until now, I was very capable for this (*i.e., to do somehow business,* Wm. G.). I must also say the truth that it ruined my health. So it was, I can't deny it. I went on, took, borrowed, bought, and sold. If I am again at home, it probably must be so. I must write the truth even though it is something that I should swallow.

Since I want to come to the end of this part of my life, I must bring out everything. The 200 dollars that the two friends lent to me for a short time, one came right after SUKES and said to me, "Do you know what I want?"

"What do you want? Most likely the 200 dollars."

"I want them, but listen to me. I took the 200 dollars from a corporation and that you should pay eight dollars weekly. In the meantime, give me ten dollars interest. Next week you will begin to pay."

I answered him, "My dear friend, such a favor I didn't ask to take money from the corporation for going away. Such a way of going was not good for me. I thought that you are lending me for a few months' time until I collect what people owe me and to sell merchandise. From a corporation I didn't need you. I myself belong to a corporation, if I would like to take 1,000 dollars, they would give me." I concealed my anger so that he should not see that I am angry.

Although my wife interfered that she didn't like the whole favor, I noticed something worse, that the 200 dollars undermined my credit. This I experienced that you will see later. I will, with God's will, come to this entire story later.

I spoke to him so that he should not recognize anything, "Anyway, you did for me something good. Indeed, I thought that you are lending me your own 200 dollars so that I should not pay interest. I thank you anyway, even though it was not what I thought. You don't have to apologize." I gave him the 10 dollars and paid every week the eight dollars, but I felt between my good friends a change. Whenever

I asked for a GMILES-HESED, I was refused as they would never have done before. I owed to a few people money, who I used to pay interest. They urged me that I should give them back the loan. I could not understand from where this is coming. I had some people who asked me to keep their money, and suddenly it became different. I indeed paid back a lot, but to take out at one time 1,000 dollars and to pay back I could not, especially to those who are not doing anything with the money.

I must mention here Mr. FRANK and Mr. FEFER—they are already in the true world (*deceased,* Wm. G.), who didn't need the money for business. There used to be times I said to them, "Maybe you need the money?"

Their answer was, "You fool. What are you? I will take back from you and give it into the bank or to another? It is better that it is with you" …when they came in the time when I could not answer, "What happened to you?"

"Just at the time when I am not well and had just returned from MONTCLAIR, you want the money? You know that my health is affected when you demand your money is due from me, and I don't have immediately to answer. Be patient, I will, with God's will, give back to you. Only wait a little bit."

Instead, to soothe me, they made me angry… "No, we want the money."

But I was so far away in my thoughts, this means that, not that I was not honest, but ignorant, also crazy. Instead to ask as a businessman, may I say the truth about myself, I got afraid of them. I took (*i.e., borrowed,* Wm. G.) from the corporation, and I gave them back a small part and every month to give back in time.

I wanted to show that I am an honest man. If one demands his dues, you have to return. I want to prove that I am giving back money even though I am not well now. I didn't want to take treasury money. I gave back, and I didn't want to do something with synagogue money, also with good friends who did me favors in the synagogue, also not from the board. Now everything is different. Not only inside was so bad but also in the bank, all over. I gave back to everyone as much as I could. I never stopped.

Business was my hobby. It was my hobby and also exciting. Not so is doing an honest man or a businessman. This I understand only now, but not then. The more I wanted to show how honest I am, the more they took advantage from all sides. So bad it came to me that I didn't know from where it was coming. If I gained something from my going away, I lost it now. The banks canceled little by little my credit. So did private persons. I didn't have money to do some business. Also, the house with the store, which had a lease for a year, came the time to renew. I paid 60 dollars monthly. So came the "nice" Jew, the owner, the SHOYHET, Mr. RABINOWITCH, and he wanted seventy dollars a month.

"What are you talking, I don't make a living. I am being ruined. And after all this, you are raising the rent? You wanted to sell me for 6,000 dollars. I am giving you now, 7,000 in order that I should not be afraid for more rent. I lost here a lot of money, but I hope to God that maybe it will get better. I already lost. I tried it. Whether I have it or not, I will buy it."

Here I must stop and not to write anymore. It is so aggravating. The rest, the house, they ruined me as well as my having believed everyone.

He promised me that the house will be mine later, for now, he can't sell it because of his children. I installed electricity with my money and brought the building in good order. The end was that I remained there by paying rent. I could not help myself. In the meantime, they already knew about me all over in case if it was enough for me (*i.e., about his financial troubles,* Wm. G.). How can the other know how and what I am going through? After all, if I would have help from my children, if they would be supportive of me, maybe it would be good for the store. I was always carrying in my mind that the clients should come into the store.

My wife had, K'AYN HORE, enough work at home with, K'AYN HORE, big children as well as a little one. After all, she is a new one and not long in the country. Across from me lived a man who used to be a jobber. He used to always come to me and envy me, only I didn't know. But it was so. His house was also rented and also had a store. But he didn't use the store. He rented it to an eye doctor who moved out from the store, so he also wanted to move because he lost his tenant. But with him, it was different. I asked the owner to sell it to me. They didn't want to sell it to me. He didn't want to buy but they convinced him to buy it for a few hundred dollars cheaper.

When he already had the house with the store, he chose to open a store the same as I had; a window opposite a window. It is easy to write, but this is hard to describe; the pain that we went through and lived through, but it was so. God should still help us because I didn't know how because I didn't have any more health and mood. What could I do to him? He was a young healthy man with a young wife, healthy and three fine boys and rich parents. He, himself, was not poor. He bought the house and arranged a nicer store than me with fresh new goods. It was natural that it affected me very much. It was already bad for me before, and even more now. A Christian world would not have done this. And now I have a competitor across the street, a Jew who does not care much for SHABES, and I have a landlord, a SHOYHET, who should have high ethics. I had begged him to sell me the house before, and he wanted 6,000 dollars. Now I wanted to give him 7,000 and to arrange something else, and I want to know whether the house is mine not to wait-wait awhile, with God's will, I can't now. He was afraid that I will move. He saw that on the side opposite they opened a store.

My heart was crying in me how everyone harassed my poor innocent feathers while I, God forbid, didn't do anything wrong to anybody. In the end, everyone wants to ruin me, not to buy out or to spoil. Why does it happen to me?

I spoke to the SHOYHET, "Have pity, I am giving you as much as you yourself want. I lost here so much. I am sick. I don't want to move."

Then he answered, "If you lost so much from where will you get money to buy? What is this your business?"

He didn't believe me. He only looked at me as a constant complainer. I made enough money. The best proof is that I established such a store.

I told him the truth that I intended to make, to take in other goods, drugs and notions, and other things, perhaps it will be better. What else can I do? If I want to arrange such a store, so only the fixtures will cost me 200 dollars. I continued to believe him. What could I do? In the meantime, I got ruined. The customers had other places they could go, especially the ones who owed me, certainly left me and, in particular, the tailors. Thus, I began to feel my poor circumstances. I was only afraid that I should not lose, God forbid, my mind. With whom could I talk if not with my family? Look how unfortunate I am. For me and my wife, it was very painful to move from 5th Street amongst Jews who know us for the three or four years since we lived here. Strangers believed that the house is ours because we installed electricity and placed in lamps, we papered and painted and fixed it up very nice. After we did all of that, there were many buyers, customers, people used to come. Now, what are we going to do?

We have to look for some remedy, and who has to look if not me. So, I said to them, to one of my boys and a girl who needed to always take medicines because of continuing illnesses, "Listen to me. I don't want yet to sink. I still want to take a heavy load on me, but see to it that you should be faithful to me and support me. I don't want to let myself down, and I will try to get money and credit. After all, I didn't take away from anyone, God forbid. I don't know a true answer for the business, and a solution is hard to find because I am so exhausted. Maybe, we can take on selling drugs, notions, ladies' things and such."

"Yes, yes, Father, I will try," answers me the boy, also the girl. So, it was said and done. It again cost me fixing as well as trimming. I did it very nice. I didn't let it down. Also, in the street, I put a lamp. It really made the store stand out and informed customers a little bit.

Now, I want to mention again that the sun again began to shine for me. Not for me alone but my family and especially for the others. They thought that I gave back the 200 as well as to everyone in the synagogue. I didn't want to accept any more the job of treasurer. It was the same with the banks. I was in debt to Peoples' Bank for 1,500 dollars. I went to the State Bank and took immediately there 1,000 dollars and gave it to Peoples' Bank, and I again began to work although I was very much afraid not to lose again. I was plenty in debt, but I must. Perhaps they will try now differently.

I must call your attention that at that time I was again active and once again obtained money. I got again new good friends. They thought that I will go broke and here to many surprised people, in the end, I was able to establish a new store, full with goods. What is the matter with this man? My landlord came clapping his belly that the house will bring him now 100 dollars a month. After all, why does he have to sell it? I understand it very well. Let it be this way. The main thing is that I should make a living. I got money from other friends and a few other banks. So, came to me a good friend of mine who lent me 200 dollars. If you recall from my writings, a certain Mr. Greenberg. He wanted me to do him a favor. He went to his bank and wants credit of 500 dollars, but they don't want to give it to him. He wants that I should take him in, do this favor for him, and endorse for him the 500 dollars in my bank. How can I refuse a man who did me a favor in his corporation? If God helped me, why not? I signed for him, and he received 500 dollars. I was satisfied because I accomplished the task, but I didn't know that anyone is such a fool as I am.

He gave back and did the same thing several times, taking again and again. I was convinced that soon he will not need me because he had a big balance. What do I know? I don't want to go further into it. He cheated and swindled me and established himself that way in the community. It was not a small thing, a president of a synagogue, a young man with a good (*i.e., big,* Wm. G.) mouth. He could speak very nice and was learned. He was proud of his Jewishness. What could I know? As a matter of fact, he used to say to me quite often, "Mr. Rosen, do you need a couple of hundred dollars?" I used to take from him. Why should I not do it for him? Later he came to me and said that he bought a house with a store between 29th and 30th on Columbia Avenue, but he is short 1,000 dollars.

"What do you want, Mr. GREENBERG?" He wants me to take 500 in the corporation. I could not take it, for not long ago, I took from the corporation. But he came to the corporation and bought shares and at the same evening, took 500 dollars which I had to sign, and he left satisfied. I was also satisfied that I can do something good for the other. This was my life for I was always doing MITZVEHS (*Hebrew/Yiddish term meaning good deeds,* Wm. G.) for people.

But it was regrettable not just for me but for my family, as you will see soon. And so it went. He already had a nice house, also a store, and he goes to paint and paperhanging the entire house, and he told me of his luck (*in Yiddish GANTSE GLIKN,* Wm. G.). God should help him, why not, I think this way. But he doesn't think the same as I. Listen, as soon as he took, he had in mind to make me unfortunate, which you will see in due time. I have in mind to tell it a little bit later. It didn't take long, and once again, clouds came with a heavy storm from all sides which made holes in my ship, in my life, which indicated that I must get ruined, that I can't hold out anymore. I was careful not to reveal to others, I was afraid. I didn't think much about my own people, and it came with a big storm. Suddenly, I was broken and thrown back. I became a helpless man and could not get any more aid.

My cries I kept in me, that my younger boy of sixteen years, HERSHELE, made me so unhappy. I am ashamed of myself, and you should know that it is my fault. I write everything for myself. In the summertime, I used to take care of my health and left the home for a couple of weeks. At that time, my boy took care of my store. He bought goods, and my wife and daughter were in the store. He took merchandise under my name, and he didn't bring the goods to the store. He sold them to a shopkeeper for 50 or 40 percent of what it cost and so it was going for weeks. During that time, he took goods for a couple of hundred dollars and had a good time along with his friends.

At that time, they (*the wife and daughter,* Wm. G.) noticed this, but I didn't know anything until I came home and encountered so many bills and statements. A darkness covered my eyes. They told me a little, but most of it they didn't say. I will tell it short, although it did happen, and there is enough that it would suffice for a book about this theft. I will bring it out quickly. I will point out the most important. A part of the bills I paid and a part I asked to cancel. We began to ask him to tell us to whom he sold so much merchandise that made me poor and the other one rich? He didn't want to say until my older boy, Max, began to beat him and there were screams. Then, he told the truth to whom he sold. For me, it was a great shock hearing from him that he sold so much merchandise for nothing, and I will have to pay.

I became interested, "How can you do this to your father?" I could not stand on my feet financially, and I asked him to go to this man and perhaps I will be able to get back some merchandise or money, but he refused.

Then something happened, which is still in my heart. They all screamed. My heart was in pains that a child can make a father so unhappy. But it was already too late. He ruined me for a few hundred dollars. I saw that I have to give up everything. I can't any longer remain in business. I thought that I will improve, but it still got worse. I didn't even know what to do, where I should go. It was very painful for me, that I invested so much strength and money. How miserable, how bad it was for me. Nevertheless, I strongly believed that the house will be mine. With God's will, I will remain here, asking him to sell me the house, and I will pay more than it is worth, more than its value, only that I should not have to move.

But for this, I didn't have luck. He didn't want to sell it to me, and even not to return for what I have invested so much in the property. He did not say it in a good way but not in an angry way either. He just was not acting as a man of honor. The end result is that I went broken with everything. My boy saw that he did something very bad to me, and that he could not any more remain at home and he suddenly disappeared from the house. For two weeks, we didn't know where he is. I was not too much worried about this. But my wife suffered a lot until we find out that he enlisted as a soldier. They sent him to California. I can't say that it didn't aggravate me, the fact that a boy who could help me so much, brought to me such a misfortune. What could I do? How could I help myself? I thanked God that at least he went into the army. There he will learn something, and he will become another person. I will leave him for the time being. Let him be there.

At home, it became worse for me from all sides. He raised my rent, to sell it to me, he didn't want, and across from me stood a fresh and healthy man with a pious and faithful child, with fresh money and also a lot of merchandise. I realized that I must abandon the wheel of my heavy ship, for there were many holes full with water, which goes down, and it is too much and too depleted to save. She must sink. It is no more for my strength to undertake and continue to lead. I was sick, poor and broken. I didn't want to sell goods for nothing (*i.e., cheap,* Wm. G.). At that time, my older boy, Max, became engaged, and he looked for another store than where he was managing for four years with my girl, as you already know, and almost didn't make out,

The Inheritance (Yurusha)

anything. So, I took everything upon myself. I had to pay his bills, and we moved from the store; we took our goods together, but there it was entirely different. I and my wife were not qualified, only my girl, HAYKE, was able to do business amongst Christians. How will we have at least an apartment? Perhaps God will help us, and it will get better when we will be together. What could I do? I continued hoping and tried and wrestled with the world and the world with me.

At that time, we used to receive letters from the boy in the army that we should rescue him, to take him out from there that he will already be good. If not, he will throw himself into the water. I didn't mind that much; why, yes, that a child should bring such misfortune upon a sick father and a sick mother and on everyone to take and give away to a stranger, everything for nothing. I listened to his cries very little. But she, a mother, is after all, not a father. She constantly cried and begged me that I should try for him and get him out. To tell the truth, I didn't want it very much. I was very angry with him; not him alone but my whole family. I saw their behavior, and I constantly asked them, "Have mercy on me and help me out, everyone a little bit so I will not go down."

I explained to them that every father is the leader, not, God forbid, the misleader. He must be at the top as a captain on his ship, and the wife and children should take care of everything and supervise so that holes should not be created in order to hold all together, strong and healthy. But this I could not obtain. What could I do since they, themselves, made the biggest holes, and I realized that, in the end, we will suffer, and others will suffer because of us. Regrettably enough, they didn't listen until the sinking came, gradually. More than anyone else, I suffered. I was always on the guard that I should not, God forbid, take away from anyone while I remained sick and poor and broken after so many efforts for four years' time. Now, I had to move far, between Christians, while I had always lived amongst Jews. But this is not yet all, what about the main thing, PARNOSE? What was lacking was health and PARNOSE.

My wife annoyed me very much. It was unpleasant that a woman had always to do, to scream and cried that I can get him out, but that I don't want it. Also, I, as the father, was thinking he is young. He was misled. Maybe he will be better, and he will make good his wrongs. It is not so easy to do as it is to write. I began with a lawyer and also with politics. I will not take up much space, but there is a lot I could write. It didn't come easy, but I got him out. He came back home. Altogether he was eight months in the army.

Imagine that my life was easy and that I should live peacefully and to write, thanks God, but it was just the opposite, filled with pains, sickness and poverty. Yet everything was dear to me and looked upon with open eyes and courage. I don't know how I could endure all that happened to me, but so it was. Now, when I am writing and telling everything, it is understandable that I am emotionally and especially physically weak. My eyes are dark, my hands are shaking and my thoughts are especially very weak. I don't remember what happened yesterday, actually an hour before. Therefore, my writing is not so good, especially my spelling. Everything is weak. I must gather strength to continue to tell my story.

I realized that I am far behind. I would hide everything, take with me into the grave that nobody should know about my life. I see that I owe a few hundred dollars and see that I will not be able to pay, it will have to be paid back after my death, and hence I decided that I must describe everything. My own family should realize what a martyr I was for them and also for others.

When I was already in the store of my older boy, far from Jews in a Christian neighborhood, not able to go to a synagogue, to see people and to talk to them and also to do business, I entered another world. It should not have been necessary. If my family had been supportive, we would not have had these difficulties after staying in our house with the store where we stayed for four years. I continued to have faith in God that with his help, I will soon regain my position, and I will try to do it, but it is not going so quick. I was tired and exhausted of my life. I felt very weak, as if I would have lived in my older years already. I was plenty in debt, so I sold my merchandise little by little. After all, I did not want to go bankrupt. To lower myself, I could not. To work hard further, my health did not permit me. To enter my clips business as before, to continue doing business in wool and trimmings, only selling out little by little was my only option, and I paid back as much as I could.

It continued to affect my heart. At that time, my oldest son was already married, and the second boy was back from the army, but not yet as it should be. Everything came in one time. I remained in bed the whole winter. I felt that if I could go away, I would, with God's help, be recuperated. This would be, for me, the best medicine. To my deep regret, I didn't have the money to go. I knew that it will help me only if I would be there, and when I will be back home, it will be the same. I am broken by the circumstances, and I need help; faithful help from my sailors from my own ship, that they should repair the holes. But how to do that? Talking to them, teaching them, will not help. To make scandals that everyone should know I didn't want. I had, K'AYN HORE, grown children; girls, one is already going out with a boy, the other one will, with God's help, soon go, so I didn't want our family's stories to be in others' mouths. I kept silent, and my life became worse every day.

My only cure was to go away. My family didn't want to tolerate the way things are going, nor did I. So, when I left home, I made up my mind that it would be better if I don't return, for them and for me. After I was away for two weeks, no one could recognize me. I was feeling so much better. After the first two weeks passed, I began to write letters to them and they sent to me and then me to them as always in the past. It was the same as before. I went away and began to feel better, but I felt that to go home is not very good. I reconsidered it and answered myself, no, I don't have to live only for myself but only for my wife and children. The only thing is that they don't understand me and that they don't try. Perhaps it is not better for other people either. I would like to go through my poor life. Maybe the girls will get married soon, then everything will be good. This way I felt in my heart that I left home forever.

I wrote to them, and they answered me that it will be different. I was away for six weeks' time, and I would have felt very good if I would not have taken an account of my life. I put myself in the shape of a little man, and I asked myself that I, a small, weak, poor human being, needs to be isolated from people and separated from family life, almost from everybody. I regained my mind, and I understood that everything is because that I am weak since my birth and that I wanted to do everything above my strength. Therefore, I paid with my poor blood that everyone took advantage of me and my feeble needs, and I remained helpless, broken my bones as well as my spirits over and over again where it would take weeks to pass until it grew back again, but not for long and this is the way it is until they were again separated from me.

Everyone liked and believed them. I was truthful to everyone, whoever did me a favor. I appreciated it. Here I would like to mention, Mr. GREENBERG, the one who did me the favor with the 200 dollars when I went the first time in my financial crisis. It appears that he took me into the corporation, where I paid eight dollars weekly. Nevertheless, I forgot it, and I did him a greater favor, and I endorsed a note for 500 dollars in the bank and also in a corporation. Also, 500 dollars from a private person.

The end was that he got bankrupt and brought me a misfortune which undercut in the banks and corporation, my credit. They didn't want to lend me money anymore. It can't be described. A man asked me, "Mr. Rosen, how come you believed this man so much and do for him so much?"

I answered, "It is because that this man helped me once with 200 dollars."

The man answered me, "I must tell you the truth that at that time with the 200 dollars, he didn't do you any favor. I must tell you that he did to you some evil. He made you ashamed and deprived you of your credit."

"How, please tell me what you know?"

He told me that my "friend," "came to the synagogue at a meeting and reported that you are very sick and that you should be able to go away and that you told him that you don't have the financial means to travel. He requested from a few brothers (*i.e., synagogue members,* Wm. G.) that they should give twenty-five dollars each so that it should amount to 200 dollars in order that you should be able to go."

At that time, this "friend" was the president of the synagogue, and I was the treasurer. The brothers were surprised, first of all because I am sick and secondly that a man who owns a store with good merchandise and, K'AYN HORE, grown-up children should be so broke. Well, why was it their (*the members,* Wm. G.) fault? Just to the contrary, when I write about them, I have the greatest respect. They all responded with their help and would have given 500 if they had been asked. But some of those heard and gave, I owed them already. One I owed 500 dollars and the other 300. Many had their money with me, for which I used to pay them interest, just like the banks. Some just were lending to me whenever I needed. They were very good brothers. I also had synagogue money, where I was the treasurer of the synagogue for many years. They all gave the twenty-five dollars when they were told that they are lending me the 200 dollars for a few weeks.

After this man told me what happened, I knew I had to go to see GREENBERG. When I came, I was angry why he took it from the corporation, as I have described before, when he already had the money from the brothers, and now two years later, I have learned that he did something like this to me. What he did was that he ruined me at that time. I didn't know the reason why everyone came to me and requested from me their money back. More than that, I could no longer get money or credit as in the past. This he did to me, the man for whom I now have to pay to the banks 500 dollars for the note I endorsed for him and also to the corporation and to a private person 500 dollars. He also took the 200 dollars from the others and made for me to give him ten dollars interest and eight dollars weekly to the corporation, and that is how he paid back to the eight people.

Now you understand how this ruined me. In all truth, at the time I learned about this, I got lost with everything. How was it possible that people could do such things? My life is suffering for nothing, for a man who stole from me, who cheated me, who took advantage of me and my kindness. I, God forbid, didn't do anything wrong to anybody. I didn't take away from anybody. I was much in debt for goods. I didn't have in order to pay on time. I asked for a postponement with respect for the other and thanked for each minor thing they did for me. It seems to me that I am in debt to everybody. I don't do anything now, before I did a lot. I suffer from that time how people were dealing against me.

So, I will open my heart and will begin to talk it out so that it should be easier for me. It is not to describe, and I know that at the same time, you will not have a good opinion about me, that I have complaints to the world. If it means to people that everyone is indebted to me, then I will say strongly, yes, yes, but as a weak man, I must say instead of yes, NO, that it is my fault in everything. A man should not be this way, but what should I do? It is too late.

I am now too much exhausted, rather perplexed. Already old and weak, to begin another life, I am not in a position. If I could only do some good for mankind. I didn't do yet anything good for anybody, especially for myself. I spent my life without any real accomplishments, nothing as you can see. In short, I consider myself bankrupt. I must admit it. They laugh at me, my own wife and children. They are right that I let myself be so directed by them and others. If I could pay back the money that I owe, I would not have to describe everything, but I must indicate as others how it was all taken from me, the money, my health, my strength and my mood.

But with me, it is entirely different. While I am writing, I am very much depressed. Nevertheless, I hope to God that I will pay back everything. Then I will be able to die in peace, although I already made a will that after my death, everyone should be paid back to the cent. After my death, I will have more than during my lifetime, only not to be in debt to anybody. My wish is that after my death, a cent should not remain after me. Not to be in debt to anyone. Then it will become clear how much I went through. I am not proud of my constant complaining that people had from me. I did a lot of good for many, and I don't need to write about this, only for my family I didn't do anything. They didn't understand me. They did me a lot of wrong, but I forgive them. To everyone, to everyone I am a good friend.

I love the world and all people, no difference, a Jew, a Christian LEHAVDL (*to make a distinction*, Wm. G.), only a human being with a heart and a pure soul to possess knowledge no matter who it is; a human being with feelings, with pity. I met every one of them. How little and weak I am, like a bird who flies with the largest flock, so I was all over and saw everything. Now I feel that I am at the end. My whole body is ruined. I don't sleep at night for almost two years since I moved to work amongst Christians, and I am far away from Jews, and I am at the mercy of a child. I am not anymore any good for business.

Ordinarily, I need to keep silent, not to say a word. I am not an old man, even though I feel like one. So, you can understand how it bothers me that I must keep quiet. I see that things are not going good, and I am not allowed to say a word.

It is impossible to describe my life. I began to think how wrong I was directing, although I know that I tried, honestly. Not, God forbid, playing cards, and I did not drink, and I was honest in business, but it didn't pay. I just opened my eyes at the same time, gained my thoughts, and I look and understand something, that the world is being led differently from the way I conducted myself, and regrettably, I can't achieve anything. I am worked out physically and emotionally. I felt how bad it is for me, away from people and hated by my own family. As long as I was the provider of PARNOSE, at least they respected me as the provider of a livelihood. Now that I am nothing and don't have the ability to make a living, I do almost nothing. When I sell something or I earn sometimes a dollar, I pay back. I paid back a couple of thousand dollars, so I want to pay back still a few hundred more. At present it is very bad for me. I carry it in myself and suffer. I see that I am the most little man. I must also note in my writing that I experienced that older people in their seventies are stronger than me.

I never feel good. In the summertime, during the heat, I feel terrible. So, one summer day, I went to the park and sat under a tree to rest and read a paper. It was a Sunday during day time, at a time when many people are walking. I could not move from the place, so weak I was, and I wanted a drink of cold water, but I could not get up. Suddenly I saw a healthy young Jew, perhaps 200 pounds weight, and he carried a big gallon of water. I got up and asked him for a glass of water. He answered me, "Mr., go a little bit down, there is water, there you will be able to drink as much as you would like."

I answered him, "You will excuse me, if I could walk, I would not ask you. I am weak, and I can't go." He didn't answer me, but water he didn't give me. I can't say that another one would not give me either. How it happened, whether I got it from another or I reached the water, is not the most important thing. The fact is that a man with two legs refused to give a drink of water to another man. The same day, I went home and thought, how can one refuse a drink of water?

When I returned home, I took the car, which had to bring me to 5th Street and Snyder Avenue, and then I had to walk to 5th and TASKER, where I lived. It was very difficult for me to walk. I felt very weak that day. While I was standing at the corner, came to me an old woman, perhaps seventy-five years of age or more, and she says to me, "My dear Jew, I have to go uptown, but I don't have car fare."

I took a look at the woman, and I forgot about everything and took the last couple of cents that I still had from that day, and I gave her, and I looked after her whether she takes the car. The old woman kept going, and she stopped at every corner and asked for carfare. I was following her until 10th and watched her. When I came home, I was thinking all night and meditated for a long time and could not fall asleep trying to get an answer and until today it is not yet explained, the truth of what happened to me on only that one day, especially of all my years during which I kept my eyes closed. I now saw what people, young and old, did only to have money. They didn't consider anything or anyone. I considered all of this and gave myself the title, the most little. Such a healthy person had such a heart to refuse a weak man a drink of water to revive the soul and which does not cost a cent. I don't know whether he even thought about this. And then such an old woman of seventy-five years can go out and cheat many people to give her for car fare, she does not have it thus collecting money that it should remain in the rags after her death.

I became a thinker from that time on, after all, what kind of world it is. I am describing the smallest episode from just one day. I missed a lot. I believed everybody and worked hard and paid up everything. I never refused if I only could do something for the other person, especially for my family. Now I see that I don't deserve a thank you. For now, since I remained in such a situation, who listens to me and who cares about me? I am wretched more than anyone else. When I owed 3,000 dollars and paid back 2,900 with a balance of altogether 100 dollars, I am being bothered more than when I owed 3,000 dollars. Only now I began to understand it, but unfortunately too late. I was already a man, K'AYN HORE, of fifty-three years when these experiences happened that I am writing about. At that time, I was not old, but worked out, weak and poor.

I will not be ashamed at all to say what my wife tells me now. "Who needs you?" She is right. I worked for her for thirty-two years and for the children in the old home and here in America. Seven years I was alone and worked here, two times I brought her to America, as you already know, and the last two years I have endured the deterioration of my health, the loss of my money and especially my mood and I am getting insane from going around and thinking how I can't accomplish anything; K'AYN HORE, with such grown-up children, and I see how unhappy I am, and at the end, they have objections to me. It comes to my mind too often that I would be most happy if I would be separated from them all.

However, I continue to think that I am not a man for myself. I suffered everything just for them. Unfortunately, they can't understand no matter how I am talking to them, in a good way or angry tone, it does not help. I know that they are in a great danger. I am telling them what they have to do, for we are close to a downfall. I know how to control myself, my health, what I am allowed and what not. However, with my wife, it is just the opposite. She is very sick her whole life and exposed every minute to a danger. I love her more than my own life. After all, she has all virtues that a human being possesses. I know it very well. Just for this, I am uneasy and nervous all these years, and I try my best. So, it was in the old home and so it is in the new home, America, which I love so much. What could I do, unfortunately, she does not understand me and thinks different than I? She thinks that she is more devoted to the children and loves them and that I don't love them. Only because of this, I suffer all the years. So, it was in the old home and especially here in America.

They object to me that I am a selfish man; that I don't care for anybody. Their words hurt me very much. I think for myself that if I would not be a devoted husband and father, I should not stay with you even one day. So, I suffer, and they laugh at me, but I don't listen to everything. When I was what they call a MENTSH (*i.e., when I was younger and healthier,* Wm. G.), when I did business and worked and brought into the house PARNOSE, not being dependent on a child as I have been for the last two years, things were different for me. Now, I became so that my eyes are like curtains, as is my face before people, so that nobody should know. My pains and my sufferings are not to be describe and how exhausted I am. Every day, every day, I have to be born again. I can't get up from my bed, so tired I am from the sleepless nights.

I am constantly thinking. I make plans how to do something, but only at night. When the morning comes, I am like in a lethargy before I can regain my life. Very hard is my life. My wife and children are angry with me. They don't believe me. They say that I don't want to do anything. It angers me. "What do you say? Didn't I do until recently by myself, alone and you didn't want to help me when I asked and almost cried before you. Now, when I remained without, without strength and without money and lived, K'AYN HORE thanks God, to have such children that don't believe a father and not to help me in my present situation, while I am sick and poor and can't do anything, maybe that with God's help I will eventually achieve something. Let everybody try for himself. Take off the heavy load from me and from your sick mother."

I stood by my words, but my faithful wife interfered and ignored all my objections and said that they are right and that they are the best children. This hurt me very much. But to make scandals, I didn't want. I think what to do. I feel that I am faithful and here she says something different. This happens not one time. Always when I have an argument, I think that I should get away from them to be alone. This would be best for me and especially for all of them, and I am continuing to figure out that it would indeed be good for me and for my health that I should do this, but my heart never lets me do. I see that it still can be good. One girl already goes out with a boy, the other one would have a boy long ago, only… so the two boys; one, K'AYN HORE, twenty years who has an income and could help, but again the same, I don't have the right words. In America, the woman is the principal tenant.

When I say day, she says night, and so is it since I have her as my wife until one hundred and twenty years. Her mother was like this. I can't do anything. It is in the veins. I know it, I lost my whole life. At the same time, she didn't gain anything with her caprices. It could not be good, it can't be good, it won't be good and this is the way. She didn't understand it and doesn't understand it until today. I constantly conducted a war to achieve one opinion, especially to teach the children. She always was faithful and devoted to them. OY, it hurts me very much, and when I have to write these words, I want to blame myself.

I lost everything, first of all my health. Secondly, I didn't accomplish anything from so many efforts. Now, what should I do? I suffer a lot, and I don't want that she should know because of the children who don't understand anything. I know how much it will mean to them, and I don't want them to suffer. In the meantime, I suffer. People think that I am happy. In fact, I am, indeed, happy; a beautiful wife and beautiful children, K'AYN HORE. Not one time comes to my mind, what am I waiting for. Day by day, I get weaker, and I am getting worse. I think, however, that it comes to you that God will help and that I will still live to see and have good.

All these years were very strenuous, filled with thorns in all my roads, but with more and better mood, I expected something better and that God, with his will, he will help me, and I will live to see greater children than I (*greater in the meaning-more fortunate,* Wm. G.) and without TSORES (*Yiddish word for trouble/problems,* Wm. G.). I, God forbid, didn't expect that children should give me, that I should rely on children. It is better yes, to work easier, not harder, I and my wife, and to know no sufferings. But alas, it is entirely different than I thought and fervently hoped. It is a great pain that I can't reveal to others, so I am writing for others to know when I am gone. They should know who I was and what I went through; all my suffering, physically, emotionally and spiritually and through it all kept quiet except for my written words.

Why was I always the loser? I didn't understand, and certainly my wife and children didn't understand me, so how could they understand the real life in America?

Part Nine
My Search for a Better Life Continues

They didn't and couldn't understand what I did for them, and in the end, they expected from me and relied on me. It is true, a man, a father should do everything for his family. I did everything above my strength, above my endurance, above my capacity. How terrible I lived my life is only 50 percent of what I have described, and 50 percent is left hidden in my heart because I can't bring out to write it. I will take it with me to the eternal world, I believe so.

I was not, God forbid, the worst husband and father and a human being to human beings. I didn't play cards, also not a drunk as other people are. But I suffered anyway. If I, God forbid, would be the person I describe above, I could understand the thirty-two years wars (*quarrels,* Wm. G.) with my wife and children. I now look back all these years and see that I didn't gain anything from my young years, all got lost. And of these my older years, nothing remained for me so far. I am sick, exhausted, poor and lonesome; disliked, I myself can't look at me. I would like to live another couple of years, but I don't know how to compensate for the mistakes that I made. I can't think of anything. Thru thinking alone, one can't accomplish anything. I can't work anymore.

I am worried about one thing, that I am behind all the years a few hundred dollars to people. That I lost my deposits in not reliable banks, I don't mind. By this I mean, my family, they did not give me profits (*i.e., interest,* Wm. G.) of even one percent and also how many favors I did for people, and today they act like they don't know me. If I could only pay back what I owe, then I would greet everyone who comes and everyone I see. I would say to him, "SHOLOM" with great joy. But how, I am asking myself? I would certainly like to live without this burden. I have pity on myself. The road is full of thorns, not only for myself but for my family. Nothing remains for me but to make a step in my older years. If not, they will laugh at me.

But I was going on. It is very hard for me to do this, no matter how I should suffer, I don't care, but they can suffer much if only they could understand this. I have left my house a few months ago without saying be well. I left without saying where I go. I stayed one night with my nephew and talked there a little about my life with regret that I must leave them. I can't endure it. I don't want to leave my children, almost all, K'AYN HORE, are grown up. What am I accomplishing by being home? Nobody listens to me, nobody needs me. I don't have the right to talk to a child. So, it remained that the best would be for them that I should be alone. They were running around all over and thought as I would fall into the water.

When I came the next day, everyone asked me where I was. I could not justify it for outsiders. When I spoke to my family, I asked them, "Why did you make such an alarm? If I am so dear to you, then why when I am home and say something, you all are laughing at me and at the world? It has to be different."

When my heart is full of pains not just for me, not just for them, for all. I see that every day my ship is going down, which I was pulling and worked many years all by myself in order that I should be able to cross the great ocean of life and that I should live to the time to bring my ship not wrecked, God forbid, only intact. I was always standing at the wheel ready to repair so that I should finally reach the land and enable to get off my own passengers, I mean my children, to marry them off so that it should be easier for me to pull (*i.e., go on in life,* Wm. G.). But to my great regret, it is different.

Instead of making it easier, they make it more difficult. My load gets heavier with still bigger holes, so more water could come in with much more work and harder to pull. Instead of coming closer to the shore, so they are pushing back, and such waves are coming on, and this breaks my every bone, although I am in bed unconscious before I can regain my consciousness. From the time I had a quarrel with my family, I feel that I again forget to live separate. I must exert myself and fight with my poor strength and again accomplish something for them and try, maybe God will finally help, and I will achieve something. I began to speak out to some of my friends with whom I was in business contact and to whom I was in debt with great sums of money in the past, but now I owed them a small amount of money, that they should help me to put me back on my feet.

I had spoken to them, "You know the truth, how I was honest in business with you and with everybody separately, but my circumstances and my weakness and health undercut my feet."

One answered me, that, "Without money, we can't help you." It means that without money, I can't do anything. The other said it in a different way. So that everyone refused, rejected me. Also, my own sister with children, not rich, but they completely refused to help me. They also knew why I didn't succeed. And for this, they blame only me that I was not leading right. This means plainly that it is my fault, and my writing reveals how my family makes me unhappy, and others know it, so I annul, take off blame from everyone else. I take it entirely on myself that in my misfortune, it is nobody's guilt, only my own. I, myself, have to be punished for all my crimes. I am suffering already too much that they blame everything on me—my wife and children and good friends. I have to be blamed a lot, why should I not write it? From my writings, you will see the truth, only the truth.

I was too honest to everyone. I believed everyone, and I hoped that only by the truth God will help me and I will endure everything. Now I see more and more that the honest way is too difficult (*in Yiddish text, the author uses the proverb in Yiddish ERLEKH IZ SHVERLEKH,* Wm. G.), and so it was with whom I got in contact and with whom I was in business contact and trusted me, and I had the largest credit. But when things were not good for me and when I began to tell and indeed asked for help, everyone left me. I came to the other with courage and told them everything from my heart. As an answer, he says that I can't anymore accomplish anything, that I am lost.

In fact, I feel it, because I am not any more a young man. I am a man of fifty-three years and very weak and went through a lot. If I would have now some people who would be willing to help me, I could still achieve something. Not so much would be needed for me and my wife.

I am helpless. I feel it for two. My wife is also worked out and sick. She gave her life for the children, even then when the children gave us a lot of trouble. I was very angry at them. At that time, she fought me. She was against me because they are young children. But now she sees very well the mistakes she made, but unfortunately too late. Now it is not good for us in our older years. I lost my health, especially she, because we believed in everyone, and they all took away my toiling and especially my health.

Mainly she lost her health because she was a faithful and devoted mother to the children. Now I don't know anything. I am poor and sick. She is more sick and worse than I am. I suffer a lot. At least if my children would be married, I would not take to my heart so much. Unfortunately, they are two girls and two boys still not married. I don't care about the boys, but the girls should already have been married. Then it would be the time for us to live. God forbid to be at the mercy of children. I would not like to live for that. My writing will not help me now in my situation. I speak out what is in my heart. I am only thinking how I should make a living and, God forbid, not to need anyone's help. This sustains me that I, God forbid, don't lose my courage. My weakness, as well as that of my wife, is that we are very sick, and it is my fault and her fault.

I have a lot of pity for her, for she is too faithful to everybody, especially the children. We didn't live yet until now, as my writing shows, and I would like to live very much for myself, for my wife and for the children. For others, I already live enough, believe and gave away. I didn't want to give to them. They tore away from me my last poor feathers from my body. I am unable to describe my life with people; how much they took away from me. I am guilty because I am so weak. I didn't understand the people. I thought that this is the way for a fine honest man. I trusted and believed in people, but now it comes out different. If you pay back 3,000 and you still remain in debt of 100 dollars, and if you really don't have it, then you remain, an M'LAMED (*the term M'LAMED really means a teacher. It was mainly applied to teach little boys in HEYDER. A man who could not succeed in the world of business was called, ironically, in Eastern Europe, an M'LAMED. This described his social-economic position,* Wm. G.), and they made fun of me. They constantly request the money back and don't want to know anything.

I paid back thousands along with my health, and now I am in debt for such a small sum, and they hound me. My words don't help. They only laugh at me. Yes, yes, this is the way it is now when I describe my life. When God will help me, I hope so, and I will live to write about better things, I will with God's will, write in a better mood. I, thanks God, lived to see more good, rested a time from writing and again went through very much. I was going around hungry, suffered sickness and also my and children. I tried again and moved around in the great ocean and in the great strong stormy waves were much bigger and stronger than I drowned. I mean, in plain language, died. People who could have lived and had accomplished a lot. For they had with something to live and enjoy, and I, the poor and weak Jew (*in text YISRULIK, a homonym for a Jew*, Wm. G.) lives, thanks God, with never a cent in his pocket. I hope, with God's will, to live a healthy and happy life.

I see how great his power is. I look to him with my open eyes. I don't keep them, God forbid, closed. The more I suffer and being neglected, the more hope and love I have for him and his world and his creations, and it awakens in me a love to all people without exception. Even those few who don't understand me and think about me, God forbid, what, I don't even know, I love them also. They think about me in evil terms, I not. I don't feel any guilt. For I think I am right. I always mingle with wealthy, healthy people, and I talk to them words, which expresses my love to them and I want them to understand. Unfortunately, I am being insulted and berated. It is also my fault; I feel it very well. But the only one is God, who knows the truth that I mean everything good. But again, the same, it is my fault and not anyone else when I, such a little human being and weak and poor, who can't explain to the other in the right way. I would not have to come between them. It hurts me later, and I suffer because of this. I keep forgetting, and I don't stop, and I suffer for this with my health, but at the same time, I am satisfied for I mean the truth which will be seen (*It seems to me that the whole paragraph reflects the author's attitude and dealing with people not related to him*, Wm. G.).

Now I again gained courage in my life, although, as I have mentioned, that I became poorer and weaker, but I lived to continue writing, and indeed, NACHES came. You should know, from my writing, about what I went through with my boy who ruined me, robbed my business, and because of him, I had to give up my store on Fifth Street and that he enlisted as a soldier and went away. I spoke to him. H,e used to help me with ten or fifteen dollars weekly and promised to help me in my present situation, but he didn't keep his word. At a certain day, I was told that he got married in court. This blow was for me very heavy and unexpected, and much bigger was the blow for my wife and for the two girls older than he. I quickly regained my peace after I found out that he, God forbid, didn't marry a SHIKSE (*a gentile girl,* Wm. G.) only with a fine child of decent Jewish parents. So, I was satisfied. I was, but my wife was not. Just to the contrary, she had so much aggravation that from such worries, she got sick. My talks with her didn't help, and I truly believed it was her fault.

He used to beg her to permit him to bring the girl to the house. Instead, to talk to him in a good way, she rebuffed him and hated them until he did it (*i.e., married the girl,* Wm. G.). Here I would like to write a lot for the simple reason that I was satisfied, and my wife was not. It took a long time until it came to a peace that my wife should go to his HUPEH (*religious marriage ceremony,* Wm. G.) to be officiated by a Rabbi. Thanks God, everything went through.

This already means good. I live for his marriage. He is now nineteen years (*which would make it 1925.* ER attribution) and his young wife, seventeen. He makes thirty-three dollars weekly, and about his sick father and mother, he does not want to know, not to hear, even not to help with a cent. Ordinarily, it annoys me as a father, for I went through with him so much, and now he deserted us at a time when I need his help. On the other hand, I think that it is good so. My wife is different, devoted as she was, she gives her health and life, which she doesn't have anymore, and cries and complains what is HERSHELE doing; maybe that he does not eat at the right time and works hard and now at this time when he does not even think about his mother.

It hurts me from another viewpoint. I, as her husband, am talking to her, "Look what you did to me all these years, and I feel your devotion.

It is already time that you should understand. Look in the mirror to see what you, yourself, created, then you will see everything. So is being wasted your health. I see what the future can bring and what it brought. I love you all the years. I went through a lot. At the same time, I have complained that you don't understand me; therefore, we both suffer. I am at least happy that he married a Jewish girl of fine parents that I have somebody to talk with. More fortunate than I, they certainly are in all ways, which I don't have. You know, I am telling you this, my wife."

But her answer is different. If I want it is bad for me. Also, if I want it is good for me.

So, I live my life. I feel that something good must happen to us, I mean with me and with my wife and children. It should, with God's will, come such a time that it should sweeten all our lives. I can't bring it out with my present writing what I feel, in one word. I am satisfied that my younger boy got married. It became easier my load to swim in the ocean. Perhaps, I will, with God's will, finally be able to swim to the shore and be able to live a couple of more good and healthy years. I don't mean in poverty, only to pay back to everyone to whom I owe and to marry off my children and to live and see that they all are happy and satisfied. That's all that I am asking from Hashem.

I believe that I wrote before that I was forced to move and go to the store where my older boy was managing, even though I knew that the store does not give any profits, but as you know I always had hope and courage. I tried and didn't let it down. My girl was very skilled for this, but again the same, without money, one can't achieve anything. She, as a child, tried like a child, but at that time, I was already exhausted and abandoned. I was very much in debt for the other store. I didn't have any more strength to take upon myself more challenges. I tried in the street to buy merchandise and to sell, but my earnings were very small, and this store also didn't give much. With very high rent and, K'AYN HORE, a big family, one can imagine what is being needed, and I couldn't keep on or rather to maintain, I couldn't do either.

So, the time was running. My girl, the one who was the whole business lady, got acquainted with a very fine boy already when we were on 5th Street four years ago, who studied pharmacy and indeed became a pharmacist. He bought a store and requested to get married.

In fact, they should had married before, for to go around four years is too long. I, as the father, ought to be the guide. But here, was entirely different. They were very decent children, very careful about everything. I have an older girl before her, also her fiancé had an older sister, and therefore, they were going around so long. They gave a chance, he to his sister and my girl to her sister to get married before them. Also, he wanted to have a store first that he should be able to make a living for her. A very decent child. If I could give ten-thousand-dollar dowry, she would not need a better young man as he is.

In short, two weeks ago, on November 28, 1926, they got, in good luck, married. Thanks God for this. Only yesterday, December 10, I and my wife also my children went to visit them. How happy I was feeling that I lived to this moment what I am writing now with great pleasure. Of course, my heart hurts me that I am so poor. You should know that I am not afraid of anybody about the wedding, that I didn't have the few hundred dollars needed for the wedding expenses, not clothing for the bride also not for my wife also my children. It should be known that we lived, thanks God, to marry off a child. I didn't have what to make a big meal, not even for a small one for the people that was requested from us by the groom's side. They gave everything to fix up the house, and here I can't even make a supper for them.

> There are three pages of drawings; the last one is followed by a narrative. They were drawn when he was seventy-five years old, and he is fifteen years older than he was when he said he began his earliest recollections at the age of sixty at the beginning of the book and about twenty years older than he is in this part of the story that has been interrupted by these three pages of drawings. ER

> **First drawing:** The frame in printed letters says: As you see, children, I had fought all the years in order to reap the fruit (could also be splendor) of life.

> LEAH until hundred and twenty 72 years.
> YISROEL, K'AYN HORE 75 years.

The names in Hebrew are in the drawings with an animal, fish, birds and Jewish symbols. The names are in some of the birds.

Second drawing: The frame is the Hebrew alphabet which also indicates numbers. Thus, the frame begins with an ALEPH, i.e., number 1, and ends with LAMED ALEPH, i.e., 31. Inside is the name YISROEL two times, and one time the diminutive form used in Yiddish, YISRULIK, which are printed inside fish. There is also the figure 75 years K'AYN HORE, and on the right side, the Hebrew work ZOKEYN printed inside and animal.

It means an old man. Again, there are birds and fish and Jewish symbols in the drawing.

Third drawing: The frame says: THANKS GOD, I went through everything and lived a good and beautiful old age K'AYN HORE. Inside is twice the Hebrew YISROEL 75 years.

Inside the drawing is a lion and fish and birds, and his name is inside two birds.

The writing under the drawing is: At home during my young years. It is true that my life was very hard. I didn't buy out anybody, plainly speaking, I didn't spoil anyone's business. I looked for my bread as the bird in the woods, as the little fish looks for the worm in the water. Also, here in America, all my years, I didn't look at others who got rich, and they did everything in order to get rich. I could also do this, but I didn't. It is also true ERLEKH IZ SHVERLEKH. I didn't have it good. Not only me, but also my wife and children. They didn't have it good because of me, but I could not help. This was my way even though I suffered a lot because of my family, but thanks God, he helped me in our troubles, sickness and poverty, as I described everything in our life. Now, thanks God, when I am writing these words with my sincere heart, I thank the Master of The World for the kindness he bestowed upon me and to my beloved wife—companion in my life, and to my beloved children and children of my children that we lived to such an old age and for all that we have, K'AYN HORE, everything; that we are old and sick, it has to be so: YISROEL and LEAH ROSEN.

The Inheritance (Yurusha) 201

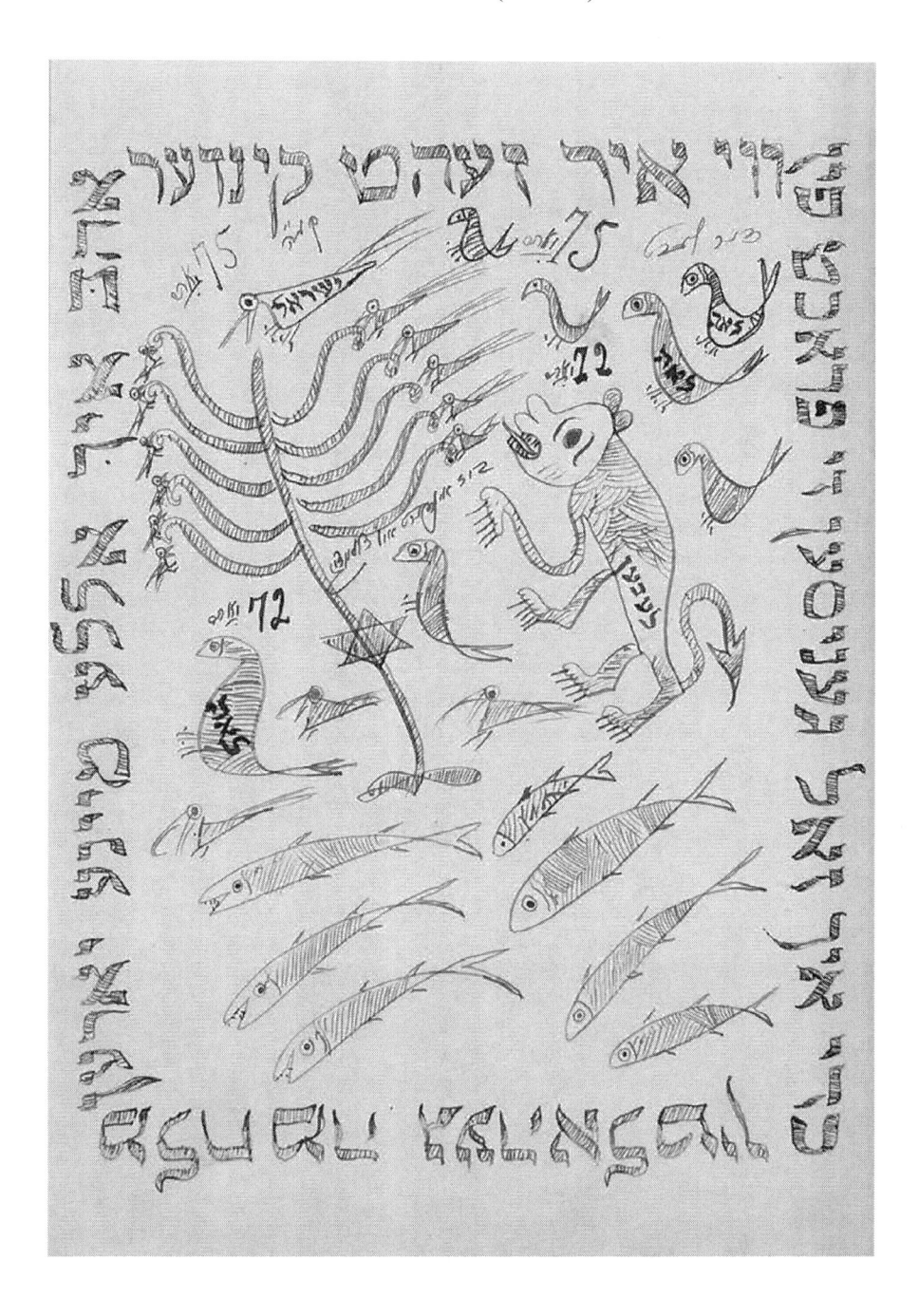

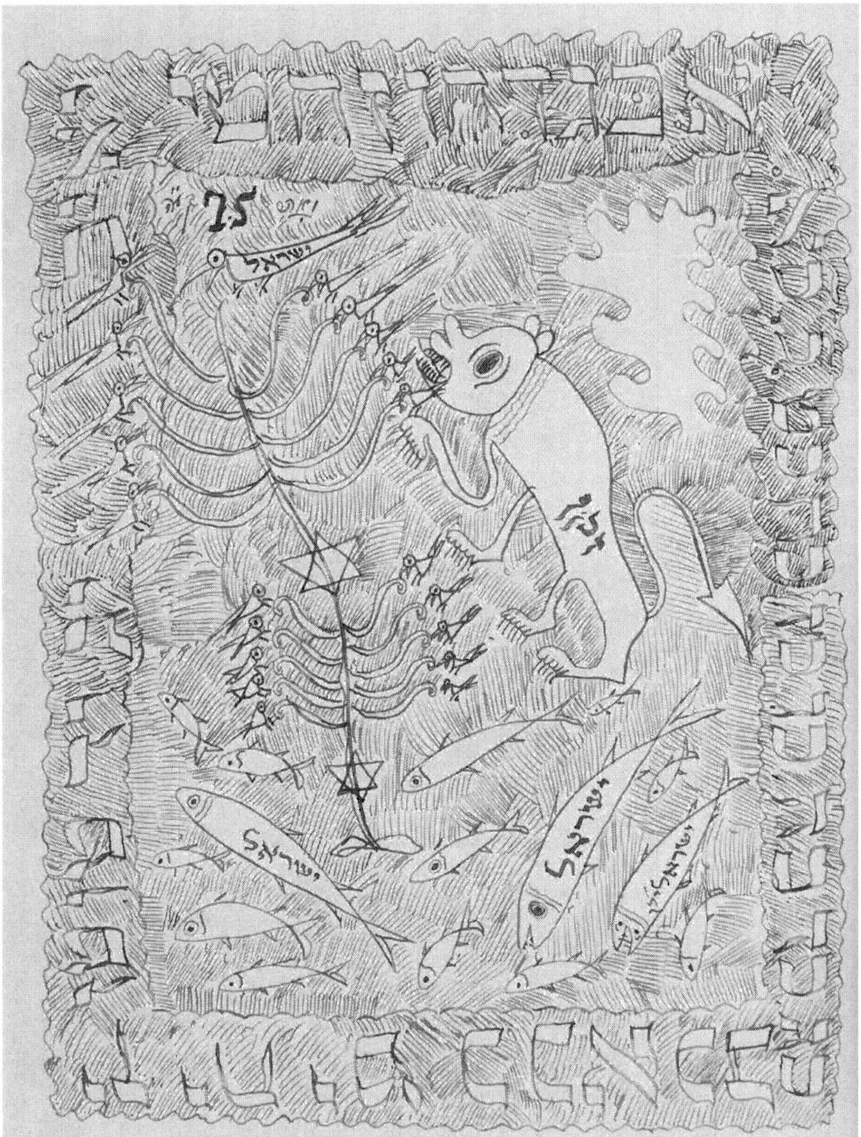
ישראל
ישראל
ישראל
ישראל

The Inheritance (Yurusha)

In the old home everything was done for a child, but here it was entirely different with me. I was so depressed by my life and by my business, which I didn't understand and I could not help myself. We didn't want that anyone should know it. When I used to need a couple of hundred dollars years ago for myself or someone else, I used to be able to get it. Now, no, because I am still in debt to a few where I didn't put back. In places where I owe twenty dollars, I could not come to ask for one or two hundred.

In addition to this, Mr. GREENBERG killed me with the money that I guaranteed for him and he didn't pay back. I also didn't pay back the full sum. When I used to need 200 or 500, I used to borrow from the corporation. Not now. So, it was very bad for me, but I made every effort and I must say the truth, I borrowed from a man 100 dollars for a month and arranged the HUPEH in the synagogue to enjoy our celebration and tried to make as beautiful as possible, and thanks be to God, it was as I wanted. Everyone was satisfied, and many envied me, even those who don't understand me and criticized me.

I am writing everything that I know, and maybe I should not write so much. But I must as I undertook it. I hope to God that with His will, there will come such a time when you will be able to see it. Yes, here my writing is full of joy and pleasure even though I had to call your attention that I didn't have the hundred dollars for the expenses, and from the groom's side, they were insulted. They didn't believe. How could it be that a man like Mr. Rosen should not make even a full supper? They were talking whatever they wanted, but only one, God, knew the truth.

It never happened in my life that I live that I should not have in my pocket two cents and not to give away one cent if somebody asked it from me, especially that God helped me that we lived to marry off a child. After my wife, is God who I love. Indeed, the man who ruined me married off his daughter, and it cost him 1,000 dollars, and I didn't have the hundred dollars. Now, rather a few months before, our younger son got married and left us, the one who helped us with the ten dollars or so weekly and also the daughter who was four years the storekeeper and the provider of a livelihood. Now we are left with nothing. My wife worked without strength, let alone I. Nothing for the older years. We still had to marry off an older girl also a young boy of almost twelve years, and we were much in debt. In short, it is good and bad. I am not giving up my hopes, and my mood still exists in me.

I suffer because my wife is upset since the children got married, she feels worse. Her talk makes me sick. I don't sleep at night and think from where will come my help (*the author uses the Hebrew sentence M'AYIN YOVOH EZRI,* Wm. G.). How to make good that my wife should be satisfied, that she should be able to revive, but this is all that I can do. My constant thinking exhausts me so much that I don't feel that I will be able to do anything. Day by day, I am walking in the streets. Sometimes I earn a dollar, but more days, I don't earn anything. The more I don't want to let myself down and be strong, I feel that every day I get more tired because of pains and thinking, as long as I am not at home, I can bear it. As soon as I come home, I am getting depressed not because my own family know what is happening, but especially that outsiders know.

I am strong enough to go around and talk to myself and think. Not one time, I embrace my head thinking that I am going to faint. It is very bad, and I am relieving my heart with my writing. I feel that it is getting worse, but the writing itself, I feel that does not me good either. Not one time I think, if God should pay attention to me so that I should be able to say my last goodbye and an end should come to such a life as I live. I am just carrying a mask. I suffer, my wife is suffering more, because of me. Maybe they, my years could still be happier. Yet, we are getting along. Everything is for me a gift. Yes, my father's words "donated years" still haunt me. I was about to die so many years ago when I was a little boy, only my mother, blessed be her memory, donated me her years which I feel now that such years with such a life are indeed only donated. They can't be better. I have to be satisfied with such a way of life to be always sick and poor and to suffer.

But, should I have affected other still decent (*the author means his wife,* Wm. G.) and bring children into this world, to suffer? For what purpose all this was needed? The truth is that I am thinking different, that I am not a falsifier. I believe in God. I love the world with everything as it is, that it has to be this way; everything is from Him… we should be grateful for everything, for it could, God forbid, still be worse, and there is a lot of worse. I can, for the time being, make my balance. I am in such a situation worse than one who comes as a GRINER to this land, but only in financial matters. But the right account, I, thank God, many times made profits. I am indeed poor, but at the same time, rich at the age of fifty-five. Thanks God, I lived to marry off two daughters (*one daughter from his first marriage,* Wm. G.) and two sons, K'AYN HORE, which is for us dearer than money. God should help us still this year that we should marry off the third daughter, so what more do I need?

Thanks God for this and all these blessings. I thank Him with all my pure heart. Give me only health, that I should still be able to make a living for my wife and small child and to pay back to everyone to the cent. Then I will be the richest and most satisfied. I hope that with God's will, it will be so. Regrettably, my talking these words to my wife does not help. She says this is not everything. In fact, she is right. I would not be better. We need for everything. We would like to live and give thanks for the life, but what to do, we are so exhausted and overstrained. We went through so much all these years.

When I write these lines, I feel depressed by everything, not just health, not just PARNOSE, but my present worries, and this is above all, mainly that my wife is very sick. No one knows so much, not even my children, she herself also not. Only I know how very sick she is from the time I am watching her. I am very much scared. I am afraid. I must say here, the whole truth, that her illness will completely destroy me. I will not be able to get up anymore. It could also be that my scare can turn out to be good. In the meantime, I am very much depressed and especially nervous.

I write these words Tuesday, December 14, year 1926, eight o'clock in the evening in bed. I am dizzy almost darkness around. My head is knocking as with a hammer, my hands are trembling, I don't know what the matter with me is. Neither can I take her to the doctor, nor can I go myself. There is not a cent in my pocket. It is very bad, and no one knows what is wrong with me. I can't tell it to anyone how our life is diminishing. If we live to the time and we will be able to do something; she for me and I for her, then I will have, with God's will, something to write. For the time being, I don't have anything good to write.

I feel that I will still write a lot. I am not dying yet, and I am trying to be strong even though I don't have the strength to hold the pen in my hand, let alone to talk, but my mood is still strong and so my life. The more I suffer, the more I want to live. My heart is telling me that something is waiting for me, for all of us. The will for life, to live is great. In the meantime, we suffer a lot. It is I who suffers more than anyone else. It is because I understand, thanks God, life and appreciates life. I can do it just for myself but not for my wife and children.

It is hard for me to figure out how much people owe me, especially my children, for what I did for them. It is only my fault. I don't have the right to demand anything from them. I, therefore, will not write whose fault it is any more. I, thanks God, did help everyone and sacrificed with my health and my last dollar. In business, I was too decent and didn't understand the world, the people, and at the same time, my own family. I didn't know how to conduct myself, and it was nobody's fault, only my own. It was already written much. I don't need to write now because my thoughts are too weak, especially now when I don't have the strength.

I am now in bed and thinking, not about the other world, for this I don't have the understanding. My judgment has almost deserted me. My whole body hurts me. Nobody owes me anything. If someone owes me, then I request that after my death, it should be advertised in the papers who owes me the greatest debt, not so much as how much money he took as much as how he robbed and took away my health. This one is Mr. Greenberg, the SHEYNER YID (*literally Yiddish for "pretty Jew," but here it is being used very sarcastically.* Wm. G.), who introduced himself to me in a mask as the best friend and ruined me and broke me (*i.e., deprived,* Wm. G.) from my credit with my whole life. I don't forgive him, and the world should know what he did. I am not, God forbid, anybody's enemy, even those who owe me.

My heart is full of pains. What is the matter with me? If my writing has become such a sickness (*i.e., a hobby,* Wm. G.), which is a fear, although I don't know why. I am my own martyr, and no one else. Nobody knows, and nobody feels as I always feel; not dead and not alive, but this time, if I succeed and survive, it will be entirely different.

So, I am concluding my writing. If I have to write, then I will write episodes of various people with whom I came in contact during my life. I will write much, much if God will let me live. Usually, I will still mention my life, but my heart is telling me that I will still live and, with God's will, also write only good things about my family, especially about myself.

(At the bottom of the page, there is a marking that almost looks like an infinity sign, which indicates the end of his writing. Wm. G.)

I still had to marry off my girl, who was going with her steady boy for several years. He was still attending college and was to graduate as a pharmacist. He was a very capable boy of very fine parents. They were from my SHETL. I, myself, was the matchmaker. As you know, I could cheat (*in the sense of delude, trick,* Wm. G.). I, unfortunately, tricked him. In fact, I didn't want to deceive him, but what could I do because I didn't have money for dowry. But, because of this match not being dissolved, God forbid, although there were many "good friends" (*sarcasm,* Wm. G.) who wanted to see this and were jealous, not begrudging the poor and sick ROSENS, who God helped, to have such fine and decent children and that they took fine husbands and my sons, decent wives. At the same time, the in-laws were all from fine families. They envied us. In addition to this, we had, thanks God, MAZL (*Yiddish for good luck,* Wm. G.).

But it didn't come easy. Thank God we overcame everything, and we married off the daughter. At that time, we lived in a private house in Strawberry Mansion and paid forty-three dollars monthly rent. I could not earn anything. First, I was sick. I experienced everything. Secondly, I was broke in my business, even though I didn't fail to pay back the big money, but a small amount, not. So, we suffered and kept silent. We thanked God that we married off our daughter. They both were working, she in a shop and he attended as a druggist for a doctor. They didn't make out much, and they lived together with us.

The Inheritance (Yurusha)

Still with us was our dear youngest son, DAVIDL, who grew, K'AYN HORE, nice and decent, and he is very good from his infant days. He just went through the public school. He, however, earned for everything: at an office of a doctor, five dollars weekly, and also in the movies for 10 dollars weekly and more. When he got older, he always found for himself always bigger and bigger earnings, and he, indeed, earned more and more and, K'AYN HORE, he grew nice and decent and strengthened our life. If, God forbid, not for this child, we could not know what would happen to us. After all this, our situation was not good, to maintain a house, even with everything the child brings in. We suffered very much and kept silent and hoped for better.

During this bad time, I went through three operations, which I don't need to describe what this means for me and for my family. My writing is not for outsiders. It is for me and perhaps for you, my oldest son, Max, you should outlive me. All my children, you are very dear to me. You may, perhaps, be able to read after I leave this sinful world. I didn't have anything, and you, children, could not help me. First, God and next good and faithful doctors who all liked me, why I know and you know too, were the only ones who could help. The main thing is that I never lost my mood and hope and prayed to God that he should help and give the doctors all ability to help me.

Life was always dear to me. I sacrificed money for life. Not to live for the sake of money as so I live to this very day, and I wish this would be until my end comes. Thanks God, I managed everything, and he helped me and I remained alive (*i.e., physically and also spiritually,* Wm. G.). I had all kinds of sickness, especially poverty. I didn't have with what to pay rent. And so, it went by, a couple of years. My daughter already had a child, a little girl, and lived with us together, and we suffer together. The young man wanted to achieve something in order to be able to open a drugstore for himself.

So was the time running, and our poverty had no end. I and my wife were sick and certainly poor and all kinds of happenings with our children and all kinds of sicknesses and operations. What this means for us, I don't have to write more. You all know it very well. I must stop. I don't have anymore the strength to write. I only pray to God to give us all health, and I with their mother, my friend in my life, we should, with all of you together, live to see only good with you all. Also, for us, a couple of more good years so that I should be able to describe the good years.

And with this episode, I want to conclude my bad writing, especially about my life. I recall a man who is already in the TRUE WORLD (*i.e., dead,* Wm. G.) more than fifty years, but what he told us, I remember as if it would be yesterday. This man's occupation all the years was an M'LAMED. He was teaching grown-up children. A Jew with all virtues, mainly he was very wise. His name was R'ITSHEL HOFFMAN, but he could not make a living, for he had a big family. So, he additionally used to do business a whole year to buy various skins and produce from this, leather. He took the leather to the YARMILINTSER Fair near us, if I remember correctly, which lasted, every year, a month long. I don't remember which month, but this is not the main point.

Merchants used to go to YARMILNTSER Fair from all over Russia. So too, did R'ITSHEL, blessed be his memory, go every year. Sometimes he made out good, and sometimes not so. Thus, he conducted himself all the years. So, it happened he came home, as in all the other years. The first thing was that he was called to the TORAH, suddenly R'ITSHEL blessed GOMEL (*the blessing said by Jews after escaping a great danger,* Wm. G.). When he went down, as is the custom, everybody greets him with SHOLOM, how he made out at the fair, and why he blessed GOMEL? "If you want to know my beloved Jews, come to the table, and we will rake a drink, and I will make with you, L'HAYIM, then I will tell you everything that happened to me at the YARMILNSTER Fair."

All wanted to hear what happened to R'ITSHEL, but I can't describe everything that he told the Jews in the old home. It is too much to tell even though it is very interesting. I will call it in the American term, kidnapped. He was kept in a forest for a couple of days outside of the town. He was endangered along with all of his belongings, particularly with his life. So, we were drinking, and he told everything to his Jews in the synagogue. It was terrible to hear, and especially to think of what he went through. The Jews looked at his face and listened to every word. In the course of his talk, a few Jews could not restrain themselves and asked, "R'ITSHEL, how could you endure all this, the pains and could escape from their hands with your poor belongings and especially with your life?"

His answer was with a smile. "Yes, yes, we have a good God. The greatest miracle happened to me. If not, God forbid, not for this miracle, who knows where I would be." They asked all at one time, "What miracle?" "My dear Jews, the answer is that I, myself, rather I alone was not there."

He was speaking as an example of the danger that we all could have confronted in the old home. It is the kind of episode I wish to write, that I described before, after I finish about my life. My dear family, what I went through and described and a lot I didn't describe as plain as maybe I should, for it is impossible for me to write down everything, and thanks God, I have lived until now. I still hope to live and be able to describe good things. I was present at all these happenings. How do you like it? Especially you, my oldest son, who is able to read Yiddish, what would you say about your father, and thanks God, I am proud of you and children's children and with my wife, my friend in my life. She devoted to me all the years. But, unfortunately, she didn't understand me.

I pray to God that all of you should outlive my bones and you, LEAH, should at least, after my death, live fifteen years; then you will understand me. In the meantime, keep well, and we will, with God's will, see each other very soon but in a good way. I will write only about good, only good. In the meantime, live and be happy.

Your father and grandfather, especially a man!
YISROEL AYZIK ROSEN

(Thus, it appears that this was going to be the end of his story and only episodes [short stories] would follow, but after a period of time, he began writing his story again. ER)

Part Ten
My Life Becomes Beautiful

I want to keep my word that God let me live until now, even though life is still very hard for me and my wife, with many hindrances that are always coming. From this child and from this child, from this son-in-law and daughters-in-law and grandchildren and friends, we also had much good, K'AYN HORE, and we would live like this, happily. I recognize that all of this is thanks to God. We, therefore, ask God that our children and children's children should be well. I said that I will not write any more bad. So, I didn't write for almost eight years, for it was the worst crisis in our life. It is called the Great Depression, but it is not to write about, for nothing was good to write.

I again began to write about my story from the year 1939, and we have had a lot of NACHES from our children. My first son-in-law had already a drugstore a long time ago, and they made a nice living and, thanks God, also a child, a girl. My oldest son also made a living with his own dry goods store, very nice and also good. The son who got married at a young age, also made a living. The daughter, who just moved, also they bought a drugstore, K'AYN HORE, each child has PARNOSE. Even the daughter from my first wife is also well up and has, K'AYN HORE, six children. In short, all is good. With us remained the youngest son, David, the only American born about whom I wrote when he was named at his BRIS, and we didn't even have for a bottle of whiskey to buy, let alone everything that we needed.

From the time he was named, David has brought light to our home, especially to our hearts, so handsome he was and especially good. He gave us mood to live until this very day as I write everything. I will indeed continue to write and dedicate my whole writing that I committed to write only good things with God's will. It will be only devoted to everything that is, K'AYN HORE, good before God and man. This special child, when he reached only the age of twelve to fourteen, he already helped us, that was at the end of the 1920s, before the Depression. He did everything, various things, and every time he earned more and wanted that all of us should live happy and better.

What he did, I need not write; you know it yourselves. For my writing is not for outsiders. He was already, K'AYN HORE, a young man when he worked recently on Market Street with a distributor of novelties. He was twenty-three years old (1938) and earns very well, nice grown-up, K'AYN HORE, with all virtues and qualities, well excuse me, not everybody has all virtues. I don't think I wrote about this, that when he was a child and walked on Wolf Street amongst the GOYIM (*gentiles,* Wm. G.), a boy unwillingly by accident hit him with an iron pipe on the leg, and from that, he almost became a cripple and until today he has a shorter leg and walks with a slight limp and is suffering. But, thanks God, this didn't harm him from being a good businessman and not to find a good match.

He was very popular with the girls. I knew he would find a very fine girl, even one with money. Whoever saw him got interested in him. People came, from parents to me and told me this. But he was always such a child and now a grown person that everyone liked him. He does not let himself, God forbid, be driven by anyone, even by his parents and especially outsiders. So, he was and so he is, thanks God, until now when he is already married, until 120 years, and he already has, K'AYN HORE, two children, boys; one of five years and one two and a half.

Why am I telling you this? I want to tell you his story from the time he worked on Market Street. He got acquainted with a poor girl in the store. She was a bookkeeper and was older than he by almost two years. She didn't have a father. He died when she was a young girl. She only had a mother like we. The main thing was that she was a very decent girl, a wise one and beautiful. When I saw her the first time in the evening, I almost didn't see her, but heard her talking, and she was to my liking. In the morning, when he asked me, "Pop, how do you like my girl?" my answer was, "Well, my child, if she is to your liking, then

The Inheritance (Yurusha)

certainly to me is good. She is poor, to be rich is not the main thing. The main thing is that she is a decent person."

So, it didn't take too long. He even tried a new business before the wedding, but unfortunately, he failed and lost a few thousand dollars, but this didn't prevent them from getting married. In short, they got married and made the most beautiful wedding, which I never had for my children and especially never saw at outsiders. It brightened our life in our older years. The HUPEH was in the large and beautiful synagogue, B'NAI YESHURUN, at 33rd and Diamond Street. To describe everything, I don't need. It didn't cost me a penny (*notice this is the first time the author doesn't use the word cent, but he uses the term penny.* ER).

They deserve all of the credit; he, his wife, my daughter-in-law, she arranged everything. I didn't ask whether he gave the money or she. It was so, and it was nice and good until this very day. It is already six years since they got married on LAG B'OMER , (*the 33rd day of the counting of the OMER and is a day commemorating the end of a plague that killed 24,000 of Rabbi AKIBA' S disciples.* ER). They should live until 120 with health and with much luck. They live with us together in the same poor house, although they could already move long ago, but their devotion to us is not to describe. The credit I give to her, to Vera, my beloved daughter-in-law. For no matter how good he is, if she would not be in favor, it would be different, but she is an exception. This I say from my true heart. If I would be, she, it would not be so. Yes, six years elapsed the 26th of May, 1946, was their sixth anniversary.

It is not too hard for me and for my wife even though we don't have because, thanks God, we don't lack in anything. We have everything to eat and drink and clothing, everything that our heart desires. So, is he, and especially she taking care of all that we need and want? I went through an operation, the last I went through, and I pray to God that this will be the last. I needed this operation long ago, but I was in such condition that I didn't have the strength to even go to the ward, and I didn't want to have it, and I hoped that perhaps I can avoid it. I suffered from serious nose bleeds and sometimes coughing up blood, so to say such hemorrhages, losing my poor blood, which I didn't have enough until one time I had to remain in bed. That time it was entirely different. It was June 26, 1942, my beloved child, DAVIDL with his wife, they were the first who tried to take me to the biggest doctor, Dr. ROSEFF (*It is not clear what the operation was, but we know he had breathing problems from his youth when he had pneumonia and from the dust when he slept in the shop as well as the problems that resulted from swallowing the wrong medicine that must have affected his esophagus and digestive system. I also know that he had heart problems. My guess is that he might have had an ulcer and possibly a hiatal hernia.* ER) My oldest son knew him, for he went through a big operation before on his thyroid because he had a goiter and on something else that is not important to describe because we all went through it.

Actually, it didn't do for me any good, but as I wrote, I want to stop writing bad, only about good. The professor examined me and said that the best thing is to remain in the hospital in order to be operated. How the operation was and after it is not necessary to write. What I want to write is how my family and mainly my wife and all my children and especially my youngest son with his wife devoted their lives to me and showed me much love, care, and concern. It was not too hard for them to do everything for me. I felt, even outsiders, love and affection. I felt a rush in my body, mind and soul. This encourages my mood, spirits and hopes and I thanked God for his kindness that I went through and survived this terrible operation.

I was, nevertheless, very sick and felt that I am dying. I asked my family to take me home. It was the fourth day after the operation during the morning hours, so that I will die at home in my bed. The doctor permitted. When they brought me home, I felt entirely different and thought to myself, after all, I am, thanks God, a man of more than seventy years, and thanks God, married off all my children and have NACHES from them and prayed for recovery whenever my children were so sick or needed operations, and that they lived, and that I have lived to see all of this NACHES that I must be satisfied. Yes, I will die with joy in my heart, and indeed, I was very sick, which everyone could see, especially that I could feel it so much. But I wanted still to live to see Hitler's defeat. Yes, I will live, and I will see it, that the war should come to an end.

This gave me new courage to live. They brought me to the doctor who operated on me and examined my hands and my feet, my nose, and my ears, listened to my damaged heart but mostly looked into my eyes and said to my family, "Yes, it is true your father is very sick, but I don't see that he is going to die." He gave me over to our family doctor, Dr. Roth, and that he should take care of me and said that I should stay in bed for six weeks and after that to send me to a convalescent home. And so, it was.

Now it was entirely different than all the years before. Everyone was dear and faithful to me. My wife was different, all my children and my children's children, outsiders and various people came to help me recover. I would never believe it, but it was so. I was encouraged and gained strength. Not I, God gave me strength and gave me new power and mood and life and saw to it that now I have something to live for. After all, I didn't live yet (*i.e., he didn't have a good life,* Wm. G.) all my years. Now, thanks God, nothing, God forbid, is lacking to me. My youngest son always comes to me and says, "Pop, how do you feel?" and he looks in my face. "I want you and Mom to live. This would be my greatest pleasure." He and his beloved wife showed us such love and devotion, and it is so even until this day with the greatest respect. This made me healthy.

My youngest son, DAVIDL, with his wife, they took good care of us and relieved me from everything. Before, I paid some rent and other expenses. They took everything upon themselves, for he already did some business. Here, about him, I would have to write and write how he, himself, K'AYN HORE, without anyone's help, God helped him for the privilege, what he did for his father and mother before and especially now, which you will see in the further chapters of my writing.

I began to feel better every day from day to day. I used to earn, but now I was free from that pressure. He made sure that I always had a dollar in pocket. So, my first task was when I already had a few dollars, the first was that I paid back to good friends where I was in debt all these years, small debts. I had paid back the big debts, but the little sums, small bills, and also the debts to friends I didn't have the means, as you already know. I wanted, but I didn't have, to my deep regret. Now, since God helped me when I have a child who provides everything, so my first duty was to pay back. The next thing I had and have always such a heart to help the other. I helped when I had. When I didn't have, I had aggravation. Now, when I have the dollar, is the first to give to whom I owe, and the second is to help, and so until today, when I write thanks God and lived to have it so good, I keep paying back. I was in debt a few hundred dollars that I never thought that I will pay back to everybody during my life. Yes, I wrote in my will that after my death, all should be paid back, but thanks God, I lived to do it myself.

I still earned a little by myself, and little by little, along with the help from my beloved son, I am able to pay back to whom I owe for almost twenty-five years from one dollar to 100 and some even more. All together, it is four years that I have good, thanks God, from 1942 to 1946, and it is the 20th of June 1946, that I am writing my good times, and I am now in Atlantic City with my wife and children that my beloved child, DAVIDL, rented a house for all of us; for his beloved wife and beloved two children, one is five years until 120 and the other boy two and a half years until 120 years, K'AYN HORE, dear children who are giving us new life to me and to my wife. We are the most happy father and mother that I lived to see it in our older years, K'AYN HORE, to have everything.

Personally, I say with the truth from my heart that I am lacking in nothing except health, but my dears, at the same time, I understand that it can't be different, for when I was a young man, I was weak and even more as I got older. Outsiders don't want to understand it, but thanks God, I understand. I understand at my younger years that it is bad for me and that I have to try not to get lost and that, with God's will, a better time will come. If I lasted too long, I suffered too much. Not only myself but also my friend in life also my family, but it probably had to be so.

Now, when I write that, thanks God, it is good for me, it is not because of my goodness that I got money and some luxuries. No, I don't have money now either. I don't have now, even my own hundred dollars, nevertheless it is good for me now. I don't wish better from The Master of the World. I only beg for health for my family. Nothing, God forbid, is lacking to me. I have the dollar I earn, and if not, my child DAVIDL gives me, also another child, all are good to me. Even my son, about whom I wrote so much, what he did to me is good. He doesn't know what to do for us. He does not have a lot; he makes a living for himself. He has, K'AYN HORE, two nice children; a boy of fifteen years and a girl almost seven years and a nice house, everything is fine. We lived to have from him much NACHES.

I must write the truth for you that first God and next to Him, our child DAVIDL have made our lives beautiful, and my son tries and does for the whole family. He makes, thanks God, a nice living and took HERSHELE in. Perhaps if he would have money also, but it is still far to this, especially for his wife, he will do more. It is good that we lived to see this and have NACHES from each child, also from my oldest son, we have great respect. He also has a decent wife, a loyal one and two children, boys. One came home a few weeks ago from the Pacific. He was there for two years and will be twenty-one, until 120 years, in a few weeks, and the other child will, with God's will, become a BAR-MITZVAH next year. They are fine children, and my son Max is, God forbid, not a poor man. We have every right to be proud of him. The main thing is that he has a good name in business. We have a lot of NACHES from him. We pray to God for their health.

And about my daughters, I already mentioned about them and their families and their success and, thanks God, they are all good. They both have one daughter; more they don't want. America is not Europe. If one does not want, then he does not have it. They have very fine and decent husbands, druggists. One got tired of it, so he sold his business and works with the other in the business and makes, thanks God, a fine living and we have from them much NACHES. A few weeks ago, they moved to their new house, which they bought in WYNNEFIELD. Telling the truth, I and my wife didn't see it yet. We wish them that they should live with luck, health and long years. Isn't this NACHES, which is the main thing; dearer than money, which I prayed for all the years and hope for and He indeed helped me. What more can I ask? Who can compare himself to me? This means for me riches, wealth. The other one also just sold his drugstore where he was ten years between many blacks and made nice living and saved some money. Unfortunately, a few months ago they made a holdup so he didn't want to stay there anymore and he sold it. In the meantime, he works for somebody, but he will with God's help buy another store in a Jewish neighborhood. Also, here we lived to have NACHES.

So, I am happy and also my wife. This is my wealth. What do you think, not so? I am proud of my children. I was proud before also, during the times when I made every effort and did everything. Unfortunately, they didn't understand me then, but I think they do now. I suffered then because of that, but now it is entirely different, everything is different. I am loved by my wife, loved by my children and children's children. Nothing is too hard for them to do for us. Even by outsiders. Everyone looks at us with different eyes. We even have NACHES from our daughter of the first wife. She has, K'AYN HORE, six children, two daughters already married off and already has two grandchildren and they are all well up. Alas, she is as she was although she is already a woman of fifty-three years, until 120.

I suffer because of her until this very day, but this does not mean much. The main thing is that she is well. Perhaps someday she will understand it. In fact, it is a great pain for me. All the years since I brought her to me and knew her, I have only aggravation. She gossips about me and about my innocent wife, who was, for her, better than a mother, especially to her children. We forgave her many times and begged for peace, but we never succeeded. Nothing helped, she poisoned the children against us. I suffered, and I suffer until today. Her husband was friendly to us and us to him. She saw to it that he should avoid us. In short, it was bad, which brought me grief and sadness.

She told people things, which is not fit to describe, and I suffered until a certain day a few years ago when they moved to Washington, and there, they made a business. In fact, we thanked God, for she did day by day gossip about us (*in Yiddish FARSHVARST UNSERE PENIMER, literally it means made black our faces,* Wm. G.), for far from the eyes is far from the heart. At that time, she already married off a daughter, and indeed let her live in her house; also, not better than she, maybe worse. She attended school here and was a bookkeeper, and she also married off a second daughter. She didn't invite us. She poisoned the children against us. If one of her children passes by on the street, they will never say how are you to me or my wife or to any of our children. It hurts us, but it is so. We can't help it. After all, there are bigger and more successful people than I who also suffer, perhaps more than me.

Now they are back in Philadelphia. Her husband, my landsman from home, is the only one who began to come to us almost every day to our house, and he really wants to do a lot for us, his father and mother-in-law, as well as for all the children. He loves them with all his heart. Even for the years before, he asked us that we should forgive him. It was not his fault. They were well up, and they made, thanks God, a nice living. They were not poor. I may say that I have NACHES, but at the same time, there is aggravation, pain, and sufferings. Only God knows the truth that it is not my fault. After all, it cannot be good with everything. I hope that they will reconsider that they made a mistake. In the meantime, I don't have any pleasure at a time when I should have pleasure.

I am ascribing it to the good life we have lived to see, thanks God, and I have from her NACHES. I hope to have more and pray that she will get understanding and be human, and that is not my fault, and that she should be able to recognize all that I did for her and that I went through everything with her. I don't regret that I brought her to this land even though my wife told me many times, "I wish that you didn't bring her, you would not suffer so much because of her." However, my wife is not right. I am satisfied despite all the suffering she caused to me. I thank God that she is in America.

In short, I am satisfied that I lived to see this day. I have NACHES from all my children, they should be all with long, healthy, and happy years. I am now all right in my older years, K'AYN HORE, it does not need to be better and always a dollar in my pocket; whatever my heart desires. I can help a needy poor man with a dollar, and so I am happy. I have what my heart desired when I was a young man at home, and I wanted to live to have for myself as well as for others and could not achieve because I was always sick and poor.

With great joy, God helped and gave me a child here in America who does and can do what I wanted and could not do. He does it with his pure heart and especially with his pure soul. He's not only good to outsiders, but in particular, he good to his father and mother and sisters and brothers. Thank God I lived too, to have from him a lot more NACHES with a fine wife and dear children who prolong our old and broken years. They make us live, and we want to live now. For we have, thanks God, something to live for. Our worries were taken away, the burden was taken off. First, thanks to God and then to our child, the youngest, and I may say that thanks to you, DAVIDL and your wife that all our children became different than before; even your mother, my wife, rather my friend in life. All is good, everyone is good, and all people are good. The whole world is good to me.

Somehow everything changed as my heart told me that we may expect good and that we have lived to see this day. All the years, I was thinking and begging many times and for many things, especially for PARNOSE, but to be able to marry off children and to have such NACHES is the greatest answer to my prayers. Today I am thinking about one thing mainly and pray daily to The Master of the World that he should give us health and long and happy years. I am grateful that I could live to the time when I could be able to pay back every cent to all the people to whom I was in debt, and for so many years, was not able to do. It caused me much pain, but today, thanks God, this pain is gone, and it makes me feel a success, even though I am not the richest man. The Master of the World and DAVIDL have saved me and my wife.

As I have written before, we lived together with my son and his family. They could have moved to a nice house with all of the conveniences years ago, but they didn't move because of us. In 1945, they rented a place for the whole summer in Atlantic City also because of us and for the entire family. He does not live for himself only; he wants that everyone should live and have happiness and enjoy and to be together as a family should. This is what I wanted and could not achieve, so God helped me to see that he is able to do this.

How fortunate I am that I lived too. I am already old, and I can't take advantage fully of all this new way of life offers, but I appreciate everything he does for me and the whole family. Telling the truth, I could never buy a new suit. Today, I have the best suits and the best shoes and everything that my heart desires. It can't be better. This winter, they made us buy the house on Westmont Street, where we have lived for many years. If yes, I really didn't care, but he thought it should be so. He bought the house for us and for everyone. He is not a rich man. God should help him that he should have as his own as much as he is in debt. However, this is the way it is with him, and his friend is the same as he.

Well, bad we had many times, but now we have only good times. I had a lot to write when we had bad times, but since God helped and DAVIDL grew up and we lived to have it good, so I have to write less. For the words, themselves, have answered it. In short, it is good, I don't desire better. I think that my wife feels the same way. We only ask God that they should all be healthy and live happy years. We hope and pray that we will still have a couple of good years to repair the years we didn't get to live in the right way and that now we can live as MENTSHEN.

When I write these words of joy and contentment, we are in Atlantic City for the whole summer, but in a better and nicer house, almost a mansion. I must write, from the very first day we arrived, June 20, 1946, and now when I write it is the 18th of July, I didn't have yet one good day of health; so sick I am, not sleeping, not eating, not bathing almost nothing. But I am enjoying and taking in everything, even with sickness. Even if my death should come now, I thank God for all and would not mind if it came because, K'AYN HORE, I lived to see and have everything.

The world has a saying, and it is the truth, that if a man was good all the years at his parents, also himself, I mean during his younger years, and in the older years were bad, then all his good years were also bad. But, thanks God, in his old age, they are good, then it washes away all the bad years. I can't be better. I am now, K'AYN HORE, seventy-five years old. I would still like to live at least five years in order that I should be able to write more words of good, but, God forbid not, I am, in one word, satisfied.

I am very weak at present, but I understand that it can be, God forbid, worse. About four years ago, when I was very sick, I prayed that I should live to see Hitler's defeat as well as Japan's and that my grandchildren should come home, as well as everyone and, thanks God, I lived to see it. Now I am continuing to pray for something. In the last few months, a call came from my wife's sister, the only one who has survived from her big family. All were killed in the Holocaust. All were killed from LONIVITS, VOLYNIA GUBERNYE (*the author still uses the terms when VOLYNIA was a part of Czarist Russia. I explained that a GUBERNYE can be compared to a state in this country. After 1918, VOLYNIA became part of Poland.* Wm. G.). She survived by a miracle a few weeks before the war. Her only son served in the army in Poland in the city of TOMASHOV (*In Poland, there were two cities by the same name in two different regions of the country. The author does not say which TOMASHOV.* Wm. G.). He was a pilot and brought to his home his mother and his young wife. Thus, they were saved and remained to this very day.

Now, we are receiving letter from them and requests that we should save them. That's all they want. These couple of letters depressed us very much, especially my wife, who is her only sister. Reading how she survived and describes how all were killed, I can't endure to describe. Hopefully, history books will tell it in a proper way. If I were young, I could do what is needed, but in these, my older years, such a man of seventy-five years, who knows what can be done by me. But, thanks God, I have the understanding and mood, and I want to try to live to see them during our lifetime, especially since God has helped us that we lived to have a child who can do for them (*the author does not mention, but he certainly has in mind David.* Wm. G.), and he really tries.

The first thing that we did was to let them hear from us by telegram. The second was that we sent them fifty dollars, although we received another letter in which they wrote explicitly not to send them anything, only paperwork to get them out. Their only hope was for us to get them out from there still alive, that's all that they want. Her son is still there in the army, and he still has to be there a month. We filled out all of the proper papers and did everything that was needed for them, and sent it in order that they should receive visas.

When I am writing now, we didn't hear anything from them. It is already five weeks since we sent the papers. For this, we are praying, me and my wife, to live to see them. We hope that The Master of the World that he will do it for us. He helped us so much, and he will continue to help us. As you see and hear, I am always turning around and asking for His help. I always seem to want something else, and he obeys us. My heart is satisfied, especially my soul, although my body interferes in everything. But who cares, even though the body can be weak, as long as the soul is here? However, it is better to have a healthy body.

I am satisfied with my life, as I said before. I used to think about many things. Now, I am only praying to God that my children and my children's children, that everyone should be healthy and happy, and that we should have NACHES from them. At the same time, it creates me pains, and I don't sleep exactly at night, if a child, God forbid, does not feel so good or just something or if it is not so good in the business, especially my DAVIDL, if he does not feel as I want, or his wife or a child, I am scared, and I am nervous that nothing will happen to me.

It has been my custom all my life to DAVEN, to pray day and night, and in my prayers to ask for good health for all. I never pray only for myself. I always pray also for my family, friends, community, my fellow Jews, and all humans. I know that I am not the only one who suffers. There is not a human being in the world who is completely satisfied with his life. Yes, I can live and be satisfied, but life doesn't let me; always a scare about the next day, so is the human being. As I write, I am satisfied even with the pain I have every day. I am taking everything with love.

I felt that all my prayers are answered, and then came worries for us again. It is now a few months ago that we received from the old home the letters from my wife's sister and her family to rescue them. It has been very difficult to accomplish. This great country is not as it used to be with immigrants. Our worries about them breaks our mood. It is very difficult to read her letters. We are not concerned about money. What we are concerned about is that we can't figure out how to bring them. We will keep trying and pray that God will certainly help.

When I am writing these words, we received from them three letters, which are impossible to endure. They suffer there, and only that we should save them. What can we do, we sent them the papers, we took care of everything, but only there they have to receive visas? They didn't receive them yet. We hope they will be able to receive the visas. I wish that we will live to see them, but I am getting weaker from day to day. We can't rest until we have achieved our goal. I hope, as does my wife. She has been aggravated since she began to receive the letters. From such a big family, she is the only one who remained. The tragedy that Hitler and the Nazis have done. I wish we would have her here very soon, but we can't do any more than what we have done and tried. Now we can only pray and hope that God will help us bring her to us in a good way.

As you see, it gives me always mood and hope and desire to live and to live for a purpose. If not, life would be miserable. And my spirit and mood is always lifted when I turn to God. Yes, I had much bad. I was sick and weak and poor my whole life. I struggled, but I refused to give up. Yes, I almost threw myself into the waters more than once, but my will to live was very strong. God never abandoned me. I almost abandoned myself, but God always came to me and guided me. I always live for something good, and as I look back, good was always there. Better, yes, it could have been, but I thank God I have lived to see this day. Today is, K'AYN HORE, good for me in my older years.

It is true that it came too late, but it came. Nothing is lacking to me. I think that my beloved wife, Leah, will say the same thing. Riches has no limits, particularly luxury, but this is the way it is and for us, K'AYN HORE, very good. We have everything that we want and need. The only thing lacking is something that only The Master of the World can provide, and that is health. Wickedness, poverty, and sickness, which always befell us in various ways and caused me to write, every time, more is no longer the main thing. I didn't bring out everything, almost 50 percent, but since God helped me, I lived to have much NACHES from my children, their children, and many friends in my older years, especially these last four years.

I'm seventy-five, soon to be seventy-six, and these last years have been more than good to me and my wife. I lived to pay back all of my debts, including the last couple of hundred dollars that haunted me all of these years. At the same time, to be able to support with a dollar a poor man, or else an important cause, is a big thing to me. I don't desire better, and I am happy and satisfied. I thank The Master of the World, my guide in life, and my partner in TIKKUN OLOM (*repairing the world*), for all he has done for me, my wife and my family.

The Inheritance (Yurusha)

I am concluding now my writing with joy and satisfaction. If I will write, I will only write episodes that I remember from my old home when I was a child and various stories that I heard from all kinds of people; learned men. Also, about America from various people with whom I came in contact. Thanks to God, I have lived to see the defeat of Hitler and the Nazis and if God will give me a few more years to live with my wife together and to live first to see, with us, her sister with the children and also to live to see that the Jewish people should be redeemed from the whole world and that they should get, ERETZ YISROEL, where they should be able to live in peace, we would be the most happy people. We hope that it will be this way, with God's help.

Family portrait, ca. 1946. Left: Theresa, Vivian, Harry, Leah, and Israel.

POSTSCRIPT

Sometime after I had my Zayda's autobiography translated by Dr. Glicksman, I was given an envelope that contained several folded and yellowed handwritten pages in Yiddish that were in my Zayda's handwriting and very fragile. There was also a smaller document written in Hebrew script under the letterhead of Grand Rabbi M. H. Twersky, the Tolner Rabbi. I gave these papers to a local Rabbi who held them for several years but was never able to translate them. After I finally completed transcribing as well as editing the handwritten translation into my computer, I asked the Rabbi to send back these documents so that I could try to find someone who could do the translation. My cousin, Kathy Liss Drew, recommended Rita Ratson, who had translated many letters and documents that Kathy's husband Jerry had from his mother and other relatives.

I finished my initial draft several months ahead of my schedule, having taken advantage of the isolation brought on by the COVID-19 pandemic, and began the first read through editing in December 2020. I contacted Mrs. Ratson and gave her the documents. I told her that I thought my Zayda's papers were his will and that the document from Rabbi Twersky was the purchase of graves. I have no idea how I came up with this, but as it turned out, I was correct.

Mrs. Ratson told me that she had projects ahead of mine but would get to it as soon as possible in about a month. I had originally hoped to have finished transcribing the autobiography by Pesach 2021. It is now three days before Pesach, and I have just picked up the translation of these additional papers from Rita Ratson. She told me that my Zayda's handwriting had become very difficult to read. I assume it was because he was very frail. She said that he tried to embellish his writing and make it fancy and artistic. That certainly was in keeping with his artistic skills, as is evidenced in his book and the kvitlich we have that he drew. She said that there were some words that she could not make out and left that space with dots. The will confirms some things and leaves me with other questions. Some of the names of shuls (synagogues) are not recognizable to me, and quick Google research does not show any results. However, the essence of what he wrote all makes sense and is part of the completion of his story.

After you finish this postscript of the purchase of his burial plots and his last will and testament, I will have completed bringing his story to his decedents as he wished but also to the public to understand one man's journey from the "old world" to the "Golden Medina," which is the story of a majority of our people at the end of the nineteenth and the first half of the twentieth century in these great United States of America.

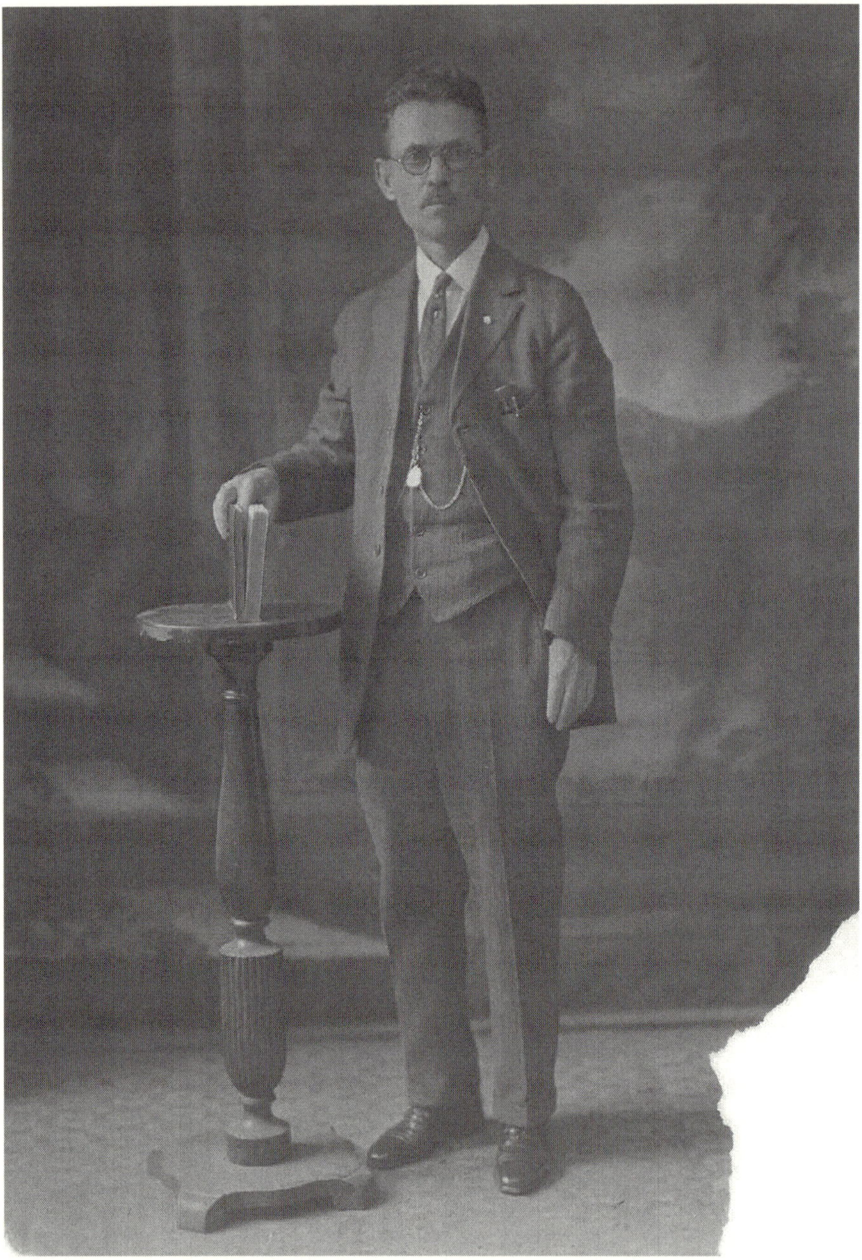

(MY CONFESSION OF SINS, BEFORE DEATH) BETTER EXPRESSED: MY POOR TESTAMENT?

My last words, which will possibly not be able to be said to beloved wife, my friend in life, as well as to all of you, my beloved children, and to all my beloved grandchildren, and to all my good friends, I want to tell you all here, you should know what I wrote a long time ago, that great testaments have no value now because I now possess nothing. You know it well on your own. I feel that my days are nearly very few. I cannot eat or sleep. To walk in the street (*outside*) for business is now impossible, even to go to synagogue, I strain very much to accomplish. I suffer a great deal of pain in my body during the day and at night.

But this is not everything to me yet. I have already been accustomed to it all my life, also I understand that I am older. The older one gets, the weaker one gets, but the main reason that I am suffering now is, that you children have started to suffer for a period of time now from various sorts of illnesses, especially now that you, my oldest son, may you live in good health, you are not well, and I will not be able to endure it already. I cannot express it, how I feel. But I accept my dying as love for all of you, as long as all of you will live and be well. This is why I am asking you all to listen, to pay attention to what I am writing to you all. I owe money now to B'nai Jeshurun, on 33rd and Diamond Streets, for which I have just taken a loan without interest, in the amount of 100 hundred dollars, you must exceed that amount when you repay them.

To go on, you all know that my wish (*request*) of all of you, for all my life, was to lie in the Rezushtshizer Shul's cemetery. I belonged in this manner for many years in this shul and belong, thank God, until this day, and my friend and I were treasurers for sixteen years, and I was given the greatest respect. The treasurer's job cost me much money, as you know from my writings, particularly, much health. This is the reason I want to lie there. I have, however, for many years already, not paid my dues. I have a word to say, a thought to leave to you still more at any rate. But now, as I am leaving this sinning world, so poor, so my request of you all is that all of you should give them not less than one hundred dollars!

I am asking of them, that they should give me two beautiful graves, as I have earned. Others took on their own, not I; even though I was one of the only ones who bought the ground at the cemetery for the shul. Also, they all know well; my love and my devotion to the shul for all the years!

Also, I know well, that your mother, beloved children, will not be able to say Kiddush (*proclamation of the holiness of the Sabbath or of a holiday over wine*), so that you must protect her and be there for her, and I further ask all of you, better expressed to you, my beloved wife, that you should not worry that they will not say Kaddish for me. You must tell my best friend, this is what I believe that he was toward me, Mr. Kruger, the Shammos (*the sexton*) of the shul; he will say Kaddish for me. I think that I have earned this from him, especially if you will pay him a few dollars for this good deed. Also, I am not requesting (*asking for*) any sort of eulogies from any rabbi who takes money for this. You, my beloved wife, and you, my beloved children, you knew me well, with all my virtues (*merits*) and faults. Your eulogy and your truthful heart will be good for me, especially for all of yourselves.

But, if by chance, it will come about that a true friend is found, who knew me well, or a Rebbe who will want to say a couple of words about me without money, then you should allow it. Even though I do not believe that there is anyone like this, and maybe yes, that I have earned it. Actually, this is what I am requesting of all of you, my beloved, for you to advertise in the Jewish as well as in the English papers and place my picture as well. You know the plan I had, the business I did for almost thirty years with English people equally with Jewish ones, and there are many still who are connected with me until the present. They liked me as a human being, and I like them. I have customers who owe me a debt. Maybe some of them and maybe all of them will repay you, in order that you should be able repay those who I owe a debt to.

I do not mean those big debts that I owe the world, better expressed, to humanity; and humanity's debts to me, this remains for the true world to come…

All this, as I am writing these words, I am feeling very bad about many things in my life and my poor health. But my beloved, you should not think, God forbid, that I am writing with an attack of fever, chills or some sudden illness, as some may say. Thank God, I have clear thought and pure gratitude and love and appreciation for the life I have lived and the way I have served and revered God.

I want you all to be well and joyous, and may you all live a long life. Sadly, I was not able to do for all of you as another man and father might have done. You all know how weak I was, particularly for almost all of my life, also I was not able to accomplish as much as I wanted for humanity. Be happy and enjoy your life with loved ones you hold dear to yourselves, and love toward all people. I was satisfied with my life, even though I was ill and poor. I am dying with love, one who is content and satisfied. Maybe I will simply be allowed to live a couple of years more; if God will not want it, may I have at least the rare honor, privilege to say farewell before my death. But as I am not able to know, I am writing everything to all of you now, how to manage with all of this!

These words are mine, truthfully. I am asking of you, my beloved wife and beloved children and grandchildren and my entire family and friends and those with whom I did business, in the street, and those few who are without fault, all people equally, you should all forgive me (*pardon me*).

After all is said and done, I was, nevertheless, not a person who had all the best of virtues. Ah, every person has his own failings; if he does not, then every person would be a king and would need to be in heaven and not in this sinning world! Well about this, I would nevertheless need to write another book, but now is not the time to write. Everything will come out of these words to portray what I thought. I made the mistake of arguing with the greatest (*most important*) people who wanted to humiliate me and to myself, I was the smallest (*lowliest*) and the weakest and the poorest, but not for the other person, then I challenged them and chased it, which cost me my health. That is the big fault I had.

Yes, my beloved, you all know it well. I want all of you to forgive me. I forgive everyone, yes, to those who brought me pain for no reason, to those who have stolen money from me, as well as energy, my writing is with love to the world: this means to me more than everything.

From me, your devoted, faithful, loyal husband and devoted, faithful, loyal father, to all you children and grandfather to all my grandchildren. Also, to those who were friends toward me for all those years, and to those who brought me pain, they did not understand me. I forgive them: may God forgive them…

ISRAEL ISAAC BAR ZVI HIRSH ROSEN
3117 Westmont Street
Philadelphia, PA
Then in calligraphy in large bold black ink in Hebrew:

ISRAEL: ISAAC: B"R ZVI HIRSH ROSEN

I am asking you all not to be alarmed; you should take time to certainly inform the Rezushtshizer Shul even though I do not want to be lying there with them. After my death, the funeral should take place at the house, not at the undertaker. To go on, my beloved ones, still after all my writing to you all is complete, so I am leaving it to you all, oh, as you all will understand it best that is the way you should do it, whatever will be better, nicer for you all. After my death, I will need nothing: I thank you all for everything you did for me during my life, and I will see you all in the true world.

This was all written in Yiddish on three 8 ½-by-11 sheets of paper and on the back of the third sheet of paper were two additional notes, one written in 1945 and the other in 1947 so the body of the will had to have been written before September 1944, because in September 1944, Israel Rosen purchased two graves from Rabbi Twersky, the Tolner Rebbe, which means the Rezushtshizer Shul must have denied him the graves in their cemetery section. The 1945 note references the purchase of the grave from Rabbi Twersky.

ADDITIONAL NOTES

Night before Shavuot: May 16, 1945

It pains me, my dear son Max Rosen, that my testament to all of you, which I wrote, is not good, but as you told me, that it will not put me in jail. I do not feel very good these days to tell you the truth, my child, since I received the unexpected letter, so I do not think about the shuls (*synagogues*) any longer, if whatever must happen with me happens then I leave everything up to all of you and do whatever is better for all of you. And what is nicer (*more proper*). The Tolner Rebbe will give me two graves at Mt. Sharon Cemetery near the Kremenitser Rebbe and if you want, you will inform, especially you will inform Ursh, who will give the same amount of dollars that I thought I would give to them. But go on, the same, I am leaving everything to all of you. You must try to be good people, with compassion toward everyone, but you should run away from those who can do harm. I gave away my life and time and money. What did I receive in return? Heartache, not more…

August 6, 1947: Atlantic City

I am asking you all, my dear children, to obey (*follow my advice*) about what I am writing to you all. You should give the sum of a hundred-$100 dollars to the "Galut Chesed" (*charity to those in exile*) where, at one time, we raised money in shul to Moshe Alper. Also, you should (*must*) give, and not more than, the sum of 100 dollars to the Kifter Shul. To Mr. Israel, you should all give to charity, Tzedakah, in the same amount on my behalf. For this, I will gather joy with this endeavor, to help with good health and with making a living and gather great joy from your children.

    Your father, Israel Rosen

The last document is the purchase of the graves from Grand Rabbi M. H. Twersky. Below is the translation of the handwritten Hebrew document under his letterhead:

Grand Rabbi M.H. Twersky
Tolner Rabbi
4900 N. 8th Street, (N.W. Cor. 8th & Rockland Sts.)
Philadelphia 41, Pa.

As evidence and by my approval-
Israel Isaak Bar Zvi Rosen of 3117 Westmont Str. My letter to him- 2 graves from the house of the Kreinitser Shul at Mount Sharon Cemetery.
Grave #673 (grave #1 and grave #2)
A cash receipt in the amount of $100.00

Two graves are for him and for his wife, may God bless them in life. May they be blessed for a long life and may their days be blessed for good ones.

Signed, day 5, passage 18 days: Becha'alotcha
Month of Sivan
September 18, 1944
Moshe Zvi Nachum Twersky
We also call him, known as: Beloved

That completes my documentation of my Zayda's life. He died on August 24, 1948. I came home from my first overnight camp experience at Camp Canadensis, and my oldest cousin drove my mother to pick us up. I don't remember if it was from a bus or train. My brother Lewis was four and a half, and I was seven, and my mother told us that Zayda had died. He was buried from his house just as he wished the day before, and we came home to a house of Shiva. I remember the conversation in the car, but I don't have any memory of the Shiva. I do remember bits and pieces of scenes with him, and I know that his soul is within me and this Yurusha (inheritance) is worth more than money. It is priceless: I can picture everything in my mind's eye as I read and re-read the stories of his life, for it isn't just one story, and it isn't about just one man. It is about you and me, our fathers and our grandfathers, our mothers, and our grandmothers, our hopes and dreams, our successes and our failures. It is what we inherit from one generation to another, and now my Zayda's story is reaching into the sixth generation.

David and Israel Rosen, ca. 1946.

EPILOGUE

I was told that just before my Zayda died in his bed at 3117 Westmont Street in the Strawberry Mansion neighborhood in Philadelphia, surrounded by his family that he looked up at the ceiling as if he saw his beloved mother waiting for him and said the Shema Yisroel prayer and breathed his last breath. Thus, his life in this world transitioned to the life in the world to come or, as he wrote many times, "To the True World."

It was just a couple of months past my seventh birthday when he died, and I only have snippets and a few brief memories of him. There aren't many photos of him. I do remember watching him working with pen and ink, drawing in the book. I don't know if he was also writing, but I do remember the drawing of birds, fish, and lions. As much as I try, I can't recall his voice. Did he speak English to me or just Yiddishe? Was his voice raspy, weak, or strong? I just can't remember that kind of interaction. I have a slight remembrance (*which was reinforced over the years by my mother*) of him teaching me the Four Questions (*the "fir Kashes"*) in Yiddish for the Passover Seder. I must have been three or four years old. I remember watching him play dominos with a friend. I remember he used to have rock candy which was white and connected on a string, and he always had a tin of Sucrets which were wrapped in foil and were green. He seemed to always be sucking on one. I remember him in the large shul, B'nai Jeshurun, watching him in his seat as I was with my mother in the women's section behind him on Simchat Torah. That was the first time I marched around the synagogue with the apple on the top of the stick with the paper flag attached. I remember seeing home movies of a Seder on Westmont Street that he conducted, but those movies are long lost. How I would love to see them again. I remember walking with him very slowly to a small shul in a row house (*many would call it a Shtibel*) on 32nd Street, a few blocks from our home. I remember a very small Sukkah in our backyard that maybe three or four people could stand in.

These are all fleeting memories. Flashes of scenes. Oh, to be with him for just an hour. I have so many questions, so many blanks to be filled in. I hope you have been able to get enough from this book to let you into the world of "MY ZAYDA" and understand that it is not just HIS STORY, but it is the HISTORY of that generation, the refugee experience, life in the "old world" (*with the poverty, the pogroms, the antisemitism and the heroism to leave*).

I believe the essence of his message is his love and trust in God, his love and belief in this great country, his love and commitment to Judaism and ritual, and his deep desire to be a good person and help in repairing the world (*Tikkun Olam*). People constantly disappointed him, his health was always a factor, he had an inferiority complex, and yet he accomplished more than I think I would have been able to achieve.

I grew up observing deep respect and feelings of love and loss from my Bubba (*his wife*) and his children. They did not exhibit any of the lack of respect and devotion that he suggested in his writings. My Bubba was a wailer, especially at his gravesite. I believe she mourned for him every day for the rest of her life. She lived for twelve more years and died on August 4, 1960. I don't know if she ever knew what was written in his book. I don't know how much my Uncle Max was able to read. If anything, he never appeared to have shared it.

It is now more than 150 years since he was born. We Jews have traveled from life in the Shtetl to the immigrant world of "The Golden Medina," endured two world wars and so many other conflicts, lived through pandemics, survived the great depression and many other economic catastrophes, agonized through the Holocaust, seen the creation of a Jewish Homeland, morphed from the industrial revolution to the technological revolution, become accepted in mainstream society and became one of the most upwardly mobile communities in the United States. And yet, we see a rise in antisemitism that, in some ways, is worse than my Zayda ever experienced. I do not know how my Zayda and his generation of immigrants survived, but they did, and we all have benefited from their perseverance, endurance, survival instincts, and strength. Many experts have written that the children of that immigrant generation were the greatest generation, but I think they were the greatest generation.

I know that I am biased, but my beloved father, David Rosen, was really the patriarch of our family. Yes, he was the youngest, but he was the one who made the end of my Zayda's life so wonderful. As my Zayda said, if your whole life has been great, but the end is bad, then your life has been bad. But if your life has been bad and challenging, but your end is good, then your life has been wonderful, and his writings stated more than once how satisfied he was with his life and how wonderful the last years were.

A year and a half after my Zayda died, we moved from the house on Westmont Street to a much larger single home in the Wynnefield section of Philadelphia. My mother was pregnant (*sure she would have another son*) so that the new baby would have my Zayda's name. Well, as it turned out, that baby was my sister Sharon, but she was named after my Zayda, with her Hebrew/Yiddish name being Sora Pesa. Even though my Zayda's Hebrew/Yiddish name was Yisroel, everyone called him Srul. Our home on 56th Street in Wynnefield was the place the entire family would come to. My Bubba lived with us, and everyone wanted to see her and my father's business was the place where many members of the family worked. Not only was my father the breadwinner for our immediate family, but he also provided the livelihood for the majority of the family at one time or another and was the anchor for the entire family. And my mother, Vera, whom my Zayda adored, was the wind beneath my father's wings.

All of my Zayda and Bubba's children, as well as their spouses, are in the "true world." And of the next generation (*the grandchildren*), my cousin Aaron and his wife Myrna and the widowers (*Mort and Ronnie*) of my cousins Evelyn and Vivian are the only survivors of my cousins on my father's side of the family. The only other grandchildren alive are my brother Lewis and his wife Leslie, my sister Sharon (*her husband Arthur died in 1996*), and my wife, Maxine, and me.

We are now in the sixth generation of our family in America and owe it all to Israel Isaac Rosen. His courage, perseverance, love of

Judaism, and belief in God gave us the foundation and opportunity to fulfill his dreams and let us experience "The Golden Medina" of the United States of America. Yes, it was my father and mother who really established the building blocks for our future, but it was Zayda who had the courage, gumption, and foresight to take those first steps into the unknown. I know if my Zayda were here today, he would be a most happy Jew to see grandchildren and their spouses, great-grandchildren and their spouses, and great-great-grandchildren living such active and practicing Jewish lives and serving as leaders in their synagogues, Federations, Jewish and communal organizations as well as national and international Jewish organizations with some of them being Jewish educators. His dream and love, as well as support of Eretz Yisrael (*the Land of Israel*), resonates within the family and has been passed on from generation to generation.

Every bone and fiber of my being as well as my soul and spiritual essence are in constant touch with the gifts that he has left us. May his soul be bound up in the embrace of his mother and HASHEM as he continues to bless us every day with this incredible INHERITANCE (*YURUSHA*).

David and Leah, ca. 1946–47.

ZAYDA'S BOOK EPISODE ONE
The Blood Libel of R'Yosele

The first episode, which I'll begin to describe, is when I was a child of eight years when my beloved mother, may she rest in peace, was still alive. I remember this as if it was yesterday. It is very interesting to describe because I can't forget it. There was a very decent family in our town by the name R'MOSHE TSIVYOS. They descended from RABONIM (*Rabbis*). This R'MOSHE was a LAMDON (*the Hebrew word for a Talmudical scholar*), a Jew, a very pious man. So, he, his wife and his children lived behind our house. Our house was in the front of the market. Their house was next to the butcher shop. Their PARNOSA (*livelihood*) was from a mill that produced buckwheat and other products. If you remember from the old home, a big wheel driven by a pair of horses, and this way they made a living.

There were more of these Jews in our town who had larger or perhaps smaller mills, and they lived happy and satisfied. They were older people, married off their children. They had in their family an orphan, a young man who lived with them. They gave him to a MALAMED (*a teacher of children in the traditional HEYDER*) who taught little children. The young man who lived with them was taken by the MELAMED to be a helper, to bring children to the HEYDER. For this, he received his daily meals and also a garment. I remember him as today a short one and a weak one, also bad looking, by the name ITSIK. He was my helper (*he took me to Heyder*) and was also a neighbor because he lived with R'Moshe. All of a sudden, we learned that this young man together with two similar young men, left for PITSHAYEV about two miles from our town VISHNEVETS and that all three got converted (*in PITSHAYEV was a famous Russian Orthodox monastery*).

Ordinarily, in the old home, if a Jew got converted, I can't describe what that meant for the parents and the whole family, particularly the young man ITSIK, who was R'MOSHE's nephew, a descendent from RABONIM. You can imagine what was going on in our town, for every Jew in general and especially for the families that three Jews should get converted. I saw them when they came back in town. One was a red-faced young man, a healthy one, my helper was a heavy one of eighteen years, and the other two were also of this age. They caused pains to all the Jews, particularly to their own families. But what could we do, those years in Russia, we were afraid, and we kept quiet.

So, time elapsed that they suddenly disappeared from the city for a long time. We all got relieved. But suddenly, two of them showed up but not the helper, and the families already had plenty of TSORES (*trouble*) from them as well as all the Jews from the town. We could not do anything. And so a long time passed. We almost forgot about them. Suddenly before Pesach, when the summer comes on, and the snows are melting from the sun, and the frozen rivers begin melting, and in our town, almost like in all small towns, was a big river and also a deep one. All of a sudden, it could be seen at the shore of the river a rotten bag, a sack, and feet were sticking out from it. When they further continued to touch the bag, it could be seen something more terrible, a whole body rotten and pale from lying the whole winter in the river falling apart. People from the whole town got together, old and young, Jews and Christians, men, women, and children. Almost nobody remained at the homes. One woman kept lamenting that he is her husband who disappeared from her about a year ago, and she doesn't know where he is. Another surmised that it is her father who didn't remain in town since long. There were all kinds of cries. As a child, I also was there. To the bag was tied up, I mean to the corpse, a couple of big stones with heavy ropes, but it was rotten, the torn sack. The bag was immersed very thoroughly with the kiss from the river where the buckwheat was produced.

And this led to recognize that this comes from a mill where they produce buckwheat. After an exchange of words, it brought children should look and recognize that this is ITSIK the helper, the nephew of R'MOSHE, the convert. Yes, yes, this is he. In the meantime, in our

The Inheritance (Yurusha)

city there was an official and another few converts who heard what we were saying to one another. In the end, it was stated that this was he. So we went with them to the mill taking them all together, first the uncle and his wife and all the children and the children's children, whoever was found from their family. I remembered this as if it were today or yesterday. Until it came that on a certain day in the evening before blessing the SHABBES candles they took out from the house the great TSADIK R'YOSELE RADIVILER may be blessed his memory. They carried him in the air to the jail. The TSADIK was of a small body, thin, almost all bones, but a great soul and the greatest TSADIK at that time. Incidentally, I saw everything. They carried him in front of our house. Darkness befell over the whole town that the great TSADIK was arrested, and here began very bad days and weeks in our town. Everyone was afraid to go out in the street because of the goyim, particularly before the two other converts who demanded that a pogrom should be made on all Jews from our town. I will never forget it. I, therefore, want to describe it to the end, which came out very bad for everybody, especially for the TSADIK, blessed be his memory.

When they were kept under the lock, the TSADIK and the whole family, I remember that my mother, may she rest in peace, cooked food for them every day, and on Shabbos, I used to go with my mother carrying whatever was needed for the family. The great TSADIK, R'YOSELE, was separated in a room. But it did not last long that my mother should cook for them. It was said that she should not do this because we will also be considered as their family. Hence we no longer carried food from our family. The few days passed, I remember, all the officials from KREMENETS, also the head (*The author calls him Pope, which in Russia a priest is called "Pope." In Russian, he is called "Episcope" or "Patriarch," which is equal to a bishop or one of his hierarchy.*) and many priests from PITSHAYEV came to us in the SHTETL to attend the autopsy on the young man. I can't forget my whole life as the autopsy was performed behind the dike of the river where almost the whole town attended and from the small shtetls and from many other villages. But this is nothing.

The main thing is how the great TSADIK was. They also brought him from the jail, not talking about his family, where he supported himself under a tree, his head on a side and his little and weak body shaking. It was terrible for everybody. It affected me as a child as well as older Jews. It began with his procession; this means with the burial. To call it an L'VAYAH, the Hebrew term for a funeral, is too good for him. But it was so. He was lying in the casket many days before his ceremony took place, almost from the whole GUBERNYE (*state*). All the big people came, the governor, the chief of police, goyim from all the villages and all of the priests, which is very understandable because they called him by the name of Jesus. A few days before the Jews of the whole town remained in their homes, they were afraid to go out in the street, especially on the day they carried him, and this is understandable. With thousands of shmates, flags and songs they marched.

I have in mind that the chatter (*the author uses an insulting Yiddish term PLAPLEN*) could be heard miles away. It was a fear that, God forbid, there should not be a breakout of killing the Jews. People were afraid to look out of their windows. But a child didn't understand so much. I remember and looked at the street and saw how they carried him. I can't describe it, until God helped and the procession passed by. They buried him and made on his place erected a big stone. And indeed, his corpse tied up with ropes full of blood around the stone. On the stone was written with big golden letters, that here rests by the name they gave him ANDRZEJ MATSHNIG, this means plain in Yiddish that he was killed. (*The author misspelled the Slavik term Matshnig. It should be in Polish MECZNIK, which means a martyr.*) He was before GEMUTSHET (*tormented*), and he is a holy man. And from this very day, they, the goyim, in our town, made a holiday every year. On that day, there was a fair in our town called by his name ANDRZEJ MATSHNIG. When everything was over, the town began to try for the great Rebbe to get him out from prison before the trial will take place.

For it could be seen that he will not hold out. About the family, nobody thought, or it was impossible for the Jews to give so much (*bribery*). Also, for the Rebbe, the worlds of our town were shaking, as well as from other towns. I remember they requested 200,000 rubles (*about $100,000*). It could not be done so quickly. In the meantime, he was sent to a larger prison, but the Jews from all over did not rest. The sum was raised, and he was taken out, broken and sick, and he could not be anymore in our shetl. He was sent across the border, GALICIA, to his family, who were from the greatest TSADIKIM. But it didn't take long that he was there when he died before the trial began. A trial took place later, and they all were found guilty. It came out that they lured him to them, not forced through a girl, where they killed him in the mill and then put him into the sack and tied it up with the big stones and threw him at night into a meadow in the woods for the river was frozen. In order that he should remain there, that he should not be able to come up, and this brought that they were sentenced to slave labor for all years. They all, indeed, died there. Only one from the family came back. He was still a young man. He got married and had the same mill for buckwheat.

He didn't live long; he died in his young years. This was the end of the great family, and to the Jews of VISHNEVETS, it was not much help that they proved the Rebbe, blessed be his memory, died before the trial. They traveled all over. To the governor, they wrote even to the Czar. The Jews had to pay, even the ones who could not. From some the houses were sold, everything, not one year, but many years. But it was paid with pain. I remember that the police commissioner and the city attorney of our town, who treated the Rebbe very bad, were punished very well. The city attorney committed suicide, and the police commissioner became insane. He was running in the streets screaming, this is because of the Rebbe, i.e., that God punishes him for the Rebbe, he used to run around barefoot and naked, always drunk. He was not any more police commissioner. The end was with him that, in a certain morning, he was found in a gutter stone. So I remember the story, for I was altogether eight years old.

Here in America, they don't make an issue from such things if one gets converted; not saying anything about the marriage of a Jew with a Christian, but it was this way. Now that I'm in my older years and weak and I don't have anything to do, it comes back to me everything that happened in my younger years in the old home. So, I took upon myself the duty to describe all episodes and stories of all the years. The only thing is that my writing is weak, especially my spelling is not so-so. But it is better than nothing. Furthermore, I don't write it for anybody, only for myself and my children who will have to read something about their father's silly things. But from silly things, one can also learn. I hope that the coming episodes that I will write will come out better, for I was older and perhaps I will remember it better. This is the end of my first story. There were many other converts in our shetl, smaller and bigger.

But nobody paid much attention and didn't make so much alarm like this man, the helper, who the goyim made out to be another Jesus, almost as their god.

Leah and Israel, ca. 1944–45.

ZAYDA'S BOOK EPISODE TWO
The Two Rich Men from Our Town Vishnevets

The second episode that I want to describe took place in the time when I was already a boy of thirteen years, which lies in my memory until this very day, from which I learned a lot. First, I will describe the ordinary rich man, a Jew by the name of R'TEVYEH. He almost knew how to pray (*in Yiddish, if you say about a man ER HOT GEKENT DAVNEN does not mean that he knew to pray for himself, only that he could lead a congregation, a minyan, a group of worshipers. This was a very common appearance in a Jewish community*), let alone write, and he was blind in one eye. Instead of wearing glasses, he had a black piece of cloth over the blind eye. I remember him as if it could be today, because my sister, blessed be her memory, lived in his house for many years. He and his family lived in a village in the country a couple of VIORSTS (*Russian measure, 7 VIRSTS was a mile*) from town. He was a farmer and had an inn, and he was well situated and had PARNOSE.

He had a second wife and children from both marriages, fine children, mainly boys, and he had for them the best M'LAMED. He was from the inn keeper's family. Since the innkeeper was a Jew and had some money, he lent money on interest from twenty-five rubles to 100 rubles, and he used to come every Friday and Sunday into town to give loans and collect. My sister and more neighbors lived at his house, a big and a nice house. But he had for himself in the front his table and chair and also a couch painted black with two covers which could be opened from both sides with padlocks. It also served as his bed, for he used to sometimes stay overnight. He was there always. He did not leave for a minute and managed his bank (*loan*) business.

I used to watch it, he was holding (*or keeping*) paper money sorted by denomination of rubles (*twenty, ten, and singles*). He also had coins (*kopeks*) in all the denominations in silver and copper. This was on one side along with the promissory notes (*VEKSLEN*). On the other side, it was always standing a few bottles of whiskey (*SCHNAPS AND BRONFN*) and various sweets (*lemon cake, cookies and white cake*). He had a long ledger book to write in the name and the sum. Nobody could read it. Perhaps he himself also not, but how he conducted his business and notations with sense and carefulness.

How he gave the money is worthy to describe, for I learned a lot in my older years and I think that it is worthy to describe everything for you children can learn a great deal from this. And this was his routine life. When a poor person came to him to borrow on interest, rich men didn't come to him, one would get twenty-five, the second fifty, the third 100, they all were equal. First, he took out the bottle of whiskey with cake and gave him and drank with him L'HAYIM and wished him luck that he should succeed with his rubles and make profit and have PARNOSE, and it should not be too difficult to pay every week the payment and he kept wishing him well. But what could he do this R'TEVYEH this one or that one had bad luck or, God forbid, a child got sick, and the few rubles had to be spent for a doctor? Or it happened something else that the borrower bought merchandise and lost money or had to spend a bit for his household or that fairs and market days were not good? There were all kinds of happenings that could affect the poor man and he suffers and could not pay.

Everyone was coming to R'TEVYEH'S house to make his payment. This was his conduct. Yes, indeed, in the time when he began his business on a small scale, this was when he lived in the village. But at the time when Jews were restricted from living in the villages (*during the reign of Alexander III, which comes under the political history of the Czars*), it is understandable that R'TEVYEH was sent out (*a sense of such removing of Jews from the villages you have in* Fiddler on the Roof, *TEVYEH the dairyman being sent out from his village*). Since he had a house in our town and, indeed, more money, he now devoted entirely himself to lending money on interest. He already gave bigger loans and, indeed, already employed a bookkeeper, who was none other than the M'LAMED, who taught his children, already grown-up young men, fine children, he enlarged his business.

What he used to do if one took money and didn't pay the installments, he used to wait a couple of weeks. After that he used to send R'SIMHEH the M'LAMED and secretary of the business and to go and ask the borrower to come or send someone to R'TEVYEH. When he came, R'TEVYEH greeted him as a guest. Nor, God forbid, with scared eyes and, first of all, asked him to sit down. He asked before anything to come to the porch.

"Tell me, R'MOSHE or R'YISROEL, what is the matter with you? I gave you a loan which is set with such payments to pay every week. At the end, you don't pay the whole time almost. It is not good for you and certainly not for me."

This Jew or another, they really wanted to pay, but at one happened a sickness at the other something else. What did the ordinary rich man R'TEVYEH do? He listened to everything and understood the one or the other's situation. He, unfortunately, knew the truth. Do you know what he did to the same people? For not one time did this happen almost every time when the poor man has such MAZL several times. He used to give to one and to the other five or six times a loan on time, and he was not afraid. With the words, "God will help you and that you, with God's will, will return pay back the old debt." Not all the times are equal again to make the same L'HAYIM with him.

And indeed, it was so, but it didn't work out. He took and took, and the other could still not pay back. So he (*the NOGID*) used to turn with these words, "Well, I can't give you any more. God should help you, and if he helps you, don't forget me." This was his conduct with the honest poor man. This way, he could help them a lot, and they paid him back, but there were also a few swindlers who attempted to take from him. The first time he gave it to him. But he (*the NOGID*) was smart enough and understood that he will take away from him. So, he used to say with the words, "Well, you can't pay back. When God will help you, you should not forget that you owe me. Keep well and be happy." So that almost the worst paid back. And so he grew in our town with decent children and gave charity. Nothing was lost ever to him. This is the story of the ordinary rich man, which I read many times, for I also was conducting myself so with my customers. It is understandable that to become a rich man, the interest grew. And it also grew at me what I have paid to the other... but this is the truth.

When I left for America, I left R'TEVYEH a rich man. He married off all his children and his children's children, very fine children. Now it is most likely that he is not anymore on this sinful world. But a man as he was, you can never forget. So lived in the old home an ordinary but faithful Jew.

Now I want to describe the other NOGID from our town. A Jew, an HADRES-PONEM (*a person of stately appearance*), a good-looking, honest and learned aristocrat. Also, a Hasid Jew from TRISK (*Hasidic Rabbinical dynasty*). He had a few sons and also a second wife. From the first children and usually from the second children already married off, all decent children. His name was MEYER FRENKEL, and his wife's name was Yette, a beautiful woman. Her weight was almost 300 pounds. When she was walking in the street, she used a cane. He lived on the outskirts of the city, almost in a palace, and the children lived near him by themselves. Near him also lived the police commissioner and the druggist, only landowners, the richest in town. His business, rather his dealings, were woods, possessions, and mills on the rivers. He was a rich man. He had good horses and a coachman. Even to the bathing house, they used to bring him by coach.

He was entirely different from R'TEVYEH the blind. I remember him praying in the synagogue where my father, blessed be his memory, prayed. He had the whole East (*i.e., the first rows in the synagogue, which is called in colloquial Yiddish DI MIZREH VANT, meaning the eastern wall*) for K'AYN HORE, his children occupied the East. He had eight sons. Plain he was the greatest NOGID in our town, and he really threw light on our shtetl, he with his children and his children's children. He gave charity, everything good and fine, but it was not so easy to reach him. First of all, he was almost always very busy. A whole week with his big business, Saturday was for him and his family SHABES. They never failed to come to synagogue on SHABES whenever he was at home (*not out of town*). He conducted a fine life, very Jewish and aristocratic.

The Inheritance (Yurusha) 255

I remember as a boy from the same thirteen years R'MEYIR FRENKEL, during the winter, came to the synagogue on SHABES in a new marten fur just put on for SHABES. He used to come to the synagogue late before the K'DUSHE (*the prayer the Cantor recites with the congregation during the Amidah*). I remember that on this SHABES he came to the K'DUSHE and suddenly he fell to the ground. It came as an alarm, R'MEYIR FREKEL is fainting. The children all and the congregants took him and put him on a big table and immediately brought the greatest doctor in our town, and the doctor declared that he got an attack of epilepsy. It was something to do with the bloodstream in the head. He was still alive, the tongue out, but he could not talk anymore. And so he was lying in the synagogue the whole day covered with the same fur coat, which he had worn for the first time that same SHABES. As a child of thirteen years, I witnessed it. He died, and indeed, Sunday was his funeral. All the Jews were there. It is clear that this was a great loss for the town. So lived the greatest NOGID in the city, but his dying was not good.

But not about his death, I wanted to bring out. I want mainly to describe his widow, Mrs. FRENKEL, the 300-pound woman, who survived so rich with a lot of money, but without business, for the children divided it among themselves, the one with the woods, another with the mill and so on. But she was still young. She still had a few children to marry off. So she took a look at R'TEVYEH the blind. Why shouldn't she make such a business, perhaps she had more. She can give a loan of 500 or 1,000 rubles, and so will grow interest and interest. It didn't take long, and she made in town and in other smaller towns. It didn't take long until she was making business in town and in other smaller towns, but listen how she gave and didn't wish success and not with whiskey and sweets. And here it happened with a Jew, the same as with R'TEVYEH. Either sickness or something one could not bring his payment.

So, on the next week, she took her big cane in hand, and she herself went to demand the payment. Usually, when YENTA FRENKEL was seen going in the market or in the street, it was already known for what she was going, especially the poor who noticed her. When she goes to him, he got scared. For her, there was no excuse that a child or he himself was sick or just something else. He knew one thing that he has to hide. But how many times can one go into hiding? Before her two times, three times but in the end she met him in the home. "Why don't you pay your weekly payments?"

"I couldn't. One, God knows my truth, I don't lie, and I will not take away from you. But what could I do? Even now, what can I do? I went through all the time sickness, or I lost everything. I ate it up (*in Yiddish, it means that he used it for food*). I will give it back to you. If I would have now a couple of rubles, perhaps I could do something with a few rubles."

But not YENTA FRENKEL, she had a mouth, she should forgive me, and you can imagine that her screaming could be heard in the street. But in the end, what could she do. You may yell GEVALT, but actually, he doesn't have it. So she made it this way with great understanding. She gave him or to another a week or two more time. If they will not bring, then she will scream in the street that they took away from her. So it was. Ordinarily, one could not escape her regardless how one wanted to do. Still, they (*the debtor*) didn't have to give it to her. So she kept her word. So she went in the street and screamed, "Jews, this thief, this charlatan" and many other names, "He stole from me my blood, which I need in order to live. I am a widow."

The people heard everything. As you know, the small towns and shtels are not America. Here when one falls in the street, he could get credit and so the other, but not in the old home. A bankrupt man was like a convert. You want to know what happened? Neither she helped nor did she understand to help in order that she should not suffer. Her money got lost because she was malicious, and she remained in her older years poor and her children poor.

This is the story of two rich men, who I remember, from the old home. The ordinary R'TEVYEH the blind, blessed be his memory, and the richest man's wife, blessed be her memory. This is what I had in mind when I was doing business in the old home and especially here in America. Constant honesty and character, it pays off. Yes, yes, my dear children, there is a God who leads, not the human being.

Leah and Israel, ca. 1940.

ZAYDA'S BOOK EPISODE THREE
A Man in the Middle Years with all the Virtues by the Name of Leyb Mazer

The third episode that I remember from my birth shtetl is when I was already a boy of twenty years, which has remained with me until this very day. I am K'AYN HORE, a man of seventy-five years, but I remember as if it took place only yesterday. I remember that in our shtetl, they elect every year or two a Starosta (*a head of a district,* Wm. G), a Jew. Almost everyone wanted to become the rich Jew, especially the poor. The rich wanted mainly the honor, and the poor wanted both the honor and the Parnose (*income*), an easy one also. When it came before elections, everyone had its time, and all the parties like the Democrats and the Republicans and many others. I remember in our town as a child that the main factor was the guilds. Shoemakers, tailors, furriers, all kinds of craftsmen, laborers and also the biggest hoodlums. Ordinary Jews and less ordinary Jews could not help with money.

It used to be a joyful couple of months in the winter. They were drinking day and night in the bars. They were fighting and screamed every Shabbes in the synagogue. I remember that for a couple of years, there was one Starosta, and they could not dismiss him, so great was his politic. He was a plain-looking man with a big red nose because he used to drink a lot of whiskey. He used to make his Parnose from being a bookbinder. This was his trade. He was acquainted with all the important people in the town, the city officials, attorneys and police commissioner. He was a good politician. They needed him. He was doing for them good business. He could not do it himself, so he employed a man as a secretary, and they conducted their business. Then he was out. No longer the Starosta. I don't remember if he died or they didn't want him anymore. Anyway, there was a need for a new Starosta.

There were many who wanted to be elected, but I want to introduce you to the man who a few young men wanted to be the new Starosta. First of all, he had all of the virtues: he could write good Russian and particularly Yiddish, let alone speaking like the greatest speaker, a nice man from a fine family. But the man had no luck. First, his young wife died while giving birth and left him with a few small children. So he married her sister and had children with her also. In addition, he worked for many years taking care of landowner's properties, but he was fired because a Jew wasn't allowed to do this. So I remember as today when he came into the town poor, naked, with little children. He didn't have subsistence for the day. He used to stay day and night with good people.

I remember that he used to stay with a friend of mine by the name of Avraham Vitels, a secretary, almost a lawyer. I used to see how good looking he was, particularly how he was talking. A brother of mine used to help with a ruble, and so did a few young men, the richest in town. Since the town (*Vishnevets*) has to elect this year a Starosta, so all would or should try that this Leyb Mazer should be elected. First, the town would win that it will have the right man who could speak to the government officials, like a governor, the police commissioner and others. After all, it is a town and many different things happen. Furthermore, it would be a good deed for the man with a wife and children to have Parnose. How was I, still a boy of twenty, going to able to help? Everyone said that they would try. One undertook to see the head of the tailors, the other the shoemakers and so on. For a couple of nights, we were meeting with Avraham Viterls, blessed be memory. Everything was ready. There is money as much if it will needed. So they put on his candidacy all at one time—MAZER the Democrat.

But the opposition put on the candidacy of a republican (*the author took the American terms Democrat and Republican to illustrate the two opposing candidates in his hometown,* Wm. G). Who he was, I will also describe for you. An ordinary Jew but rich. He had in town a hardware store. He could not read or write, he should forgive me. He is also dead a long time. But what I remember as if it was yesterday, his name was R'Shmuel Mamet (*the first letter of the last name is not clear, it could also be Samet,* Wm. G). This name he received when he was already rich, but the name from before I will not write for it is not necessary. What for he needed to be a Starosta? But it was so many of our Jews all the years in the old home and certainly here...

Well, both were working day and night mainly with the guilds. I remember that every evening they used to come and report how is the situation; good, very good, we have the guild on our side so he could be elected with 95 percent. I used to listen to everything. In the meantime, the man is almost dying for a slice of bread let alone to pay rent. He used to come every evening naked and barefoot. It was terrible. Only his wise eyes were visible. He is also not alive. My brother, blessed be his memory, helped him a lot. All together, two weeks before elections, when everything was all right, they (*the author doesn't say who,* Wm. G) let him know that he can't run for the office of the Starosta. Why, because he does not have his own house, and the one who does not have his own house can't be elected. This affected everybody's mind. What to do? But immediately was a created suggestion. This came from the lawyer Vitels. Since we are good friends (*in the text brothers,* Wm. G) and also rich, so one should write off on his name the house...

And this was accepted by those who suggested it. Yes, everything now is all right, almost hundred percent. All decent young men and all the guilds and it comes the day. I mean the evening. All got together in the synagogue, all citizens of the town, everyone, even the strangers who don't have the right to vote they belong to another town also were there. I used to help out. They called out before they began to vote in order to hear who has more, whether the rich man R'Shmuel or the pauper Leyb instead to call we want Leyb Mazer. The whole screaming from all came out suddenly from the guilds. We want Shmuel Mamet (*see earlier note about the name,* Wm. G), not Marzaviden (*an insulting term,* Wm. G). Instead of we don't want Mazer, they called him by such a shameful term, Marzaviden, if you knew what this meant for a Jew, particularly for the man Leyb Mazer. Now you understand that the rich man became the Starosta, not Leyb. I will never forget how we all felt, especially all those young men who tried for him with money, with everything, but it hit mainly him.

I remember that for heart-breaking and shame that he could not endure any more the pain, shame and poverty, to see how his wife and children have no bread are walking naked and barefoot: so he left the town. Where did he go? Where used to go our people? To America. He didn't have so much, so he left for Odessa. Well, I will make it short: what he did there, I don't know. I only know that here his wife and children died from hunger. My brother and others had watched it. But there he didn't have any better luck. How long was he there? I don't remember. I only remember when he came back, he was worse than when he departed, broken and old. He came again to his "brothers" (*good friends*) for help. But in the end, something had to be done until God helped. Indeed the same man who tried for work, tried again. They took him to a big mill where buckwheat was made along with other products. His job was to travel and buy buckwheat (*in Yiddish, it is RETSHKE*) and PROSE (*this is the original Yiddish, I can't find the English term*), everything that was needed for the mill. They gave him a horse and wagon to get to the landowners or just rich Christians who have for sale the products that were needed. And for this, he would get five or six rubles weekly, and that he should have bread. And so he began. I watched it very careful, only to have bread and a garment. He became another man, and so he used to travel in the small towns and villages for a long time.

He was wise. He could talk to all kinds of people, and he got acquainted with many landowners. When he came to buy the RETSHKE and PROSE, they had other grains like corn or wheat to sell, but he didn't have money only for the grain, which his bosses told him to buy, so what did he do? He used to take samples and come into town and show it to Naftali Kohen, a great merchant, blessed be his memory, also to a second and third buyer, and so he began to do big business and earned a lot of money from brokerage.

So passed altogether a couple of years traveling around for his boss. But he saw that he doesn't need him anymore. I remember as today. I was already living in a small town, LONIVITS. I got married, my father-in-law of blessed memory was a merchant of grain with landowners, and we also had a lodging house. All merchants from VISHNEVETS and from the other towns stayed with us. So the same

The Inheritance (Yurusha)

LEYB MAZER used to also stay with us. But it was entirely different than before. With the finest harness, a good horse with a carriage, and he himself dressed in the best clothing, a good fur, and he looked nicer than he was before. A man. You know our Yidelech, they should be healthy, all over if one falls, there will always be who won't let him get up. The truth is it should not happen to anybody. I went through it; therefore, I feel a need to describe it.

To see that one is alive, that things are better with him, he is not any more helpless bothers others, and they want to know how he gets to wear a new garment or he bought something for the house. Everyone expresses his opinion, this is it, and so it will be as it could be seen as LEYB MAZER looks nice (*dressed*), travels nicely, and lives nicely. LEYB MAZER began to live as he wanted. I knew him very well from my home, and I knew how he had suffered. When he used to come and stay with us for a few days, one could spend time with him. I even remember he once came to us, and I wanted to go home to see my father, of blessed memory, and my brothers and sisters. And LEYB was already traveling as a rich man. So I said that he should take me and he did. As we were traveling, I took a look at my side, and on the ground was an antique ladies umbrella. How could you leave this? And I said to him to stop, that I see an umbrella. He stopped and picked it up. A very good one with new silk, only a princess could own such an umbrella, but to whom it belongs? I say it belongs to me. He says that it belongs to him, for he took me without pay. When I came home, the verdict was so. Only what I want to bring out how I remember everything with LEYB MAZER. I want to describe until the end what happened with him, well he really, within a few years, became rich from trading, very big, already not for everybody, only for himself.

He lived in almost the biggest in town. He didn't have his own house, but he used to sit (*he rented a house*) in the nicest house in town. He had a maid, married off a few children (*this is inconsistent with the previous writing that his wife and children died. It could be that some children had survived.*) So he took to build his own house, almost the nicest house in VISHNEVETS. My brother, blessed be his memory, used to stay overnight in his house. It used to be joyful. He was his best friend, you know. Well, the house was finished, and he made good business and indeed, became a rich man. And this is true. Now I remember they began to bother him that he should become the STAROSTA in town. Not anybody else. He answers, I don't need it. I am busy in business, thanks God. I am older many years. But they don't let him rest. After all, who does not want such an honor, especially someone who has a business? It will make him more famous (well known) in his business here he didn't need anyone.

Almost all Jews from the town, big and small, agreed and LEYB MAZER became STAROSTA, and he was for many years. He didn't travel any more, but he did business. When I used to come to VISHNEVETS, I used to come to his house. He married off the children beautifully. It is certainly fifty years, perhaps more. What happened to him you certainly (*or most likely*) know? He is a long time in the true world. But it was so with Jews in the old home. Money, and money, and so it is here and this way it will be. Perhaps when it will be one world, and everyone will live as brothers, but I think that will be never. Furthermore, what can say such a little man as I, even bigger, but it angers me, children.

ZAYDA'S BOOK EPISODE FOUR
Shabes in the Old Country

Did you hear that a rich man in the old home could have a disturbed SHABES? A poor man or a pauper, yes. This was nothing new that poor men, paupers, could have disturbed SHBOSIM, but not rich Jews. So, it happened once that a rich man had it. And the whole town was on wheels (*a Yiddish saying implicating the effect of the happening*). But before I want to describe how poor Jews had disturbed SHBOSIM. That they had disturbed weeks, even years, we know, but even if one was poor, when the SHABES came, everything was done in honor of SHABES; to prepare everything so that on SHABES morning, there would be something to eat. They used to make (*in original SHTELN*) CHOLENT (*a baked dish of meat, potatoes and legumes served on Sabbath, kept warm from the day before in view of the prohibition against cooking on the Sabbath. The pots with all these foods were carried Friday afternoon to the bakery and were there in the oven until Saturday noon time*). Some did it at home. Some didn't have the firewood or the straw, so they took it to a close neighbor and even sometimes to a far one. But even the woman who made it in her home sometimes it happened that the food was burned from the extensive fire or raw, not ready or when she wanted to take it out on Saturday morning, she turned it over, took off the lid, and there was nothing to eat during the whole SHABES day. It is clear that the husband, and wife, and children were not happy with such a life. They used to mourn everybody with such luck.

But many Jews used not to have a piece of firewood, and the women were forced to carry the few pots to another. This was shameful for them that one should look what the other is preparing. But it was so.

266   Israel Rosen

The CHOLENT was prepared mainly in the winter. When they came home from the synagogue, the mother sent a child, a boy or a girl, a little child. An adult was not allowed for it was restricted to carry on SHABES (*This refers to the eruv, i.e., wire or string on the circumference of a town or neighborhood to classify it as enclosed private property in which objects may be carried on the Sabbath according to Jewish law.*) When the child was walking with the pot, he fell in the street, or it was slippery, and the lid fell off, from the snow or rain and everything that he was carrying came out or the pot broke, and when he came home, you may well understand how one felt the whole SHABES: all were fasting. The mother cried, and the children and everyone argued about the poor luck that even on SHABES they have to go around hungry. Such things happened.

This happens only to the poor. I remember when I was a child of poor parents. Before my father, blessed be his memory, was rich, but not for me. So it happened also with me that I was walking on SHABES with the pots and I fell, and it broke, and the food remained on the street, and I came home with nothing, and our SHABES was disturbed. But who knew that of the rich Jews also (*the CHOLENT accidents*). No, for a rich Jew, never knew about this.

But it so happened in our town that a rich Jew had a disturbed SHABES, rather a shameful one which bothered him for a very long time. He would not see anybody because he was ashamed. First, I will introduce you to him. I mean both the couple, people in the middle years, rich, never had any children. He was a common man, almost didn't know anything. But as you know, in the old home as well as here, the main thing is to have money. If one has money, you can have everything, particularly the one who pays for this. And so was with the rich man who I want to describe. They lived in a nice home, and their conduct was very fine. But understand that besides money, he does not have anything. This he didn't understand, certainly she not. Ordinarily, he had an eastern pew (*a front pew in the synagogue*). Equally, she was a woman going almost every SHABES to the synagogue, a nice couple. Her weight was perhaps 300 pounds. Why not? There was no lack of anything (*in their house*). Sometimes they took a poor man for SHABES or just gave a few dollars (*in the Yiddish, rubles*). But they were disliked for their arrogance (*it may also be vanity, snobbism*). They only wanted honor and to be recognized. But for everything comes a time. Listen, what happened to them that they had a disturbed SHABES, particularly a shameful one.

It is already sixty years, as the couple, on a SHABES in the winter when there was a great frost, put on for the first time (*in the text BANAYEN, i.e., to renew*) he a modern fur, equally his wife in a mink coat. People were talking that they cost at those times fifteen hundred dollars (*i.e., rubles*) together three thousand dollars (*3,000 rubles*). In those years, it was a lot.

And when God helps when you are well and rich, so one demands honor more than one deserves. So the couple felt very good at that SHABES. They decided that on that Saturday, they should go a little bit late to the synagogue, in order when they came in, all the Jews should already be there and all the women. When they (*the couple*), he to the front pew and she to her front pew (*needless to say that the women were separated, usually they had a balcony*) so that all men and women could see what kind of furs they were wearing. This was important, and when they were walking in the street together and came to the synagogue before the reading of the TORAH. He was so busy with himself that he forgot at what place they were reading. He used to always have SHELISHI (*the third*) or SHISHI (*the sixth*) ALIYAH. But he was so carried away with his thoughts that he didn't realize that it was already up to R'VIE (*the 4th*) as if he was passed on purpose. So he yelled at the GABBAI (*a trustee*) rather than to the sexton, why he gave him R'VIE? So the SHAMES (*the sexton*) answered him word for word. He gave the SHAMES a slap. Of course, the SHAMES and the trustee and the congregation did not remain silent, why he slapped him for nothing, unnecessary, a Jew and at the SEFER TORAH?

His answer was because he was given R'vie. This angered everybody. For everybody knew that they gave him SHELISHI. And the answer to him was that he is a rough person and you don't know the difference. Do you need to beat up a Jew, a poor man, you are so deeply occupied with your thoughts about your great arrogance, so you made such a scandal and this which happens once in many years. His wife noticed and heard what her husband did, that he slapped the innocent

SHAMES. The women also understood what had happened. If he is such a rough man and doesn't know R'VIE (*the 4th*) from SHELISHI (*the 3rd*), so why did the poor SHAMES have to suffer. So, his wife was very ashamed and grabbed her fur coat and left the synagogue and didn't wait for him. She went through the side streets so that no one should see her, so did he. When he came home, then it began. His wife screamed that she will take her life, rough man, if you don't know which ALIYAH they gave you, then keep silent. They gave you the same as always, at the end, you made a scandal and slapped an innocent Jew. Such a thing never happens. I will not be able to go to the synagogue. I never knew that you were such a rough man.

In the synagogue, there was prepared everything for KIDDUSH—whiskey, wine, and good cake. There was plenty of food. It was not necessary to send a child for the CHOLENT. However, they started arguing with each other, and he didn't want to listen to her. Their argument became so intense that they threw plates at each other and broke everything that was on the table. They didn't eat or drink the whole day, and this brought them to a disturbed SHABES and disturbed weeks and perhaps years. The whole town kept talking, but he deserved it. I remember it as it would be yesterday indeed in the BEIS-HAMIDRASH where I prayed. They should forgive me; they are already in the true world. But it is worth describing the memoirs from before as a child, and you will be satisfied to read that something like this happened. Yes, yes, children, it is true. Some Jews did not conduct themselves decently in the old home. They disliked each other for nothing, even brothers and sisters. It was terrible, certainly here, and we want other nations to like us while we ourselves hate each other. As long as there will not be unity among ourselves, we can't expect others to like us. Perhaps one day may come when we can all live in harmony, and I want you, children, and your children to experience that."

ZAYDA'S BOOK EPISODE FIVE
The Story of Binyomin the Convert

I now want to describe, my dears, is from forty-eight years back. At that time, I lived in the village of MEKELVETS (*the writing is very unclear*), you remember, in the inn by the name ZABNA, which is in my taste until today, near a monopoly. Our PARNOSE (*livelihood*) was derived from drunkards, GOYIM, which is not to describe. But here, I don't want to describe our life there. I've already described it. I only want to describe the great episode what happened there during my time when I lived there. There were a few Jews in the village. One rented the mill, another something else. We were six Jews. There was also a Jew who leased a property. There was employed a Jew who had the place as here in America. They call it a manager who supervised the workers, also as a bookkeeper. He was married. I remember him very well, a wife and children, already married off two daughters. Truly, his wife was a very ugly woman and not a good housekeeper. Her name was ROKHEL. His name was BINYOMIN. I used to see her almost every day standing near me with the GOYIM. He was a good-looking Jew with a long beard and broad shoulders, a strong one, he was a BEN-YOHID (*the only son*), a KOHEN, a learned Jew with many virtues, had come from a small town near us and near the border by the name of LEKSENITS.

I knew his mother, an old woman and a sister who had five children, a few daughters and one boy, very bright. All of a sudden, it was heard that this BINYOMIN KATZ is going to marry the lessee's SHIKSE (*i.e., the daughter*) by the name of PRUSKE. Her father's name was KASYONEN. There was an uproar in our town, also in VISHNEVETS, all over, not just in our village. As I said that two of his daughters already got married, and he already had grandchildren. There was a lot of pervasion. I remember my father-in-law talked to him. I still was very young. I knew him very well but stayed away from him. His mother came, and they all were crying before him, you have a fine wife. She will take a divorce, and you can take whoever your heart desires. And who do you want to take, a barefoot SHIKSE, an ignorant and plain shepherd, a daughter who is standing in the city with a bag and asks for bread. What do you see in her? (*This is not clear. Above, the author wrote that the girl was the daughter of the lessee, and it is generally accepted that the economic status of such a person was not one to stand in the streets and beg for bread.*) And for her, you want to get converted?

I will never forget what was going on for several weeks in the village right next to me and in our INN. Day by day, the talk was about BINYOMIN KATZ, but regrettably, nothing helped. They went to PITSHAYEV, also not far away from us, and he got converted, and he came back to MEKELVETS and married PRUSKE. I and my wife witnessed it, and another couple of Jews from the village saw when they were driven to the cloister and from the cloister. Musicians played and danced in the streets. He probably was fifty years old, she perhaps was eighteen. What could his old mother do and his family? Well, the mother, because of her sufferings, died soon after. His two daughters with the husbands left for America because they were ashamed. They could not remain in LONIVITS. Only the wife and a few small children remained, and their grandfather, their mother's father. He stayed in the village as always (*the convert*). He became an assistant to the priest, this is called an IDOK. He knew all the ceremonies, and even they did not favor him, they honored him. And so bypassed a year or two. In the meantime, she had from him already two children, a boy and a girl.

All of a sudden, he lost his permanent job as a manager, and he didn't have any work. Then he looked around where he is in the world, disliked in town by the Jews and in the village by the GOYIM. Healthy he was and the few children in America wrote to friends and to him that he should come to them. There he will make a living and to leave his PRUSKE, and he will begin a new life. America wipes out everything, a thief, a murderer, especially a convert. If one comes here, he can even become a REBE. Not so quick it was done, for he loved very much the healthy PRUSKE, indeed healthy as a horse, that's all. In addition to this, they have for bread. In short, at a certain day, he left as others do it, left her with two children. He came to New York, to his daughters. He didn't have any worries.

He learned to be a cutter of cloaks at that time and began to make a lot of money. People thought that he will entirely forget her or perhaps will bring her and the children and make them Jews. But he didn't think so. To the contrary, he sent her money and money indeed that was the end. You know, times ago, if you sent ten dollars, it was twenty rubles, and he sent her much more. What could she do to reciprocate? She raised ordinary Christian children (*in Yiddish SHKOTSIM*). They were eating and drinking, and she didn't lack anything. She used to come to us to buy, and so went a couple of years.

Suddenly who was in the village, his name was now PETRO, he was still healthy, good looking, but without the long beard, and he had golden watch, and for a couple of months, having a good time. We used to see him every day at our INN. But the money, the couple of dollars he brought from America, came to an end. To go to work as a nothing, as before he could not and did not want to do. As everyone who comes back from America, he can't be the same then he goes back especially PETRO, who earned a lot of money as a cutter. He had her enough (*in the text, ate her enough i.e., sexually*). That is all he could have from her. After all, he had a big family in New York. Very fine children, sons-in-law and grandchildren.

I remember him saying to me before he went the second time, YISROEL, listen to me come with me to America. Such a young man as you, why should you be lost here in the village among GOYIM, drunks? There you will make a living, and he said it to me several times. But this is not the way it was. I wish I would have gone with him. But not this I have in mind. It was a couple of weeks after he left for New York. He already had a trade, and he began to work as always, and he again began to send her money and even more than before. She had a good time, became healthier every day, and also more beautiful. She dressed like a lady (*in the text, PRITSE, the wife of a landowner*).

She had everything until it came such a time that she had a child from another, but he kept sending her money. Here, however, from her side were already sleeping (*this sentence is out of context unless we assume that her side became indifferent to her affairs*) when this was heard. It was so quick when he left and not later, otherwise, it could be assumed that it was from him. So they wrote him, he didn't believe it, that they made up such a story in order that he should forget about her. How could he find out the truth?

I remember one day came to me a young man from LONIVETS who was a couple of years in America, and indeed, in New York. He came home to his family. What is doing this BINYOMIN KATZ, rather, PETRO? Since he was his friend so he asks him only when he comes home he will go to the village, to his PRUSKE and be with her in her house to see how many children she has, if two then it is a lie, and if three it is the truth. The young man wanted to know where PRUSKE lived, and he tells me he found out that it was common knowledge about her having another child from another man but that he must obey his good friend and he must see it for himself. If it is true, he should write to him so he will forget about them.

And so it was. He was at her home and saw three children, and he came back to us. He immediately wrote to him, and after that, he went back and told him in person. So, he stopped sending her money, let alone a letter, and he forgot her completely. This pleased his children, and they thought they could bring their mother and the remaining children and make peace that they should all be together. Yes, indeed, they brought her, but he did not want to be with her. She died shortly afterwards.

Now I want to describe what PRUSKE and her SHKOTSIM did when he stopped sending her money. She didn't have what to eat. The boy was already grown up, helped out his grandfather KASYONEN PASTURING THE SHEEP. She used to go every day to another Jew in the village, mainly she used to work for us. In the course of talking, she used to curse him why she let herself be misled by a Jew (*In the text, he uses the term ZHID, which is an expression of derogatory meaning if it was used in a cursing or insulting context*) and that she could take someone her equal. She already used to walk around barefoot and with shabby clothes (*as if naked*), let alone the SHKOTSIM. She wasn't too smart and remained in the village and didn't have money for bread.

So it passed another couple of years until I, myself, went to America, and when I went to New York, I wanted to see BINYOMIN KATZ, the convert, PETRO. I came to my niece, who lived on Verit Street, and we were talking about BINYOMIN the convert. So she said to me, Uncle, perhaps you would like to see him. He lives not far from me on Macklin Street 88. He has a delicatessen store. I was eager to see him. I was only a few weeks in the country. They advised me, and I went and saw on the window the letter B KATZ, KOSHER DELICATESSEN. I went in, met a few customers, and he was behind the counter in a white apron, healthy and good looking, without a beard along with a healthy, good looking not old woman with a white apron. I didn't want to interrupt him. He asked me, what would you like to say young man? I was young, altogether, thirty-seven years. I had a beard. But before I answered him, he said to me, I think that you are YISROEL LAZER'S son-in-law from MEKELVETS. Yes, this I am R'BINYOMIN, SHOLOM ALEYKHEM. YISROEL, when did you come here? A few months ago. How do you like America? You will be all right. I wish you had listened to me years ago when I went. You would have forgotten about everything. But you will be all right. In the meantime, a few customers came in. He asked me to come again, I said good day and I came back to my niece.

We spoke about him a lot, for she knew about his story in the old country. I, for myself, was thinking about what this man did during his lifetime. There, he left a GOYE (a Christian woman) with children, and here in America, children and grandchildren. And only now, he married a Jewish woman, pretty, without children, and is doing business side by side. He is healthy and good looking, and already in his older years and behaves as if nothing ever occurred before. I didn't think much about him as I began to do now. He, perhaps, is not anymore in this world. If yes, he is perhaps very old, even his children here. At the older years, everything comes back to my mind. Although, God forbid, I never committed a crime, but I am only a human being, and all these years, some things happen between people. If, during my lifetime, I said something to somebody that I shouldn't have said, it worries me now and makes me angry, especially something like this (*the deeds of a convert*). I can't understand until today. This, I remember and can't forget.

Now about another one also from LONIVITS, I remember there was in our town a Jew by the name of R'ITSHE YISRULIES, so he was called. He made a living from teaching the oldest children in reading and writing. He was paid very well. All rich men, even from other SHTELEKH were taught by the REBE R'ITSHE, a Jew, a wise man. I remember that the ROV of the town died. They want him to become the ROV, a man with all virtues. His carving and paintings were displayed to the public to admire. It was a privilege to be his pupil, to talk to him.

But he was not appointed as the ROV of the town, 90 percent were against. Listen why. He really was qualified to be. But it was not wanted because about two miles distance from us in the small town of BIATOCERKVA there lived his brother, also a great LAMDN (*a scholar in rabbinic studies*). He knew something, but he made his PARNOSE that he was the greatest thief. There was under him almost all thieves from the whole VOLYNIER GUBERNYE. He was the head. Not an ordinary thief to steal a horse or just so something else. He went out on the roads to kill (*in MORDEN*). And he was a Jew, a HOSID, yes, he prayed every day. People knew about him. This prevented his brother from becoming ROV in our town, but he became the ROV in another city MEKELEVETS.

His brother ruled many years until he was caught at a murder, which was committed in the field. They were cut off from the woman the diamond earrings together with her ears. Then he was sentenced to slave labor. How he escaped, I don't know. But one thing I do know, when I came to Brooklyn and saw the convert BINYOMIM KATZ they called attention to the great rich man R'ARELE, so he was called all over, and I went to see him with the same beard and the long caftan as at home. His business was that he had a stable with horses to rent. There were not yet machines (*i.e., automobiles*) as today, and he observed SHABES. He was a GABE OR A PRESIDENT IN A SYNAGOGUE. Yes, yes, so came Jews to America, and here they became RABONIM (*Rabbis*) and so it is to this very day. I asked about this, and the answer was, it is America, she washes off. To the contrary, from decent Jews became tailors, pressers, rough people, everything... go ahead and ask.

ZAYDA'S BOOK EPISODE SIX
The Fantasy of R'Itshel

The episode, children, which I will describe for you now, was about fifty-three years ago in LONIVETS. A neighbor across the street from your grandfather, blessed be his memory, by the name of R'ITSHEL, a M'LAMED, a wise Jew. What could do such a Jew in the old home who was a scholar (*in rabbinic studies*)? So, he became a M'LAMED and taught grown-up children. He himself had a lot of children from his first wife and from his second wife. He lived very poor. Since he was wise, so he was capable for business. He began trading, for instance, with what he used to buy during the whole year, all kinds of skins from sheep and calves, all kinds. He travelled from year to year to YARMILINTSER to sell them during the summer months of TAMUZ and AV (*Hebrew names of months usually corresponding with July and August*). And so he spent about two weeks until he sold everything. Sometimes he made more than fifty dollars (*i.e., rubles*), sometimes less. So he collected a couple of hundred dollars (*i.e., rubles*) from year to year. This helped him to marry off his children. One time he departed as usual, and he came home. They gave him an ALIYAH (*called to the Torah*) as always. But this time, he made a blessing for GOMEL (*an additional blessing said by a Jew after escaping a great danger*). So the Jews asked him, "R'UZIEL, why did you BENCH (*bless*) GOMEL?" He answered, "Well my dear Jews, if you want to know, so first I will ask you to sit down at the table. When we make L'HAYIM (*a toast to life*), I will tell you everything."

This is what he began to tell them. "This year, I had a very good fair. I sold my whole merchandise with a good profit. The last day in the evening, it was almost dark, approaches a woman with two men, healthy and the woman screams to them, yes, it is he, my husband who left me many years ago with two little children. But now I found you, you murderer, take him, this is he. It didn't help my talking and crying before them, and I understood what this means for me. It is YARMILINTSER, who watches to all things being done here at this fair? One does not know about the other, even in the middle of the day, especially now that it is already dark. For me this means to take away the money from me and perhaps something more to dispose of me from this world. And nobody would know. My screaming didn't help. Nobody wants to hear my screams.

I talked to them, "You are making a mistake. I have at home a wife and children."

But my pleas didn't help. The two men took my hands and feet and put me in a wagon. I see that the woman was bigger and healthier than the men. I saw in front of me the angel of death. But what could I do? They brought me to the outskirts of the town, into a house separated from all houses in the field. They took me into a small room, there I met two children already grown up and she screams to them, I brought to you your father, the murderer who left us when you were still very young, but now he will not get away. She approaches me, give me a couple of rubles. First, I will make a VETSHERE (*a super*). Next, you know what I need, and she says to the two men, brothers, watch him until I will be back. I am thinking what to do, and I pray to God that a miracle should occur to me. But how it is possible? I carefully took out from my pocket two rubles and gave her. I thought what is going to be with me, and she said to the men to watch until she will come back."

So he was telling the story to the Jews and keep their mouths open and listen to everything what R'UZIEL tells and everybody takes, in the meantime, a drink of SCHNAPS (*whiskey*). It is understandable, they got scared when he tell the Jews this story. They asked him suddenly what happened further.

"She came home burned like a fire (*i.e., excited*). She sat next to me that I should eat, but how can I eat, although all day I didn't have in my mouth anything, while I see the death before my eyes, not talking about the money they want to take from me. And here she wants to force me to be with her and bring me to a sin and perhaps to kill me.

Who know what is going to be? We finished eating. It was late at night. She sent the children to sleep. Also, one of the men went away and the second went to sleep. I remained with her alone. But talking to her will not help me. I am only thinking how to get out, to get free from this misfortune."

All Jews listen to him and want to know the end, how he really was saved, and R'UZIEL answers, "Wait, indeed the greatest miracle happened to me what you will hear later. In the meantime, my dear Jews take again a little bit (*i.e., a drink*) for what God helped me with his great miracle." The Jews took again a little whiskey and pitied him that he had to go through so much. Now when the brother, rather the murderers went to sleep, also the children, I remained alone. She said to me, "Come we will go to sleep, it is late. I waited many years for the moment so that I should be able to be with you together as a man and a woman." And the truth I will tell you, dear Jews, when she said to me these words, I saw before me even a beautiful, healthy and young, a bad woman. A scare fall on me at this moment, after all what should I do? She took off her clothes to be naked and went into bed and forced me to lay down next to her.

I saw that nothing will help me but the fear of the strangers, the money, and also the sin, which was waiting for me to be with her. I got undressed, almost everything. But you must excuse me, dear Jews, I remained only in my pants. Here came to my mind, and I said to her that I want to be ready before I go to bed. I left the house in the field, it was dark also summer late. I began to run over the fields and woods and didn't look backwards, only kept running. How much I ran this way, I can't say, whether two towns or three until I saw when a light is shining.

And so I came to a little house, a Christian one. I went in and met there sitting a young Christian woman with a small child in her hands, a baby of a month or two or three and opposite an oven which was burning where she warmed up water that she needed for her laundry that she needed to wash. As soon as she saw me, she got very scared. But I told her that they wanted to kill me and take everything from me. They took away from me my clothing and the shoes. Only that I ran away from them in the darkness and this way I was scared. She had pity with me. Her husband was in the field as all used to be summer in the field, watch their horses. After being there a few minutes, not more, she said to me asking that she has to go out to take in something and gives me the baby on my hands and to sit where she was sitting and watch that the pot with the water should not overrun. But I was thinking, particularly scared from what I went through at night that I forget that I am holding a small child in my hands and that a big pot with water stands across from me and the boiling water come on the little child and a little on me.

But when I saw the child, I got very scared. I went out and left the child. It was still dark. I kept running more scared as before and came to a SHTETL where I bought shoes for myself and a jacket, and God brought me home. Don't I need to BENCH GOMEL for such a miracle? All Jews said at once, YES, a miracle, but R'ITSHEL, how could you endure all these things; to be with the murderers and to be in one room with such a woman as you are telling us and go through so much and at the end with the child?

"But this was indeed the greatest miracle of all miracles that I myself was not at all there." With this, he finished. A Jew, a scholar from about fifty-three years ago by himself with a child and with another woman had himself so much life and made up such a story and to tell it in the synagogue after he had a little SCHNAPS. Yes, so it was once in the old home where Jews lived. Stories were sometimes made up to teach lessons as Jews always did with MIDRASH. Since I liked what I was told, so I am telling it to you. I think you will also like it.

ZAYDA'S BOOK EPISODE SEVEN
The Lessons of Dr. Shmaryohu Levin and How I Saved a Life

The episode which I will now describe was about thirty years ago at a big meeting of BRIS-AHIM where there were about 2,000 brothers, K'AIN HORE, also many outsiders. I don't remember what the subject was, but I will remember being there as long as I live. But what I heard were inspiring words from this great man Doctor SHMARYOHU LEVIN, blessed be his memory (*Dr. Levin was one of the foremost Zionist leaders in Czarist Russia and a great orator*). I was saved, and all of you and also strangers who were desperate were saved. I think, my dear children, that this was before I brought all to America to me. You Max, was already here. I will give over the words what the great man Dr. SHMARYOHU LEVIN said with his voice, which roared like a lion. I will never forget his figure, tall and full and dark as an ARAB.

And he brought out in his tone what preachers in the old home used to preach. And this was how he spoke to my dear Jews from BRIS-AHIM. There are people who can speak from a platform before thousands of people, so strong are their bodies and personality, especially spiritually. They are not nervous, and they can influence everything which he wants to accomplish, God forbid to the evil and also to the good. This means, as our Jews understand it HAHAYIM V'HAMOVES B'YAD HALOSHOHN (*Life and death are in the hand of the tongue, i.e., in the contents of one's speech*). Words can bring life and also, God forbid, death, as our great President Franklin Roosevelt, blessed be his memory, brought life to everybody and to make a distinction (*between sacred and profane in the text LEHAVDL*). Hitler and the like brought death for mankind everything by their great influence of their speeches. Furthermore, he (*Levin*) said there is a minor one with a low voice, not so strong, who can speak on minor subjects not for so many people. They are people who can be presidents and various persons already not so, lower and lower. So he went every time lower with his voice. There are people who can talk to outsiders and to their own whenever something happens good or God forbid bad they speak out.

So he continued with his talk. Many thousands can't talk before the masses. They can, however, talk with the family, with the wife, with the children when something happens to them, to consult what he has to do or she. It does not matter whether it is a man or a woman, for there are many women who can also talk a lot. Accomplished for mankind, particularly for themselves. So, he was talking, rather so sounded his words over the big BRIS-AHIM audience until he let down his words. There are thousands of people who can't talk to anybody; not to outsiders and not to their families. However, they can talk with themselves whenever something comes up to talk to themselves good, and God forbid bad, he will not go down, and he will save himself.

But, my dear Jews, we owe something to such people who can't talk to themselves if something happens to them. They become desperate and don't talk to anybody, let alone themselves. Such a person is lost, such a man must commit suicide and make unhappy his family and outsiders. Hence, dear children, one should be able to talk to himself, if God forbid not. ... I had it with myself all my life. I only spoke to myself what befell me. Yes, I used to talk to my family in the old home, to my brothers and friends, but they didn't understand it to be a human being to another human being, especially to a brother. Also, here in America, but mainly children I spoke to myself all the time, particularly at the time when I brought you all over. It took seven years of hard work and suffering before I brought you to me, and at the end, they sent you back, and I remember standing alone at the shore of the ocean, sick and desperate. Everything lost, what to do, one truth as I already described in my writing. This is what saved me, particularly it saved all of you. Thanks God that he gave to me such an understanding and courage. Also, I have to thank the great Dr. LEVIN, with his words that a human being should be able to talk mainly with himself. If yes, he will not get lost, and the one who can't, is lost. My ability to talk to myself almost all my years, this does not mean that I didn't have fears and problems. Yes, you know, my dears, I had them indeed. I spoke to God and silently praying to him day and night that he should help me. He always helped me. I thank him I don't need , God forbid, to commit a sin, especially in my older years, he certainly helped me, and I have hope in him that he will continue to help me, this means also my family, until I will leave this world and go to the true world to where everybody should be ready to come.

All of this leads me to describe to you how, fifteen years ago, I saved a man in his middle years who wanted to throw himself into the river, into the water, because he could not talk with himself. He would do it if God would not have sent me in the right time... listen, my children, how this happened. It happened as always when I was walking in the park. It was a warm day. I don't remember the day, but the time, not winter, not summer, just a nice day. There were not too many people when I entered the park. I met sitting a man of about fifty years, very good looking and dressed in the most beautiful clothing, a Jew. That was not known to me the first time, although when he turned to me the first time when I held my daily paper (*THE TOG Yiddish paper The Day*), I noticed an attached button of BRIS-AHIM, and I asked him casually, "Do you belong to BRIS-AHIM a long time?" To this question, he said to me, "Yes, I belong also to other fraternities."

But what comes from all of this? I noticed something different about this man's sitting posture. So from one word to another, I asked him, "Have you been sitting here for a long time? It's a very nice day, isn't it?" His answers were perplexing.

"Do you live around here?" I asked.

"No, I live at 29th and Wharton Streets," he replied.

"Do you have children?" I continued. A Jew wants to know everything, I thought. Then I asked him, "What is your occupation? How come you have time on a weekday to come to the park?"

He replied, "In fact, I am busy with my business. I own a grocery store, and I am doing good business. Nothing is lacking for me. I am rich, and I have everything, but..."

His BUT was something terrible. I saw that he couldn't sit quietly; he was so nervous and upset. He wasn't holding a paper or smoking; he was just turning around and thinking.

In the meantime, I took a look into the TOG paper. Suddenly he turns to me with these words, "Well, as I see, you are a fine and a smart man, one can talk with you, and you are not a stranger, a brother from BRIS-AHIM. I will talk from my bitter heart."

I said to him to talk, and I will listen.

He began to talk with these words, "As you see, I am a rich man. I have money in the banks." He didn't wait long and takes out two bank books with thousands in them. "I have my house and more houses, in one word a rich man and healthier. You see how richly I am dressed? I have everything. At the end, I came here to make an end of such a life, to throw myself into the water."

When he said to me these words, I could not believe that I hear the truth what he says to me. I continued looking at him with my answer.

"Well, my dear BRIS-AHIM brother, you will not take your life. I will see to it, but why? I see that you are young and mainly healthy and rich. What brings you that you should commit such a crime? Most likely you have a wife and children."

"Yes, I have a second wife and children from the first and a child with her, but I can't endure it, I can't take it from her. I was away from her several times, but I am coming back after being a few weeks away from home. After all, I have such good business, and I make the best living, and what a living, I am rich, but comes out from this that life is worse than death."

I listened to everything and was holding him at the hands, and I wanted to know everything. Before he told me about everything, I looked at him as one looks at an insane person, a man, a good looking, a healthy, a rich one with two books in the banks, a business, such a man wants to throw himself into the water. I am sick and poor. I don't even have for car fare, and I am with mood and life.

"But, my dear Jew, why comes to your mind to commit such a crime?"

He replied, "But I can't take it anymore. She is very jealous of me. She makes bitter my years. For instance, how? In store are coming in various Jewish women and non-Jewish. It is a business. Sometimes you have to say a few words. You can't be dumb if you don't want. When the woman leaves, she makes me scandals day by day that life becomes miserable for me. So I was away several times so that I should not come home. I come home and think perhaps she will think it over. But when I come, she is still worse. Until it came to my mind to commit suicide. Since I see that you are a wise man, so I told you everything."

My answer to him was, "You did very well. You will know better about life if you listen to me and do whatever I tell you. First of all, I would not commit suicide because one who wants to do something like this, does it and does not have time to sit down and think. The one who wants to throw himself into the water, throws himself in his clothing. If he still has time to undress, then he is saved, especially since you took time to sit on the bench and think. But more than that, you told me the truth, and your talking is true. You will certainly be saved. But you must listen to me and do what I am going to tell you.

"That you are coming back is not good. Go home now and pack all your good suits, shirts, and underwear together so that you won't come back to her. Then go to the banks and withdraw your thousands and go away to California or to another city and forget about her if she is such a woman. Have a good time. You are young, healthy, and rich. What would you have accomplished if you would have come to a conclusion (*i.e., committed suicide*)? What would people say? You would make your children ashamed."

When he heard this, he wanted to kiss me and said that I am an angel who saved him from destruction. He gave me his hand and said goodbye. Then I realized that he was someone who can't talk to himself.

Believe me, my dears, I went a few weeks later to see if is true, the address he gave me. Yes, it is true. I saw the big store with the woman, but he was not any more there. He went away, and I don't see him until this day. Why am I telling you all this? If a man has a lot (*to worry*), he should be able to talk with himself, with the master of the world, believe in him, times change. That, my dears, I don't leave you any money, but you should understand life. Money is not the main thing. The main thing is to be happy all the time, that you should be able to talk always to yourself and to, blessed be his name, so God will help you, and you will be healthy and happy, and you will live to have good with your children and children's children to my age. How do you like my silly writing?

ZAYDA'S BOOK EPISODE EIGHT
The Message of R'Tsvi Hirsh Maslansky

The episode that I want to describe now, my dear children, happened twenty-eight years ago in our Philadelphia when they had to lay ground, it means the first stones to build an orphanage. I remember that they brought the great famous R'TSVI HIRSH MASLANSKY that he should make a speech, actually a sermon, for the Jews of Philadelphia to raise money, and the meeting was in the hall at 7th and Snyder. I was between many Jews, and I listened what everyone knows about the great ROV. I learned a lot from his thoughtful words. So I will tell you word by word, and you will understand.

He began with the words, dear Jews, did you see how apples and pears are growing on the trees? When they are growing, you will see very good apples, but when it falls down by itself, then almost 90 percent of them have holes. Worms got in large one and small one to eat them. But if you cut out the worms, you could eat them, and they are the sweetest apples and pears, for they (*the worms*) got in when they were already ripe, as one could see. But on the same tree, you could see some or more very big and good apples without any holes and grew at length and in width. Either it was taken down or it fell down by itself. Then you could see something entirely different, a big and a white worm was inside in the length and in the width either dead or alive.

So I am asking you, my beloved Jews, so was speaking ROV MASLANSKY, blessed be his memory, to all who heard him, and he explained to them why the small apples had holes and the big one not. And at the end, there was one big hole in it more than that the small one could be eaten, and they were sweet, and the big apple, when it was cut out (*the worms*), it was sour, poison to eat it. How did the worm come to it while it could not be recognized a hole in it. So he (*the ROV*) explained it this way. As soon as the leaves begin to blossom comes always for little worms. But this is known, and it is being watched. Almost 99 percent of them are falling down by themselves. But it happens that it remains with the blossoming a very small worm and it grows together with the leaf and grows together with the apple inside and grows. The apple grows bigger, so grows in it the worm. He is comfortable and good. Nothing is lacking to him, he eats and drinks. Only for himself, it suckles the big apple until, in the end, nobody should have anything, only the worm himself until the time comes either they take the apple down, or it falls down, and it is being split, fed by the apple only for the worm so that another one should not profit but the end comes.

So, my dear Jews from Philadelphia, you are going to lay the foundation for such a great purpose as such institution of an orphanage, what can be noble and more beautiful? And every Jew should donate to such an institution, an institution more needed for such a good purpose. Ordinarily, you can't argue that there must be those who are needed to try everything possible to take care of the finances. And when it is ready, it needs a very careful watch that it should be accessible for all. The first thing is to have a staff of workers, a president and officers and a director. So more and more, what I don't need to tell you. You should remember that you should nominate such people who you know as decent people with a good name, that God forbid, should not sneak in at the first stone such people as the little worms at the first blossoming and that they should grow only for themselves. Everything for themselves as the big worm in the big apple. When you will see at once something strange, you will be able to throw him out. But he will not be so bad if you see it quickly.

You will be able to sweeten your work, but if you will not be able, the whole time you should keep your eyes open on the big one for whom everything is for them until, God forbid, it comes that this institution or another is being split and dissolved and can't exist anymore and falls down being split in two and can't survive because he penetrated too much to live only for himself a good life. This is the main thing, everything what, my dear Jews, are going to do, so you should watch carefully that something like this should not happen. Only people who are honest and should be good for everybody, not for themselves only. If it will be so, you all will live to eat and enjoy, and all will appreciate your work.

ZAYDA'S BOOK EPISODE NINE
Foreman of the Jury

A very interesting episode I will describe for you, my children, what I witnessed seventeen years ago when I was asked to serve on a jury. I was already one in the year 1921, so I knew already a little the proceedings, but I was not a foreman. To be a foreman, I was scared, because, first of all, you have to know to speak English, next to be strong with strong nerves. I remember well the trial, which took place in 1930. The first day I came to court, I took my place as a jury man, was in the month of November on a Monday, and I was very scared that I, God forbid, should not become a foreman. But it happened to me. I became the foreman of a case which was very interesting.

    A wife was suing her husband that he lives (*i.e., has sexual relations*) with his secretary. Indeed, he didn't want to live with her (*his wife*). He got separated from her. He didn't have any children from her, still very young people. His name was EYKANER. He was a good-looking man, a learned one, and he held a great position in a big firm. His salary was $30,000 a year. He paid her (*his wife*) 200 dollars weekly, and he didn't want to live with her. As usually, she didn't want to give him a divorce for any amount of money, but she made miserable his years, always dragging him to the court. Besides that, she got from him 200 dollars weekly, she had rich parents and rich older brothers. She spent money, hired detectives to watch him. He himself lived in a hotel on Walnut Street. He used to travel a lot not to be at home, but he had an office in Philadelphia with an accountant. When he used to come, the secretary used to come in to him to the hotel to give over the business. As usually, he was occupied with her many hours. He went out together with her to eat or to a movie or just to spend with her. But she (*his wife*) brought people who testified that they saw how he and she (*the secretary*) were together, even looked through various ways through the window and through the lock at the door and similar testimonies, which were very interesting.

I can't describe everything, all the talks, which both brought out. Indeed, both had big lawyers. The judge was an old man. In one word, the case was interesting. It took from Monday, ten in the morning, until Tuesday at noon. In the jury, I was the only Jew. There were eight Christian men and three ladies, a young girl, and an old woman perhaps seventy-five years old, and it was because of her that the jury could not reach a verdict, which I will describe further.

I want to bring to you about the man and the secretary, also about his wife. Usually, the husband, EYKANER, sat together with her (*the secretary*) as all defendants sit. I kept looking at both of them, how nice this couple was take (*in observation*). They always talk when they were called to the witness stand. As I was looking on them surrounded with love, to the contrary, when she (*the wife*) came to the witness stand, I hated her and could not look at her. She was tall and skinny with red hair. Her talk was with poison. It looked to me always that she is drunk. I hated her from the very first moment as soon as I took my place as foreman of the case, although there were moments that her witnesses said everything about him, that he lives with her as husband and wife, so I thought and gave him some credit. And I thought, how can't you love such people and not to have a good time with such a woman even if you are an angel? I could not believe that such a man could marry such a woman. But there was money, a dowry, as in the old home it took place and indeed with myself. Well, children, if during my lifetime, I didn't have good and pleasure, so I had these days to be a jury man, especially a foreman in the case, which I can never forget. And indeed, I had 4 dollars daily, and at that time, I didn't earn a dollar a week.

But as for myself, I resolved as a jury man, especially as the foreman, that I must strain all my weak nerves since I can't talk and free this couple. She should not win. Her lawyer demanded many thousands to give to her also because he lives with her as husband and wife, not divorced. She proved with witnesses that they saw the couple (*he and the secretary*) naked together. Well, it is a lot to write. I was told that if he is found guilty, he will have to pay a lot, if not, he may go to prison. And so we left the court. I went first with the papers, and they followed, and we were taken to a closed room up as it is the custom. I was sitting as a judge at the head of the table. You should have seen me then, and I was scared, and I didn't even know how I should open the case for the gentle people to begin discussion. But God helped me immediately. A very fine elder Christian asked me if I want to be helped since he understands that I can't transfer everything as he would relay. But I asked him whether he is for her or for him, what is his opinion? When he told me that in his opinion the man and the secretary are the finest and she is not. I asked him to help me. So he took a place next to me.

Since I, as foreman, was asked so he answered and so was proceeding the interesting case and almost all on our side. First, it was difficult, but later, we compromised and talked until late at night, but we didn't finish, and could not come to an end. The old Christian woman of seventy-five years only screamed that he is guilty despite the fact that all Christians spoke to her, but it didn't help, and we came with a report that eleven are for not guilty, only the old (*was against*). And so, it remained for the next day it was too late. And so ended the case that the old woman gave in to us. So the couple got free. When I came with all to the court and reported that we all signed the verdict not guilty, a joy broke out. The old judge praised us for this. The lawyer shook hands with me and told me how rightly I conducted the proceedings, let alone from the couple (*i.e., the man and the secretary*). Even from her (*the wife*) I was greeted that we rightly conducted the case. Everybody greeted us, particularly me. I don't know who the credit altogether should be given to, the Christian who helped conduct everything or to me.

But I was the foreman and all the Christian men, all the time which we were on the jury, greeted me every day when we came in the morning. Only the old woman didn't want to take a look at me. Afterward, I found out why she was against, and we suffered a lot of time because of her (*i.e., lost a lot of time*). In fact, she said she understood that they should get free, but because that I was a Jew and was the foeman, she didn't want and thought she will bring TSORES (*trouble/problems*). But she could not do anything since all were for them.

When all of us said goodbye to each other and left the since we were together, the girl told me that she is a Jewish girl and she thanked me because that I myself could not speak a good English, but you are a gentleman with a lot of SEYKHEL (*good sense and intelligence*). You won all Christians, who liked you all the time, and the truth is that it was so. After that, we used to meet in the street with some and some kind of affection and closeness remained as if we had travelled together on a ship. Also, sometimes I saw EYKANER, and I remember also the lawyer. I remember this as a great episode in my life.

ZAYDA'S BOOK EPISODE TEN
My Atlantic City Mitzveh

What I am describing now, children, happened three years ago (*1945*) in Atlantic City. As you all know, I write the truth, so everything that I write is the truth. About a lot, you know what happened during my life, but a lot you don't know. As you know, I was always poor in living and in health. We didn't have the most important things, which are needed every day, particularly to go to Atlantic City for the whole summer. But God helped us, and we lived to have a lot of NACHES from our children in our older years, mainly from our MIZINEK David and his beloved wife and lovely two children.

    For they are our whole life, because of them, we live in our older years, and they bring to us all a lot of pleasure that, thanks God, before and after that, my dear children, David and his lovely wife, that they both should outlive us. If not for them, we don't know what would happen with our life. Nothing is too expensive for us. But we are old and weak this, does not deprive them, but if not for them, it would be worse. So we, thanks God, feel better that we have everything, so it is easier to live, although life is not very good.

    But it is so. This is not their fault the world was so created. Old is not young. Others would not understand but I, thanks God, understand; therefore, it is for me easier to live and to suffer. Your mother, she should be healthy, is younger by a few years and will not understand this. Ordinarily, I suffer for two, for me and her. After all, your mother was all the years healthy, and I was all the years sick. She does not want to take it. But this is not what I want to describe. I described it not one time in my writing. And since all together, it is three years when the summer comes, we are going to Atlantic City until after Labor Day.

While young, when and if we went, it was for eight days or two weeks, and it cost twenty-five dollars a week. But today, thanks God, if you go, we rent a very good house with everything. Nothing, God forbid, is lacking, including the best to eat and drink. Hence it should be good, but not I and not the mother, we can't enjoy… this was the year 1945 while the war was still going on, and indeed, it ended that summer. Atlantic City was full of soldiers from all kinds of hotels and many on the boardwalk.

We lived on Laclede Place near Atlantic Ave. There was no boardwalk at 4100, so I walked to the President Hotel. From there, it was not far to the Hotel Ostend, where I used to spend a couple of hours with familiar Jews and walked back for supper at five or six o'clock. So I used to walk day by day. Years ago, I used to walk a lot to see everybody, but not in the last years. The couple of squares also required strength, and I had to exert myself. On the way home, I took a look at a bench, and there was a lady's bag. Usually, behind me, soldiers were walking slowly. It is not also so as at noon, but there are always people here on the boardwalk. I took it from the bench and hid it under my jacket and thought that there is no money in it. First of all, I never had the luck to find something. To lose, yes, and indeed, I thought that I would be happy that there should not be any money.

When I came home, I met the old Mrs. Rosen and the young one. Otherwise, nobody was in the house. I went upstairs, didn't look in the bag, I took time, you should excuse me, I went to the bathroom, which is more important than everything, even as money. About the few words, children, I would like to write for you children an episode, but let it be enough. When I was ready, I opened the bag and wanted to see what was going on. As soon as I opened it, I saw a lot of paper, usually letters in English, cards and two tickets, two railroad tickets from Washington to go back, keys and paper money, ten-dollar bills, one dollar bill, and silver, together a sum of about fifty dollars. When I saw money, I called Vera to come up, "I need you." I had in mind two things. I knew that with Vera, I can talk and trust her. She is wise and understands. The mother, she should be healthy, is also very good, but it is different. But I made a mistake by calling. I scared them, but it was so, and they both came up to me. I showed them I found somewhere a package, "See Vera." She took and read everything and saw that the lady came only today from Washington and stays in this hotel. She said to me there is still a small packet, we opened it, and there was a hundred dollars in 20 dollar bills, new only from the mint.

So I asked Vera, "What I should do?"

She said to me, "Pop, don't worry, tomorrow it will be in the paper."

I answered, "Why should we wait until tomorrow?"

We knew her address where she was staying. We knew her name, so we could call her. We called, and she answered how she had just come and forgot the bag on the bench and that she would come over. I expected that it should take altogether fifteen minutes or a half an hour. This waiting made me nervous. Some children said, particularly the mother, that I should not had let the woman know. But I and Vera insisted that we did what honest people ought to do, and Chayke (*Irene, ER*) said that I should request that she should give a few dollars for the poor. So we were thinking, and it took a long time until she came. But she came and was restrained as I saw her behavior. First, I recognize that she is not poor; secondly, that she is from the German Nazis and old. But so it was, she told me that she came today from Washington, everything as it was written, also the money. I took out the bag and gave it to her. Everything was there. Nothing was missing.

And Chayke told her, "You may give my Pop a couple of dollars for charity, for my Pop is a charity man, and you are lucky that my father found it." Not anybody also so we thought she will give twenty dollars, not less than ten. But all of us remained sitting, almost ashamed, for she took out only two dollars and gave it to me.

This annoyed all, and of course, myself as well, but it was my opinion that this was the way that I should have done it. I didn't regret it, particularly now. I was angry at her. I used to go pray every day in the morning and at the evening. That evening, I didn't go, for I waited to return the money. Next morning, a few men from the congregation asked me, "Mr. Rosen, where were you yesterday?"

So I told them I found money, which belonged to a Christian woman, whether I had to return it. They told me that HASHOVAS AVEYDO (*return of a loss*) is one of the greatest MITZVES when you return. I asked, what about if she is a Christian?

The answer was that because of a Christian, the MITZVEH is greater. Any way, this was the only time I found money during my life—150 dollars. I lost many times. Therefore, I found this summer a dollar on the sand and didn't return. I know, children, what you are going to say about your foolish father, so I was all the years, and so I will die. Keep well and laugh of your father, particularly you, LEAH, I don't want to hear it.

THESE WERE THE LAST WORDS HE WROTE. THEY WERE WRITTEN DURING THE SUMMER OF 1948, AND, THEREFORE, HE NOT ONLY LIVED TO SEE THE DEFEAT OF HITLER AND THE NAZIS BUT ALSO THE ESTABLISHMENT OF THE STATE OF ISRAEL IN MAY OF 1948.

HE DIED ON AUGUST 24, 1948.

Acknowledgments
by Elliot Rosen

First, I would like to thank my Zayda, Israel Rosen z"l, for having the fortitude, courage, initiative and guts to pick up and leave his world of the Shetl and come to America. If he hadn't, in all likelihood, we would have all been victims of the Holocaust. I also want to thank him for writing his story and leaving it as a legacy for our family. In his will ("My Poor Testament"), he bemoans that he has nothing to leave. However, his memoir is the greatest gift he could have ever left. It is priceless, and it is our inheritance.

There are many other people that need to be thanked for their roles in the process of moving this project forward, even though it has been decades in the making. I want to thank my Bubba, Leah Rosen z"l, for keeping the book and not destroying it and for Uncle Max z"l for keeping it safe, and my dad, David Rosen z"l, who trusted me and gave it to me with permission to bring it from the darkness of unknown to the light of discovery. Rabbi Fred Kazan z"l connected me to Dr. William Glicksman z"l, who did the translation and historical notes and explanations and was the first to acknowledge the treasure we possessed. However, it was my wife, Maxine, who suggested, more than once, to work on the book and get it on the computer and in readable form. Of course, she used the isolation during the first year of Covid to push me into action. My cousin Kathy Liss Drew encouraged me to get it published and even offered to help fund it. She introduced me to Rita Ratson, who translated the will and grave purchase document. Kathy also connected me to a cousin of hers, Rachel Anderson, who is a marketing PR/Publicist and works in the literary world. Rachel submitted the book to several publishing houses, and that is how Calumet Editions received my manuscript.

I am indebted to my brother-in-law, Peter Garfield, a world-class commercial and artistic photographer, for his help in photographing images from the original manuscript as well as reshooting the family photos. Ian Graham Leask, the Publisher at Calumet Editions, and I connected immediately, and as he said, "I could hear your Zayda's voice as I read his story." Ian and Calumet have my sincere gratitude for being my partners in this project, and my editors Howard Lovy and especially Beth Williams, have been amazing to work with in helping transform the manuscript into a final product with the help of a very talented designer, Gary Lindberg. I am deeply indebted to Neal Karlen, who wrote the forward with his extraordinary insight, passion and understanding of the beautiful world of the Yiddish language and culture, as well as a magnificent introduction of the despair and joy of my Zayda, Israel Rosen, as a "writer of art" and "a mensch."

Along the way, my children, Rachelle and Mitchell, Samuel and Terri, and Leah and Peter, and my grandchildren, David, Naomi, Aviva, Spencer and Bayla were always ready to hear the stories and episodes from "the book" and my cousins, nieces and nephews were anxious to hear and read the stories when I shared them at Passover Seders. My son-in-law Mitchell scanned all of the original handwritten pages of the translation of the manuscript and placed it in the cloud for posterity, and my daughter Leah created the map of that part of the world, making sure his Shtels were properly identified and placed. Over the years, I would show the book to family and friends, tell them parts of his story, and quote some of the passages, and I promised that someday I would put it all in proper form. Well, that time has finally come.

The only other living person who knew Israel Rosen besides me is my cousin, Aaron Rosen, which is why having the record of my Zayda's life is so important for the succeeding generations. Finally, I must acknowledge my sister, Sharon Rosen Webb (who is named after my Zayda), and my brother, Lewis Rosen z"l, who died suddenly shortly after I signed the publishing agreement. Over these years, as I put more things together and confirmed bits and pieces of information, I would call them to share the information and discuss our legacy. Sharon was born a year and a half after Zayda died but did grow up in our home with my Bubba and heard everything about him. Lewis had only vague memories of him, but the three of us would talk about our childhood living in a multi-generation home and where we came from.

Sharon had the family photo albums at her home in Los Angeles, and Lewis was in Los Angeles celebrating his seventy-ninth birthday. Sharon brought the pictures to him to bring back to his home in the Philadelphia suburbs so that I could pick them up to be included in the book. The last contact Sharon and I had with Lewis was her giving Lewis the pictures in Los Angeles and me picking up the pictures at his home a mile from my home in Pennsylvania. He died of Covid a week later.

My Zayda and this book are the last living link between loving siblings, which means Zayda is still touching his family and descendants seventy-five years after his death. An amazing man, an incredible story, and a continuing journey for the Rosen family. As long as you're remembered, as long as you're talked about, as long as someone carries your name, you didn't die; you are immortal. May *The Inheritance (Yurusha)* give Israel Rosen the immortality he so richly deserves.

Israel Rosen was born in the village (Shetl) of Vishnevets, Russia (now Ukraine) in 1870, the youngest of nine children. His mother died when he was ten, forcing him to fend for himself thereafter. He came to America in 1906, settling in Philadelphia, and brought his family over in stages as he accumulated funds. He suffered poor health throughout his life and struggled to make a living. He worked as a peddler with horse and wagon, pushcart, and eventually in stores selling tailoring and textile supplies. A religious Jew with a deep belief in God, he married twice and fathered seven children. He died in 1948.

Elliot Rosen is a licensed funeral director and has worked for Joseph Levine & Sons for forty years. Prior to that, he was an executive at David Rosen Inc. with his father, brother and uncles. He was born and raised in Philadelphia and lives with his wife, Maxine (a talented award-winning ceramicist), in Penn Valley, Pennsylvania. They have three married children, Rachelle (Mitchell) Solkowitz, Samuel (Terri) Rosen and Leah (Dr. Peter Konwerski) Rosen, and five grandchildren, David, Naomi (fiancé Max), Aviva, Spencer and Bayla.

Elliot has been an active participant and leader in the world of Jewish philanthropy for more than sixty years. He has held major leadership positions in Jewish organizations and institutions worldwide. He is currently co-president of his synagogue, Har Zion Temple in Penn Valley. Elliot has received many honors and awards locally, nationally and internationally in Israel from both Jewish and secular organizations and institutions. He was a featured speaker and trainer for several years for UJA, the predecessor of JFNA, and he has been a guest lecturer at colleges and seminaries and has taught continuing education courses for many years. Elliot has written extensively, including articles for the Jewish press as well as secular newspapers. For several years, he wrote a monthly column for *Replay Magazine*, a national trade publication.

Elliot is an avid sports fan and played basketball, baseball and football in his youth and continues to shoot hoops with his grandchildren (he played competitively into his mid-sixties). He is very proud to have played basketball with several high school classmates who eventually played in the NBA. He has also enjoyed bowling, playing golf and tennis. He enjoys theater, traveling, and walking and taking hikes with Maxine. However, he claims that he is driven to perform acts of loving kindness, Tikkun Olam (repairing the world), and as many mitzvot as possible every day.

Dr. William Glicksman (translator) was a distinguished Philadelphia-based scholar and the esteemed author of many articles and monographs on Yiddish as a language, culture and world view.

Neal Karlen (Foreword) is the author of nine books, including *The Story of Yiddish: How a Mish-Mosh of Languages Saved the Jews* (HarperCollins, 2009), which was a finalist for the National Jewish Book Award, was named a top ten book of the year by the Jewish *Forward*, and praised by the National Yiddish Book Center as "a delightfully unconventional, unique, and brashly entertaining tale."

Made in the USA
Middletown, DE
12 August 2024